Tarik Sabry is Reader in Media and Communication Theory at the University of Westminster. He is author of *Cultural Encounters in the Arab World: On Media, the Modern and the Everyday* (2010) and editor of *Arab Cultural Studies: Mapping the Field* (2012), both from I.B.Tauris. He is also co-founder and co-editor of *The Middle East Journal of Culture and Communication*.

Layal Ftouni is a writer, research candidate and visiting lecturer at the University of Westminster and SOAS, University of London. Her publications include 'Rethinking Gender Studies: Towards an Arab Feminist Epistemology' in *Arab Cultural Studies: Mapping the Field* (2012).

'I am overjoyed to see that a collection inspired by and interrogating the rubrics of Arab subcultural studies has come to fruition and have been consistently wowed by the quality of the scholarship within. It has been a long time since I have read an anthology on a similar topic this insightful and various.'

– Kay Dickinson, Concordia University, author of *Arab Cinema Travels: Transnational Syria, Palestine, Dubai and Beyond*

Arab Subcultures

Transformations in Theory and Practice

Edited by **Tarik Sabry and Layal Ftouni**

I.B. TAURIS
LONDON · NEW YORK

Published in 2017 by
I.B.Tauris & Co. Ltd
London • New York
www.ibtauris.com

Copyright Editorial Selection and Introduction © 2017 Tarik Sabry
and Layal Ftouni

Copyright Individual Chapters © 2017 Ramy Aly, Jamal Bahmad, Donatella Della Ratta, Tarek El-Ariss, Heba El Sayed, Rayya El Zein, Layal Ftouni, Justin McGuinness, Nisrine Mansour, Augusto Valeriani, Sami Zubaida

The right of Tarik Sabry and Layal Ftouni to be identified as the editors of this work has been asserted by the editors in accordance with the Copyright, Designs and Patents Act 1988.

All rights reserved. Except for brief quotations in a review, this book, or any part thereof, may not be reproduced, stored in or introduced into a retrieval system, or transmitted, in any form or by any means, electronic, mechanical, photocopying, recording or otherwise, without the prior written permission of the publisher.

Every attempt has been made to gain permission for the use of the images in this book. Any omissions will be rectified in future editions.

References to websites were correct at the time of writing.

Library of Modern Middle East Studies 152

HB ISBN: 978 1 78076 902 8
PB ISBN: 978 1 78076 903 5
eISBN: 978 1 78672 042 9
ePDF: 978 1 78673 042 8

A full CIP record for this book is available from the British Library
A full CIP record is available from the Library of Congress

Library of Congress Catalog Card Number: available

Printed and bound in Great Britain by TJ International Ltd

Contents

	List of Figures	vii
	Acknowledgements	viii
	Introduction: Arab Subcultures and the Paradox of Cultural Translation *Tarik Sabry and Layal Ftouni*	1
Chapter 1	*Hatha al-Shibl min dhak al-Asad*: Would-be Arab Youth Studies and the Revival of 'Subculture' *Ramy Aly*	18
Chapter 2	Hacking Rites: Recoding the Political in Contemporary Cultural Practices *Tarek El-Ariss*	44
Chapter 3	Just a Bunch of (Arab) Geeks? How a 'Techie' Elite Shaped a Digital Culture in the Arab Region and Contributed to the Making of the Arab Uprisings *Donatella Della Ratta and Augusto Valeriani*	62
Chapter 4	Resisting 'Resistance': On Political Feeling in Arabic Rap Concerts *Rayya El Zein*	87
Interlude	Performative Interventions in Public Space: An Interview with Dictaphone Group *Layal Ftouni*	113
Chapter 5	Cosmopolitans, Nationalists and Fundamentalists in the Modern Middle East *Sami Zubaida*	126
Chapter 6	Mediated Imagination, Class and Cairo's Young Cosmopolitans *Heba El Sayed*	152

Chapter 7	Screening Everyday Violence: Youth, Globalisation and Subcultural Aesthetics in Moroccan Cinema *Jamal Bahmad*	177
Chapter 8	Visualising the (In)visible: The Queer Body and the Revolving Doors of the Lebanese Queer Subculture *Nisrine Mansour*	196
Chapter 9	Web-based Identity Discourse from the Maghreb: The Case of *Mithly.net*, 2010–11 *Justin McGuinness*	222
	Notes on Contributors	254
	Index	258

List of Figures

Figure 1	The 'smiley face' on the zoning wall at the intersection of El Sheikh Rihan Street and Qasr al-Aini, downtown Cairo, December 2011	20
Figure 2	*This Sea is Mine*, performance by Dictaphone Group, Ain El Mreisseh fishing port, Beirut, September 2012	115
Figure 3	Map of Beirut's seafront: ownership and private exploitation	117
Figure 4	*Nothing to Declare*, lecture performance by Dictaphone Group, Ashkal Alwan, Beirut, September 2014	119
Figure 5	*Nothing to Declare*, lecture performance by Dictaphone Group, Tranzquartier, Vienna, June 2013	121
Figure 6	Map of the railway, condition of the train stations, and their current use	124

Acknowledgements

We would like to thank the contributors for their commitment and generosity and I.B.Tauris for literally adopting the Arab Cultural Studies Project, of which this book is part. We would also like thank the University of Westminster's Arab Media and Culture Centre for its continuous support.

Introduction

Arab Subcultures and the Paradox of Cultural Translation

Tarik Sabry and Layal Ftouni

[W]hen Adorno uses Lukács to understand Schoenberg's place in the history of music, or when Fanon dramatised the colonial struggle in the language of the manifestly European subject–object dialectic, we think of them not simply as coming after Lukács, using him at a belated second degree, so to speak, but rather as pulling him from one sphere or region into another. This movement suggests the possibility of actively different locales, sites, situations for theory, without facile universalism or over-general totalizing [...] To speak here of borrowing and adaptation is not adequate [...] [T]he exercise involved in figuring out where the theory went and how in getting there its fiery core was reignited is invigorating – and is also another voyage, one that is central to intellectual life in the late twentieth century.[1]

Edward Said

Theory is no longer naturally 'at home' in the West – a powerful place of Knowledge, History, or Science, a place to collect, sift, translate and generalise. Or, more cautiously, this privileged place is now increasingly contested, cut across, by other locations, claims, trajectories of knowledge articulating racial, gender and cultural differences. But how is theory appropriated and resisted, located and displaced? How do theories travel among the unequal spaces of postcolonial confusion and contestation? What are their predicaments? How does theory travel and how do theorists travel? Complex, unresolved questions.[2]

James Clifford

Putting together a book on Arab subcultures, an area of study scarcely researched, has been a challenging but also a productive process. The persistent question that bore attention since the earliest stages of this project was: 'Why Arab subcultures?' The desire to grapple with the sense of urgency attached to this project, without falling into a presentist appraisal of subcultural practices, introduces another set of challenges. How do we historicise and write about a cultural phenomenon that permeates the cultural fabric in the region through the lingua franca of Cultural Studies? What is Arab and 'subcultural' about Arab subcultures? Can we uncouple the term 'subculture' from the specificity of its etymological roots and its appropriations in research in the UK and the US, or is 'subculture' a universal category that discloses itself in similar ways, regardless of the differences in historical moments or cultural geographies?

Studies on subcultures in the West, represented by two distinct schools – the Chicago School and the Centre for Contemporary Cultural Studies (CCCS) at the University of Birmingham – provided a rich repertoire of scholarly material and research. A paradigmatic shift can be traced from earlier studies in the US in the 1940s and 1950s, when the dominant readings were focused on 'the sociological' as a determinant factor in the study of youth culture, to the cultural (predominantly Marxist) class-based and ethnographic approaches in the 1970s. From there, the emphasis moved to semiotic readings of subcultures in the late 1970s and 1980s, then on to a post-modern, post-Weberian identification of 'post-subcultures', where society is replaced by the individual, and where distinctions between subculture and dominant culture became problematic – as post-modernism began to fragment dominant cultures into 'a plurality of life style sensibilities and preferences'.[3] Since concepts such as 'youth', 'teenager' and 'subculture' are Western constructs par excellence – ones that are determined by historical events, mediated and inflected by historical contexts and posited on a specific ideological field – can such a body of work speak to Arab subcultures without a process of translation? What would it mean, since we live in a world of mediated spaces and times of the 'other', to think in terms of a trans-subcultural theory that, in the meantime, avoids the pitfalls and intellectual impasse that result from essentialist and exceptionalist discourses?

The process of thinking and writing, as an attempt at making sense of a cultural phenomenon, presupposes the presence of an object of study that is attached to *a priori* knowledge and affective regimes. Notwithstanding the importance of recently published anthologies and edited collections on Arab youth cultures and the Arab avant-garde, this volume attempts to open up the study beyond its generational determinant or modern musical experimental aesthetics.[4] What is conjured up in the term 'subcultures' in this volume encompasses actions, aesthetic practices and different modes of being and becoming that are positioned in a differential relation to the dominant culture. Notwithstanding the universality of difference as part and parcel of the social fabric of everyday life, the volume addresses difference and differentiation as they are embodied, affectively felt and enunciated to occupy positions of order, dis-order and opposition to the social, cultural and political status quo, both within the region and in diaspora.

Little has been written about Arab subcultures. The only available work in the English language to focus directly on the topic of subculture(s) in the Arab region is a chapter entitled 'Subcultures in the Arab World' by Said and Mughisuddin, which appears in a co-edited collection by Hazen and Mughisuddin, under the title *Middle Eastern Subcultures: A Regional Approach*.[5] Interestingly, the collection was conducted for and funded by the department of the US army. Said and Mughisuddin's chapter (as well as the rest of the volume) pre-dates Dick Hebdige's (1979) seminal work and thus a whole micro-sociological, post-modern turn in debates around subculture. For the book's editors, Hazen and Mughisuddin, and unlike Hebdige, the key focus is not on *style*, but on social change: how does a subculture affect the rate of social change? The use of the term 'subculture' in *Middle Eastern Subcultures* bears the hallmarks and thus the influence of the Chicago School's behaviourist and macro-sociological approach. For Said and Mughisuddin, the study of subcultures is seen as 'a useful starting point for a noneconomic understanding of evolving societies'.[6] The aims of Hazen and Mughisuddin's volume become pretty clear once it is framed within the context of the Cold War and its politics, the aftermath of the 1967 Arab–Israeli War and growing neoliberalisation policies at both the cultural and economic levels in the region. Described as a 'cursory survey' examining 'interest groups' by US *Foreign Affairs* magazine, the book inevitably spoke the language of international relations qua US foreign interests in the Middle East.[7]

Neither the editors of *Middle Eastern Subcultures* nor the authors Said and Mughisuddin engage with subculture as a category of analysis and enquiry, let alone address the complexities of translation – cultural and epistemological – that imbue the process of thinking and writing Arab subcultures. Their work was more concerned with mapping out youth politics in the Middle East during the Cold War, and thus the collection remains – regardless of its effort to explore structures of power and the creative energies (especially those of the young Left) that marked the 1960s and 1970s – a piece of intelligence for the US army. What we find even more alarming is that up until now, there has been no critical engagement with the question of cultural translation in thinking and writing about Arab subcultures, neither has there been a serious attempt at engaging with Hazen and Mughisuddin's survey.

The growing interest in theorising and doing cultural translation in fields such as Anthropology, Post-colonial and Cultural Studies since the 1980s has attested to a methodical and analytical shift in writing cultures. This is premised on an emphasis on cross-cultural encounters and 'contact zones', to use Mary Louise Pratt's term.[8] Writing cultures becomes an exercise in cultural analysis delineating practices of borrowing, appropriating and imitation across cultures, sometimes performed agnostically, at others reparatively or even stylistically. Paradoxically, interactions between cultures and the practices of translation that they ensue are, as Clifford reminds us, 'constitutive of cultural meaning rather than a simple transfer or extension'.[9] This is further complicated by heightened mediated connectivity and communication flows whereby processes of translation cease to be supplementary acts specific to cross-cultural encounters, but rather are an immanent condition of our being in the world concomitant with the experience of globalisation.

The chapters in this volume, both empirical and theoretical, are all conscious of, and informed by, the complexity and paradoxical nature of translation as they attend to the question of Arab subcultures: both as manifest in certain practices (art, music, film, protest) and epistemically produced as phenomena to be studied and theorised. It is the epistemic situatedness of the category 'Subculture', its (un)translatability, that, as editors, drives our line of questioning in the proceeding sections.

Arab subcultures: what is in the name?

Writing from within Western academe about subcultures in the Arab region inevitably puts us in a position of unease, both regarding our place in the economy of knowledge production, and the language through which we write. The limitations imposed by language and channels of circulation are further compounded with concepts and theories whose predicament many regard as epistemically grounded in the anglophone West. When acknowledging the genealogical roots and routes of Subcultural Studies, the anglophone specificity of this area of research becomes the more evident. An anglocentric approach, one would anticipate, situates 'subculture' etymologically as a lexicon whose roots are in the English language, but also conceptually as a category linked to an emergent set of concepts and modes of enquiry emergent from within Euro–US academe. Our contention is that such a critique falls into an essentialist view of language, and a return to originary discourses surrounding knowledge and cultural formations. This critique collapses the signifier 'subculture' into fixed unalterable meanings and concepts specific to sociohistorical relations in US and British youth cultures. By virtue of this view, the revisions, transitions and translations that subcultural studies underwent within the one language and across different schools of thought in Europe and the US are largely dismissed. It is worth noting that the category 'subculture' in the Chicago School referring to delinquents, criminals and outcasts – most notably Chicago's 'foreign' Others – was then repoliticised in the British context to refer to forms of youth symbolic engagement at a specific conjuncture in post-industrial British culture. Nevertheless, we ask, can one borrow the term 'subculture', sever it, cut it off from its referents, as Derrida would say, and reinvent it anew?[10] Or do we invent a new terminology borrowing from Arabic: a name that would embody but also generate the bodies, texts and objects we attend to in this book?

What do we hear when we say the words *athaqafa al-fare'eya al-arabeya* (Arab subcultures)? What mental images, imaginings and meanings does it conjure up? What does it denote on the levels of sound and utterance? What does it connote at the cultural, historical and epistemological levels? Before attending to these questions, it is important to situate the linguistic term 'subculture' semiotically, as a sign that has its own specific cultural and historical trajectory. When uttering the term 'Subculture' in the English language, we imagine Punk culture, Teddy Boys and Mods, and Skinheads. We also see a defined moment in music production and experimentation in white, working-class Britain. However, when we hear the Arabic utterance ثقافة فرعية (subculture) what we think and visualise is absence. This absence is best understood as being a result of the dissociation between the composite signifier ثقافة فرعية and a set of ideas, concepts, theories or even scholarship. Without falling into a reductive understanding of the function of language, as being a naming process that corresponds to the thing it names, we see the Arabic term ثقافة فرعية as an emergent category which – although not already there before its appearance in language (*pace* de Saussure[10]) – is nonetheless lived, felt, embodied and enacted. However, this does not mean that the Arab region has not had waves of subcultural, transgressive and affective histories that date back to the nineteenth and early twentieth centuries and even well before (see Chapter 5). What it means is that, because of its disinterest in and disconnection from everyday life, the Arab cultural discourses have yet to systematically engage with the broader meanings and interpretations of culture.

At the risk of this becoming a struggle over naming rather than meanings, we advocate cultural translation as a way of problematising the epistemic rootedness of concepts in language and a specific locale, while being wary of their uncritical adoption as universal phenomena. We understand cultural translation to be constitutive of two different, yet relational, types of translating: one is purely epistemic – in that it occupies itself only with the sociology of knowledge (investigating thought processes that take place between the experiential and conceptual) – while the other is ethnographic.

Many of the contributors to this volume have engaged with the question of subculture through the prisms of affect and aesthetics. The pertinence of these two terms in our contributors' texts has invited two key questions: why are affect and aesthetics now emerging as important categories? How have these categories shifted the language of subcultural critique? While the Arab uprisings in the early twenty-first century do not constitute a determining rupture from a pre-aesthetic and pre-affective engagement with cultural phenomena, they have undoubtedly released creative and affective energies in the arts: music, performance, film, dance, poetry and literature. Furthermore, the resurgence of the aesthetic and affective in cultural theory can be thought of as a response to a sense of disenchantment with semiotic and discursive readings of culture. The marginalisation within Cultural Studies of the aesthetic and affective against a more pronounced emphasis on representation since the 1980s has neglected the sensorial, emotional and embodied in our reading of, and encounters with, culture. As a response to post-modernism's preoccupation with style and spectacle, or its reliance on predominantly linguistic models to analyse culture, affect and aesthetic theories have presented new modes of thinking culture as a constellation of power relations, aesthetic experiences and affective regimes. Many of our contributors are part of this intellectual project, and this is demonstrated in their own accounts of subcultural phenomena in the region.

Our attempt at culturally translating subculture is also an attempt at unlearning the associations that it evokes. It is a return to thinking the premoment. Here, unlearning is not to be confused with denouncing, criticising or even de-Westernising the already existing scholarship on subcultures. We see unlearning as an exercise in historicisation: a return to non-originary beginnings. Our emphasis on the pre-moment is an attempt to highlight the historical arbitrariness of knowledge production, and the strong link that exists between two epistemological processes: a historical, radical contextualisation and cultural translation. We see the iteration of subculture into the Arab context as a process of both accounting for its political leverage and opening it up to new meanings and conventions – especially through engagement with experiences and theories of affect, as the chapters in this book delineate.

The epistemological pre-moment: translation between the experiential and conceptual

Why is the pre-moment necessary as a conceptual exercise? Subculturing or any kind of culturing is always preceded by a moment: a pre-philosophical moment. The temporalising of conceptual work is to lay it out in a temporal epistemic order: the pre-moment, the moment and the post-moment. What is the nature of the relationship between thinking a moment and its pre-thinking, i.e. the temporality that precedes the thinking process? In its most quoted and debated subcultural analysis, subculturing in British Cultural Studies has been the product of a participatory, experiential moment. Dick Hebdige and Sarah Thornton,[11] to give only two examples, moved into thinking subculturing through a participatory and experiential phase, which they then elevated to a 'scientific' articulation of the subcultural encounter. Subcultures, whatever we name them academically, are out there independent of our thinking of or about them. For us, the pre-moment (or pre-subculturing as an academic act) is also an enquiry into the experiential moment that precedes subcultural writing. This kind of cultural translation, we argue, necessitates a study of the process or movement from the experiential to the conceptual. Since subculturing and the writing of culture, in any context, is always managed through some form of cultural translation, a bridging of the gap between meaning and being,[12] we ask whether culturally translating subcultures (or any form of culture writing from one historical context to another), in fact, requires a double-cultural translation. Although Hebdige and Thornton use the English term 'subculture' and attach academic language to it to give meaning to a British phenomenon, they still had to engage in a cultural translation from the experiential into the conceptual (a pre-philosophical moment). So, the burden of cultural translation is universal. What is universal is also its universalising paradox: the fluid and complex relationship between relativism and absolutism.[13] Cultural translation is an impossible epistemic task as long as the tools of translating themselves are universal and universalising. The only way out of this impasse is double-critique. Our relativism has to be contextualised within contemporary Arab thought, studies of the everyday, and our absolutism has to be constantly negated. To think in a pre-moment fashion is to ask (in non-academic language): why did we just ask the questions we asked? Why do we ask them now? As the reader will find out, these questions are variably discussed in different chapters of this volume, focusing on the signs of a post-revolutionary energy or chagrin: a creative disenchantment with history.

Arab Cultural Studies continued

The editors of this volume are part of a growing collective of scholars – both Arab and non-Arab, in diaspora and the Arab region, and from different disciplines in the humanities – who have been rehearsing the idea and the possibilities of a critical Arab Cultural Studies project for almost a decade. Why Cultural Studies has not been taken on in the Arab region is, for us, a telling question, and perhaps makes the project all the more relevant and necessary. In *Arab Cultural Studies: Mapping the Field*,[14] key and emerging scholars who work largely in media and communication studies departments in the Arab region and in diaspora made a passionate plea for Cultural Studies as a critical field of enquiry into Arab media and culture(s). In addition, they provided a sober account of the politics of institutionalisation in a region that is still governed largely by authoritarian regimes. One of the aims of *Arab Cultural Studies: Mapping the Field* was to engage scholars working on Arab media and culture(s) in reflexive processes of re-territorialisation and de-territorialisation – that is, to rethink media and culture(s) in the region in light of key, cultural, philosophical and sociological questions posed within an Arab context, and to undo this very process by asking: how do we free the interpretation of Arab culture(s) from its teleological discourses of historical progress versus return to tradition?

The telos of this line of questioning was never to de-historicise or depoliticise Arab cultures, but to delineate a broader definition of culture that allows us to think of cultural practices in the Arab region within, but also outside, the dominant and rigid interpretations of culture advanced by pan-Arab and pan-Islamist discourse. While the teleological historicisation of Arab culture has inspired its maturity into a conscious intellectual and political project (here we are especially referring to the pan-Arabist intellectual project), it has simultaneously alienated other hermeneutics about culture – especially those vying for broader and non-essentialist interpretations.[15] The point of dislocating the artificial conjunction between interpretations of Arab culture and historical discourses of progress and/or tradition is to open up space for less totalising articulations of Arab cultures and identities. So, rather than dislocation being a tool of de-historicisation, we think that this epistemological exercise will unveil alternative discourses of becoming, and broaden the spectrum of research on Arab cultures.

From anthropology's contribution to the colonial enterprise, to the historico-political and cultural project of pan-Arabism and the subsequent ascendancy of Islamist salafist discourse, cultures of the Arab region and their interpretations have been subjected in the main to teleological discourse. The plethora of knowledge produced has interpreted Arab cultures either through devices of temporal distancing, positioning 'the referent in a different time to the producer of anthropological discourse',[16] or has been driven by teleological discourses of historical progress versus the return to tradition. On the margins of these two essentialised forms of knowledge lie hybrid, transgressive and non-essentialist interpretations of Arab cultures that have been proliferating and multiplying. These interpretations have been unaccounted for, and relegated to the margins of debate and knowledge production in the Arab region.[17] The editors of this volume strongly believe that an Arab Cultural Studies project can only begin to have an effect if and when anti-essentialist philosophies of transgression are reinstated in Arab thought and in the reinterpretation of culture. We also believe that the everyday offers the best possible site for rethinking and broadening the meanings of Arab cultures. It is within this historical and intellectual context, and that of the paradox of cultural translation described above, that we have decided to produce a volume on Arab subcultures.

The book

In Chapter 1, '*Hatha al-Shibl min Dhak al-Asad*', Aly writes a speculative future for a would-be Arab Youth Studies: one that puts forward a new set of hermeneutics for the study of subcultures. For Aly, a simple transposition of the already canonised theoretical concepts and methods that have emerged from the Chicago School or the CCCS can be quite limiting, or even ill-suited, to the study of Arab subcultures. At the heart of this chapter is a serious attempt at cultural translation *à la* double-critique. It presents an emphatic critique of CCCS's take on youth cultures and subcultures, highlighting the internal fissures in existing studies and methods. It also points to the limitations of emergent scholarship on youth cultures in the Arab region as being somewhat fragmented, detached and overtly presentist. According to Aly, this scholarship uncritically appropriates generic rhetorical terms such as 'resistance', 'transgression', 'reclamation' and 'protest', without any attempt to rethink the local resonance and meaning of such a lexicon in the respective studied context. Moreover, the logic of causality that sees a connection between youth culture and social change not only falls short of offering adequate accounts of politicised youth formations and their modes of operation, but also in the implication of youth in a web of interconnections that include the cultures of the military, Islamists, state bureaucrats and employees and urban elites. Aly calls for a dialogue that facilitates critical engagement with Cultural and Youth Studies in the UK and the US. Apart from the problems posited by an uncritical and unreflexive appropriation of subcultural theory, for Aly, the main intellectual and epistemic impasse is that of language accessibility.

In Chapter 2 El-Ariss explores the interplay of hacking (*fadh*) and scandal (*fadihah*) as new modes of cultural production and confrontation linked to the changing technological and political landscape in the region. Focusing on a new generation of authors from Egypt and the Gulf, El-Ariss examines how contemporary Arabic literature stages the political through hacking rites – practices, attacks and manipulations. These rites re-enact a new form of *iltizām* (political commitment) in literature that moves beyond its attachment to pan-Arabism and nationalism popular in cultural discourses of the 1950s.

The new authorial position in contemporary Arabic literature, El-Ariss argues, is both 'scandalous and scandalised', moving back and forth between exposing scandals (*fadh*) in writing and being exposed and hacked as authors implicated in their own hacking practices (p. 57). This leads to instances of vulnerability, injury and threats of erasure that constitute new forms of resistance. For El-Ariss, this new kind of political commitment 'has given up on the utopia of an Arab future invested in the novel as its historical vehicle'. These texts 'open up spaces of new forms of imagined communities, political authority, subjectivity and authorial functions that require further investigation' (p. 57).

In Chapter 3, Della Ratta and Valeriani explore how an elite of Arab 'techies' shaped a digital culture in the Arab region and contributed to the making of the Arab uprisings. Their chapter follows an historical analysis that moves away from the pitfalls of technological determinism to argue that it is not the technology per se, but the multiple different ways in which it is appropriated, remixed and reconfigured, that were central to the mobilisation of social movements for sociopolitical change. For the authors, technology is not only defined by a set of tools, but also by the cultural milieux that result from the use and appropriation of those tools.

Through a political ethnography of live performances of Arab rap, in Chapter 4 Rayya El Zein argues for an affective study of the dynamics of exchange between audiences and performers at rap concerts. The chapter engages with fascinating fieldwork material from concerts in Beirut and Ramallah that document the political feelings that are generated in and around what El Zein identifies as processes of *objection, confrontation and repetition*. El Zein considers two examples, one of a concert by *Katibeh 5*, a group of five emcees based in the Palestinian camp of Bourj Al Barajneh, showing at Masrah Beirut (Beirut Theatre) in the Ain El Mreiseh area, and another of a concert by the emcees Shadia Mansour and DAM at the Shrine, a world music venue in Harlem, New York.

El Zein presents an emphatic critique against the model of subject-based agency in performance studies and political theory, and against the neo-liberal discourses that incorporate the spectacle of difference as tolerance and/or engagement with political dissent. Considering political feeling, El Zein argues, opens a space for the consideration of the marginalised processes of political engagement. El Zein warns against reifying *affect* into a mould in which successful subjective interactions take place and advances the notion that theorising politics through *affect* should account for the possibility, the chance and the ability to explain mood and feelings as they unfold.

In the Interlude, Layal Ftouni interviews Dictaphone Group, a research and performance collective based in Lebanon that creates live art events based on multidisciplinary study of space, and who have been creating site-specific performances informed by research in a variety of places such as a cable car, a fisherman's boat and a decommissioned bus. This conversation was conducted in Beirut in May 2014 between researcher Layal Ftouni and Tania El Khoury, Abir Saksouk and Petra Serhal. In this interview, Ftouni engages members of this collective with key issues including art, activism, publicness and space.

In Chapter 5 Zubaida traces the cultural histories of the avant-garde and cosmopolitanism in major metropolitan Middle Eastern cities such as Cairo, Alexandria, Baghdad and Istanbul. His rich historical narrative of intellectual formations, masonic lodges, taverns, drinking cultures, belles lettres, dance and homosexuality in the Middle East of the nineteenth and early twentieth century underscores the misconception that the Middle East always has had religion as its essence or main cultural reference point. We have decided to republish Sami Zubaida's piece, which appeared in his 2010 book, *Beyond Islam: A new Understanding of the Middle East*,[18] since it acts as an historical precursor to thinking about subcultures and the avant-garde as cultural phenomena in the Arab region. Zubaida's cultural history of the Middle East demystifies teleological discourses of becoming and their selective cultural history. While we are aware of the acute epistemic distinctions that exist between terms such as 'subculture', 'avant-garde' and 'cosmopolitan', we also are certain of the connections and intersections that exist between them. Zubaida's cultural history has persuaded us, as editors, that the three categories can and do intersect – and we argue that this has implications for both theory and method, as it opens up the discussion on subcultures to new theoretical possibilities.

Drawing on nine months of ethnographic fieldwork conducted in Cairo between 2008 and 2010, Heba El Sayed's Chapter 6 undertakes a critical, comparative analysis of the subcultural experiences of young, upper-middle-class and working-class Egyptians living in Cairo. The chapter critiques the subcultural theory that emerged from Britain in the 1970s for its class determinism and drastically undermining the importance of 'race', culture and gender. El Sayed also critiques post-subcultural studies for marginalising class altogether, while over-romanticising the cultural possibilities, choices and opportunities for agency that face contemporary youth. El Sayed takes a more critical and holistic approach to the understanding of youth cultures, focusing on the ways in which young Egyptians' 'leisure and cultural lives intersect with wider aspects of their biographies' (p. 152). El Sayed shows how 'structural inequalities related to class position, as they intersect with urban experiences, gender identity and religion, continue to play a central role in organising youth cultural experiences in Egypt' (p. 154). The chapter demonstrates how in Egypt, subcultures are not centred solely on social exclusion and subordination, but also that the young Egyptian middle classes are involved in their own class-based struggles. El Sayed's chapter demonstrates how Egyptian subcultures become 'dynamic multi-node spaces where new relations between the local and global, self and others, distance and proximity, the virtual and immediate coalesce, creating alternative avenues where national and religious particularities are (re)imagined, yet never completely abandoned' (p. 155).

Bahmad's Chapter 7 examines the location and transnational circulation of youth subcultures in a Moroccan film entitled *The End*. Bahmad explores the representation of Casablanca's neoliberal spaces in *The End* with a special focus on what he calls 'trash aesthetics', where reality is framed 'through an aesthetic that refuses to glamorise the filmed objects and subjects' (p. 189), portraying them lightly by borrowing from a collage of subcultural media texts. The chapter shows how, instead of being passive consumers of global subculture, Moroccan youth have been active post-colonial agents in the translation and adaptation of global flows to their cultural heritage, consumption habits and living conditions. Bahmad examines the articulation of post-colonial subjectivities through subculture as a transnational economy of flows. Drawing from his analysis of *The End*, Bahmad engages with the filmic text as a 'contingent experiment in cinematic realism to render urban subjectivities, and invent new cognitive maps for a post-neoliberal postcolonialism through a critical reconstruction of youth subcultures and everyday life in Casablanca' (p. 178). Bahmad argues that the subjective aesthetics that are inherent to *The End* and to other recently produced films in Morocco may be read as a reflection of the entrenchment of neoliberal values of individualism in Moroccan society. However, contends Bahmad, the focus on minor subjectivities through unconventional film syntax is not analogous to the loss of critical totality; rather, these films as subcultural texts are 'haunted by the quest for a new meaningful way of being Moroccan that is free from domination in the present and the tyranny of the past' (p. 185).

Mansour's Chapter 8 reflects on the process of understanding queer existence and subculture in Lebanon through the medium of documentary filmmaking. Her chapter seeks to tie in 'the physical and political invisibility of the body to convey the voices of individuals who are struggling to articulate their everyday sexuality within a charged social setting (p. 200). Mansour also questions 'the delineations between filmic and social visibility and invisibility' (p. 201). Her ethnographic approach, including 36 in-depth interviews with respondents from the gay community in Lebanon, allowed her interlocutors to 'embody, renegotiate and reimagine "subculture" as a multitude of discursive practices' (p. 201). Her documentary project, *Hues of Love*, sought to 'document the experiences of many individuals who embody queerness in various ways and enact it selectively within various social spaces' (p. 214). Mansour's filmic decision to do away with both fetishes of documentary – pictorialism and linear storytelling – provides the author with a vantage point from which to capture the deep existential workings of subcultural subjectivities and their fluid affective formations.

McGuiness in Chapter 9 analyses a particular form of digital discourse, that of *Mithly.net*: a website created in 2010 for 'an imagined public of Moroccan gay people, mainly Arabic readers, but also partly francophone' (p. 222). The site ran for just six issues in its first version between 2010 and 2011, and the second version ran for a further handful of issues before disappearing in 2012. This makes McGuiness's study, by default, historical.

McGuiness's analysis of the site is contextualised carefully within key debates on homosexuality in the Moroccan public sphere. Through a systematic discourse analysis, it shows how *Mithly.net* remains, regardless of its subcultural potential, conventional both in visual and linguistic terms. The most used language in the site, we learn from McGuiness, is the standard Arabic, also the symbolic terrain of the Moroccan nation state and its *Makhzen* (ruling system). Also, argues McGuiness, regardless of the site's conformity to official discourses of the Moroccan state and its apparatuses, the fact that such a digital space was able to exist for individuals to engage self-reflexively with who they are and what they think is 'already a considerable achievement' (p. 245).

Notes

1 Edward Said (2000) 'Traveling Theory Reconsidered', in *Reflections on Exile: And Other Literary and Cultural Essays* (London: Granta Books), pp. 451–2.
2 James Clifford (1989) 'Notes on Travel and Theory', *Inscriptions: Travelling Theories, Travelling Theorists* 5. Available at www.complit.utoronto.ca/wp-content/uploads/COL1000-Week08_Nov4_JamesClifford.pdf (accessed 27 April 2016).
3 David Chaney (2004) 'Fragmented Culture and Subcultures', in Andy Bennett and Keith Kahn-Harris (eds) *After Subculture: Critical Studies in Contemporary Youth Culture* (London: Palgrave Macmillan), p. 47.
4 See Thomas Bulkharter, Kay Dickinson and Benjamin Harbert (eds) (2013) *The Arab Avant Garde: Music, Politics, Modernity* (Middletown, CT: Wesleyan University Press). See also Jørgen Bæk Simonsen (ed.) (2005) *Youth and Youth Cultures in the Contemporary Middle East* (Aarhus: Aarhus University Press).
5 William E. Hazen and Mohammed Mughisuddin (eds) (1975) *Middle Eastern Subcultures: A Regional Approach* (Lexington, KY: Lexington Books).
6 Ibid, p. 75.
7 John C. Campbell (1976) 'Middle Eastern Subcultures: A Regional Approach', *Foreign Affairs*, July. Available at www.foreignaffairs.com/reviews/capsule-review/1976-07-01/middle-eastern-subcultures-regional-approach (accessed 29 April 2016).
8 Mary Louise Pratt proposes the term in her book *Imperial Eyes: Travel Writing and Transculturation* as a space where encounters between cultures occur. According to Pratt, the concept of the contact zone foregrounds the interactive, improvisational character of imperial contacts, albeit within asymmetrical relations of power. Mary Louise Pratt (2007[1992]) *Imperial Eyes: Travel Writing and Transculturation* (London: Routledge).
9 James Clifford (1997) *Routes: Travel and Translation in the late Twentieth Century* (Cambridge, MA: Harvard University Press).

10 See Jacques Derrida (1982) 'Signature, Event, Text', in *Margins of Philosophy*, trans. Alan Bass (Chicago, IL: Chicago University Press).
11 Ferdinand de Saussure (1974) *Course in General Linguistics*, in Charles Bally and Albert Sechehaye (eds) *From Notes on Saussure's lectures (1901–1911)*, trans. Wade Baskin (London: Fontana).
12 Dick Hebdige (1979) *Subculture and the Meaning of Style* (London: Routledge); Sarah Thornton (1995) *Club Cultures: Music, Media and Subcultural Capital* (Cambridge: Polity Press).
13 Niklas Luhmann (1998) *Observations on Modernity* (Stanford, CA: Stanford University Press).
14 See Talal Asad (1986) 'The Concept of Cultural Translation in British Social Anthropology', in James Clifford and George F. Marcus (eds) *Writing Culture: The Poetics and Politics of Ethnography* (London: University of California Press).
15 Tarik Sabry (ed.) (2012) *Arab Cultural Studies: Mapping the Field* (London: I.B.Tauris).
16 Here, we are referring to a group of Moroccan philosophers who call their philosophy the philosophy of 'transgression' – by which they mean the cyclical dynamic between modernity and tradition. For a detailed analysis of this school of thought in Moroccan contemporary philosophy, see Tarik Sabry (2010) *Cultural Encounters in the Arab World: On Media, the Modern and the Everyday* (London: I.B.Tauris), pp. 33–41.
17 Johannes Fabian (1983) *Time and the Other* (New York: Columbia University Press), p. 30.
18 See Sabry, *Cultural Encounters* and *Arab Cultural Studies*.
19 Sami Zubaida (2010) 'Cosmopolitans, Nationalists and Fundamentalists in the Modern Middle East', in *Beyond Islam: A New Understanding of the Middle East* (London: I.B.Tauris).

Bibliography

Asad, Talal (1986) 'The Concept of Cultural Translation in British Social Anthropology', in James Clifford and George F. Marcus (eds) *Writing Culture: The Poetics and Politics of Ethnography* (Berkeley, CA: University of California Press).

Bæk Simonsen, Jørgen (ed.) (2005) *Youth and Youth Cultures in the Contemporary Middle East* (Aarhus: Aarhus University Press).

Bulkharter, Thomas, Dickinson, Kay and Harbert, Benjamin (eds) (2013) *The Arab Avant Garde: Music, Politics, Modernity* (Middletown, CT: Wesleyan University Press).

Campbell, John C. (1976) 'Middle Eastern Subcultures: A Regional Approach', *Foreign Affairs*, July. Available at www.foreignaffairs.com/reviews/capsule-review/1976-07-01/middle-eastern-subcultures-regional-approach (accessed 29 April 2016).

Chaney, David (2004) 'Fragmented Culture and Subcultures', in Andy Bennett and Keith Kahn-Harris (eds) *After Subculture: Critical Studies in Contemporary Youth Culture* (London: Palgrave Macmillan).

Clifford, James (1989) 'Notes on Travel and Theory', in *Inscriptions: Travelling Theories: Travelling Theorists* 5. Available at www.complit.utoronto.ca/wp-content/uploads/COL1000-Week08_Nov4_JamesClifford.pdf (accessed 27 April 2016).

—— (1997) *Routes: Travel and Translation in the late Twentieth Century* (Cambridge, MA: Harvard University Press).

Derrida, Jacques (1982) 'Signature, Event, Text', in *Margins of Philosophy*, trans. Alan Bass (Chicago, IL: Chicago University Press).

Fabian, Johannes (1983) *Time and the Other* (New York: Columbia University Press).

Hazen, William E. and Mughisuddin, Mohammed (eds) (1975) *Middle Eastern Subcultures: A Regional Approach* (Lexington, KY: Lexington Books).

Hebdige, Dick (1979) *Subculture and the Meaning of Style* (London: Routledge).

Luhmann, Niklas (1998) *Observations on Modernity* (Stanford, CA: Stanford University Press).

Pratt, Mary Louise (1992) *Imperial Eyes: Travel Writing and Transculturation* (London: Routledge).

Sabry, Tarik (2010) *Cultural Encounters in the Arab World: On Media, the Modern and the Everyday* (London: I.B.Tauris).

—— (ed.) (2012) *Arab Cultural Studies: Mapping the Field* (London: I.B.Tauris).

Said, Edward (2000) 'Traveling Theory Reconsidered', in *Reflections on Exile and Other Literary and Cultural Essays* (London: Granta Books).

de Saussure, Ferdinand (1974) 'Course in General Linguistics', in Charles Bally and Albert Sechehaye (eds) *From Notes on Saussure's Lectures (1901–1911)*, trans. Wade Baskin (London: Fontana).

Thornton, Sarah (1995) *Club Cultures: Music, Media and Subcultural Capital* (Cambridge: Polity Press).

Zubaida, Sami (2010) 'Cosmopolitans, Nationalists and Fundamentalists in the Modern Middle East', in *Beyond Islam: A New Understanding of the Middle East* (London: I.B.Tauris).

1

Hatha al-shibl min dhak al-Asad

Would-be Arab Youth Studies and the Revival of 'Subculture'

Ramy Aly

In aesthetic terms, Cairo's contemporary urban landscape is a mix of dystopia and brutalism. Among the most common things that one encounters in this decidedly modern landscape are the countless miles of concrete and red brick walls encircling empty plots of land, military compounds, syndicate social clubs, embassies, gated communities, state buildings and government facilities.

In recent years, the taste for walls as the corporeal means through which hierarchies of access are regulated and signified has made its way into the dilapidated streets of downtown Cairo. The waves of protest that have gripped the centre of the city since 2011 have spawned a maze of concrete block walls which now criss-cross Garden City and Qasr al-Aini to protect the parliament, the Ministry of the Interior and the British and American embassies. The walls are reminiscent of the coastal defences that purport to thwart the sea's relentless attempts to consume and redefine the terra firma that provides us with ontological certainty. Like the sea, Egyptian protestors of all shades have shown little deference towards these attempts to regulate and control change.

On 18 November 2011, the military police and central security forces evicted protestors from Tahrir Square using disproportionate force, leading to a number of deaths and hundreds of injuries. On 19 November, 42 young Egyptians lost their lives, tens of others lost their eyes, and hundreds more were injured as protestors confronted the security forces on Mohammed Mahmud Street. The first wall in Egypt's very own 'Green Zone' was erected on Mohammed Mahmud Street to protect the hated Ministry of the Interior headquarters.[1] The following month, just metres away from Tahrir Square and Mohammed Mahmud Street, a peaceful sit-in outside the Cabinet Office was forcibly cleared, with scores of protesters beaten and arrested (16 December 2011).[2] Once again, young people refused to accept state-sanctioned violence and there were deaths and injuries, as military police officers hurled broken floor tiles and furniture from the roof of the ten-storey Cabinet Office building onto protesters on the ground, cracking countless skulls and revelling in their impunity by urinating onto protestors on the ground below. Three people were killed on the first day, the clashes around the parliament building and the Cabinet Office led to the construction of two more walls at the intersection of El Sheikh Rihan Street and Qasr al-Aini, but not before four more people had lost their lives and up to 2,000 were seriously injured.[3]

Within hours of the fighting subsiding around the concrete walls, street artists had painted one of the walls with a yellow and black smiley face, the iconic image of the late 1980s acid house and rave scenes in London and New York.[4]

What was this sign doing in Cairo at this time, and in that place? Could the authorial intentions and designs of the street artists who adorned the wall with this sign do anything to control the multiple meanings, places, people and references with which the smiley face is encrypted? Chris Sullivan, one of London's acid house pioneers, recalls that:

> The first version of the Smiley face we now know was designed by the freelance artist Harvey Ball (who earned $45 for the job) in 1963. He created it for the State Life Assurance Company, who used it as a badge to boost the morale of their workforce. By 1971, more than 50 million Smiley badges had been sold in the US, while in the UK it was adopted by the Windsor Free Rock Festival in 1972 [...] the first person I saw with a Smiley t-shirt was Barnzley Armitage, now co-designer of 'A Child Of The Jago' label with Vivienne Westwood's son, Joe Corré, who wore it as an ironic nod to the Summer of Love in '67.[5]

Figure 1 The 'smiley face' on the zoning wall at the intersection of El Sheikh Rihan Street and Qasr al-Aini, downtown Cairo, December 2011
Source: Photograph by the author

From the brief semiotic genealogy offered by Sullivan, we see the smiley beginning its life as a charm for white-collar human resource management, moving its way through the mainstream, counterculture, subculture and club culture scenes, through music, fashion and lifestyle, to appear in Cairo in the throes of revolt, carrying a similar but different message under quite different existential circumstances. To quote the late Stuart Hall: 'Its signification is rich and richly ambiguous: certainly unstable.'[6]

The smiley face is a sign that has been reiterated across time, space and context. Each time it is deployed it carries with it a situated authorial intention, and yet its past meanings can never be silenced, and the unforeseen meanings that it will come to represent can never be foreclosed.[7] Like much street art in Egypt, the smiley face staring out in the direction of Tahrir Square survived for only a few weeks: it quickly fell prey to what Mona Abaza describes as the 'Professional Whiteners'[8] of the local municipality, whose orders I understand in terms of '*sous rature*' in a Heiddegerian and Derridean sense, where the act of crossing something out on a page is intended to suppress meaning by the threat of deletion, and yet it acts only to reinforce its ambivalence.[9] The 'true' meaning behind the smiley face on the Qasr al-Aini wall is extraneous to some extent. It was undeniably sardonic, but encrypted with an anxiety, the tragic loss of life that had created the canvas for its own manifestation. Some may have considered it to be a blasé affront to the sanctity of human sacrifice for the sake of emancipation. More straightforwardly, others may have seen it as a monument to the victory of protesters over the security forces, who were forced to retreat behind a concrete wall. In my mind, I had made the link between the image and the tumultuous debates around subculture and post-subculture analysis: that this act of meaning-making could not be erased.

I take little comfort from that situated act of meaning-making, for it only emphasises the sometimes fanciful intellectual indulgences that we entertain. It is only in the eye of the decadent and privileged transnational subject or scholar that the smiley face on the Qasr al-Aini wall reads as the proverbial middle finger pointed by youth club culture at Thatcherism and Reaganism. Indeed, I must be careful not to forget that I have emphasised one use and interpretation of this sign at the expense of others, in part because of my own sensorium and because of a deep-seated intuition that signification and aesthetics can constitute resistance. The desire to find a coherent connection or an authentic, original meaning is, in itself, misleading. As Hall reminds us, the desire to fix meaning is the work of power and ideology,[10] and lest we forget as a group of professional interpreters of culture, we are implicated in both. Sometimes we 'trip the light fantastic', seeking evidence for the meta-narratives of power and resistance that reflect our politics, or provide moral justification for our careers.

One wonders what the smiley face on the Qasr al-Aini wall might have meant to the underpaid and overworked souls who were ordered to paint over it, or the shopkeepers whose businesses have suffocated because of the zoning walls on which the smiley and other street art (which we valorise) have been painted. There is little doubt in my mind that the cultural references I cite here to locate this fleeting sign are not shared by my neighbours in Cairo's Green Zone.

The transient smiley face on the Qasr al-Aini wall should be seen cartographically in relation to the other walls in its vicinity. Only 100 metres away is Mohammed Mahmud Street where, for two years, the walls were painted with the smiling faces of the revolution's martyrs. Their renditions sat alongside those of one-eyed protester-witnesses whose eyes were gouged out by buckshot fired from police rifles, and the mangled faces of those tortured and beaten to death by Egypt's security forces. The walls of Mohammed Mahmud were one of the few places in Cairo where the visual memory of the revolution's fallen was publicly recognised and preserved by young artists. After numerous attempts by the authorities to literally whitewash Mohammed Mahmud's walls, they acquiesced to the inevitability and persistence of those images of remembrance. When the images of the fallen were painted over, they were replaced only with the images of those newly-murdered and lost, layering the wall with further meanings.

The new faces were a poignant reminder of the processual nature and human cost of social and political change across the region which, in its numerous waves and manifestations, has made a mockery of the 'Arab Spring', 'Islamist Winter' and post-uprising analyses that impose the terms through which change should be framed and evaluated. Indeed, just at the moment when I (and no doubt, many others) became attached to those images of remembrance on Mohammed Mahmoud, canonising them, inserting them into grand schemes of aesthetic resistance, they were painted over by iconoclastic street artists who see these walls as public newspapers, and not as consecrated genres, renditions or spaces.

Originally I had intended my contribution to this volume to be one in which I would confidently analyse street art, football gangs and revolutionary pop music, but in truth I was not able to move beyond the implications of the smiley face on the Qasr al-Aini wall. While some will consider the account I have provided thus far to be anecdotal, I see it as allegorical in the way that it exposes the productive problems of writing about the politics of youth culture in the Arab world at a critical historical juncture.

Pseudo-presentism and the historicisation of the revolution

Across the Arab world, modes and implications of resistance, change and continuity unfold abruptly. The assertion some make that Tunisia, Bahrain, Egypt, Libya and Yemen are somehow 'post-uprising' seems woefully short-sighted, underpinned by a kind of political normativity so powerful that it refuses to acknowledge the struggle that continues to fill the streets of Cairo, Sana'a, Tunis, Manama, Tripoli and other cities across the region, with militia, protesters, riot police and paramilitary forces – as though what young people were trying to unseat were simply the regime figureheads, and not the entirety, of the socio-economic, cultural and political regimes in which they remain a subordinated majority. (I seem to lack the aptitudes required for the kind of instantaneous scholarship that quickly fell like precipitation on the 'Arab Spring'. Saying something meaningful about youth politics and social change in the Arab world creates a fear in me that I associate with Derrida's introspective fear of writing.[11] It is for good reason that I have this fear, for we may recall how Foucault's writings on the Iranian revolution were among his most impassioned, political and yet arguably his most botched.[12])

Today, I believe that those of us interested in Arab youth cultures are in a similar position to Foucault in 1968 and 1978. Pickett suggests that Foucault's understanding of transgression and the politics of resistance changed over three distinct but interrelated phases.[13] The events of May 1968 in France forced Foucault to think about the materiality and physicality of revolt and revolution. In *Language Counter-memory, Practice*[14] he argues that one of the strengths of May 1968 was that people exercised 'a power which did not assume the form of hierarchical organisation'.[15] This has quite a clear resonance in relation to the ostensibly 'leaderless' revolts in Egypt, Libya, Syria, Tunisia, Yemen and, to a lesser extent, Bahrain. Foucault's conception of power and resistance seem more reflective of the dynamics of change and continuity that we see not only in the Arab world, but more broadly in the process of social change. Contrary to commonly held belief, there is no sense in Foucault's work that resistance is futile; simply that his celebration of struggle is not punctuated with either a universal or local utopian end point – it is continuous. In *The History of Sexuality*, Foucault's scheme of 'local struggle' does not discount the possibility of the 'massive ruptures and binary divisions' that characterise revolution but, instead, sees the revolution itself as an exceptional and passing culmination of more prevalent and quotidian 'mobile and transitory points of resistance' that constantly make, fracture and remould both individuals and collectivities: 'the swarm of points of resistance traverses social stratifications and individual unities. And it is doubtless the strategic codification of these points of resistance that makes a revolution possible.'[16]

McKay has argued that the moments of the political radicalisation of young people should be seen as the beginning, and not the end, of the strategies of resistance.[17] Recognising the problems with such an assertion, if taken literally, McKay draws our attention to Esler's reading of youth resistance, which emphasises the dialectics of change and continuity of these forms over time:

> Practically everything that our insurrectionary youth have tried – from New-Left militancy to hippie style withdrawal from society, from the campus revolt to the commune movement – has been tried before. The crucial importance of the Youth revolution of our times lies not in its alleged uniqueness, but in that very continuity with history which 'the Movement' itself – and most of its critics – have so vehemently denied.[18]

Esler perceptibly diagnoses an age-old problem: namely, the way in which youth movements, their establishment critics and (we might add) their establishment advocates engage in a type of cultural solipsism, where the phenomenological and existential 'nowness' of struggle silences the historicity of power and resistance as an ongoing dynamic in societies.

In recent years, interest in Arab youth cultures has experienced a surge that is inextricably linked to the way in which young people in Bahrain, Egypt, Libya, Tunisia, Syria and Yemen have engaged in political protest and direct action that gave rise to widespread protest movements demanding political change and social justice. Young people across the Arab world have reacted to authoritarianism and inequality in novel ways, not limiting themselves to the 'imagined' or 'magical' semiotic and stylistic solutions of working-class subcultures, or to the campaigning and alternative lifestyles of middle-class countercultures and protest movements.

One of the most notable aspects of the first phase of the uprising in Egypt in January and February 2011 was the way that young people who were associated with subculture and counterculture groups – based on leisure, music, art and rights campaigning – converged with professional syndicates and trade unions, and subsequently were joined by members of the public to create a sustained momentum that galvanised a set of political, economic and social demands. I would argue that the young middle-class politicos who articulated the rejection of human rights abuses and corruption, the spectacle and carnival of protest that football 'ultras' (ultra-fanatical supporters) bought to demonstrations, the visual expressions of street artists, the folk, pop, rock and rap music that was produced or performed to reflect the uprising, and the strikes and support of both working- and middle-class syndicates were decisive in drawing in ordinary members of the public. Such members of the public were provided with a space in which they could express their rejection of authoritarianism, state violence, corruption and inequality on placards, in paintings, songs, installations, poems and chants. Indeed, thousands of people, both young and old, women and men, poor, destitute and affluent, those with long hair, short hair, beards, ripped jeans, piercings, veils, tattoos, *jellabiyas*, engaged in aesthetic and semiotic resistance to the status quo, and confronted the apparatus of the militarised Egyptian police state and paid for it with their lives and limbs – not only during the famous 18 days,[19] but also during the rule of the Supreme Council of the Armed Forces, the Muslim Brotherhood and, now, against the Sisi regime.

'Subculture lite' and the politics of resistance

For those who would strike a more sceptical chord in response to the uprisings since December 2010, we can say at the very least that young people and the cultures that they live through have played a tangible role in disrupting the status quo in their respective societies; and that their social, political and cultural praxis increasingly point to processes of social change in those societies that we cannot fully appreciate yet. While the connections between youth cultures and social change in the Arab world may be increasingly apparent, the theoretical tools that we have to understand youth cultures seem most strained. Post-subculturalists, for example, argue that the theoretical schemes postulated by the various generations and shades of youth culture scholars, such as 'subculture', 'club cultures' and 'neo-tribes', fall short of offering adequate explanations for contemporary politicised youth formations.[20] Indeed, without reformulation and recontextualisation, those theories and schemes are equally ill-suited for explaining contemporary youth movements in the Arab world (be they leisure or ideologically based), or the ways in which they interact and intersect. Blackman reminds us that as early as the late 1950s, Robert Merton argued that the attempts to study the politics of youth culture should only be considered as 'intermediate theory', in other words, while they drew upon grand theories they were grounded in everyday life.[21]

There is no such thing as Arab Youth Studies as yet, but it could not be more pressing as an area of research and theorisation. Youth Studies emerged from the Cultural Studies literature of the Birmingham School which, Hall argues:

> provided answers to the long process of Britain's decline as a world superpower. It also investigated the impact of modem mass consumption and modern mass society; the Americanisation of our culture; the postwar expansion of the new means of mass communication; the birth of the youth cultures; the exposure of the settled habits and conventions and languages of an old class culture to the disturbing fluidity of new money and new social relationships; the dilution of the United Kingdom's very homogeneous social population by the influx of peoples from the new Commonwealth.[22]

I would argue that the Arab world is experiencing a similar historical watershed: that the uprisings, revolts and revolutions that have gripped the region since December 2010 herald and signal rapid social and cultural change in a similar way to what Hall describes in postwar Britain. While the homogeneity of British society was altered by the arrival of migrants, the homogeneity of Arab societies has been altered by the demise of authoritarian regimes, which has obliged people (in those places where uprisings are taking place, and those where they have not) to take stock of the broad range of political persuasions and interests – regional, ethnic, gendered, sectarian, ideological and generational grievances – that exist in their respective societies, and which can no longer be brushed under the carpet or quelled by the homogenising force of authoritarianism. Perhaps the first question one would need to ask the would-be 'Arab Youth Studies' is whether hegemonic structures within each nation state, and in the region as a whole, have been satisfactorily theorised in terms of their relationship to youth cultures. American Youth Culture Studies, which developed from the Chicago School, have emphasised the notion of generation; while British Cultural Studies have been informed by Marxist, Gramscian and Althusserian understandings of social stratification, hegemony and the media. What, then, of the long-awaited 'Arab Youth Studies'?

If, as the title of this chapter suggests, the relationship between a would-be Arab Youth Studies and Anglophile Youth Studies is fittingly captured by the Arabic adage, '*Hatha al-Shibl min dhak al-Asad*' ('This cub is the offspring of that lion'), then the least we owe ourselves – and the subjects of our research – is a more robust account which does not assume that the insights provided by these two traditions in Youth Studies (the Chicago and Birmingham schools), grounded in both their respective epistemological traditions and historical contexts, can be unproblematically transposed across time and context to the Arab world in the early twenty-first century.

The conceptual debate in Anglophile Youth Studies is both healthy and full of contestation in the search for meaningful terms, grounded concepts and theoretical schemes. It is a field that is acutely aware of the need to constantly rethink, recontextualise and substantiate the theoretical ground that it claims. It is very rare to read any account of Arab youth cultures that substantively builds on the wide array of new readings of youth formations in the growing subcultural corpus. Instead, a 'subcultures lite' approach is quite common, lexically devoted to early CCCS terminology such as 'struggle', 'resistance', 'challenge', 'transcend', 'rework', 'adapt', 'reappropriate', 'reclaim', 'protect', 'preserve' and 'defend'.[23] While these terms and concepts are powerful and relevant, they can become generic rhetorical devices that create a rather overburdened notion of cultural resistance that often appears routinised and Delphic.

Scholarship tends to covet and celebrate resistance wherever it is palpable. For example, recent literature in Arab Media and Cultural Studies suggests that popular culture in the Middle East and North Africa is 'a form of cultural resistance against different forms of global and local domination'.[24] We also find that contemporary youth cultures, such as Arab and Muslim heavy metal and rap, are becoming the 'sites of subcultural and even countercultural production' and 'resistance'.[25] We may add to this the literature that highlights the way in which national, and sometimes nationalist, cultures can be forms of resistance to hegemonic cultural imperialism or colonialism.[26] These readings each have a legitimate place in our understanding of Arab history, culture and society, but they also suggest that we need to insert resistance into some kind of scheme, lest it become everything but also nothing, everywhere but also nowhere. Much like its nemesis, power, resistance has become 'a magic word'.[27]

For its part, anthropology has struggled with the concept of resistance since the 1970s. As Brown and Seymour argue,[28] 'resistance' was the successor of a more longstanding debate on agency, particularly on the part of Anthropologists who are concerned with Marxist or Gramscian readings of structural power.[29] Seymour[30] recounts how the desire to emphasise agency in anthropological and 'resistance studies' gave way to critiques by Abu-Lughod, who argued that scholarship tended to romanticise resistance.[31] Kellner, who lamented the way in which resistance is fetishised,[32] and Ortner, who argued that 'thin description' in the study of resistance seemed unable to rigorously account for consciousness, subjectivity, intentionality and identity.[33]

In an early response to the emergence of a CCCS orthodoxy, Stanley Cohen argued that imputing a heroic and resistive nature to subcultures as a whole seemed to ignore many of their problematic and troubling features and practices, such as sexual exploitation, racism, homophobia and, sometimes, wanton violence. Cohen argues that there was an impulse among CCCS scholars to interpret encoded and concealed meaning at the expense of surface meaning, and often to impute 'opposition' and 'resistance' uncritically to subcultural signification, discourses and practices.[34] Furthermore, the reading of working-class youth subcultures as being leisure-based, 'magical' and 'imagined' solutions, meant that it was often difficult to see how spectacular subcultures confronted the material structures of subordination. The result was a strained notion of resistance through style and leisure ritual.

Subcultures: the semiotic, ideological and quotidian

Cohen argued that the type of semiotic analysis which early subculture studies relied on was more suited to the analysis of art than to the analysis of life. Although there are intimate connections between art and life, and media and youth cultures, there seems to be a persistent slippage that makes, for example, Arab media studies synonymous with Arab Youth Studies and with Arab Cultural Studies more broadly. Hesmondhalgh suggests that the slippage which makes Youth Culture Studies and Popular Music Studies one and the same is flawed: the two disciplines, he argues, should be allowed to go their own way.[35] Hall goes so far as to say that:

> [W]hat matters is *not* the intrinsic or historically fixed objects of culture, but the state of play in cultural relations: to put in bluntly and in an oversimplified form – what counts is the class struggle in and over time.[36]

Fundamentally, the subcultures literature does not analyse style, music and art simply for their own sake, but because they say something about the dynamics within the superstructure, both local and global. We should always be conscious that Cultural Studies was a foundation stone for the New Left.[37]

Many of Cohen's early misgivings about how youth cultures are analysed still ring true today. He felt that the principal weaknesses of the CCCS paradigm was that its mode of analysis revealed little about how subcultures were lived, how people came to them and left them, and how those subcultures were related to consumption and the mainstream. His critique suggested that the principal problem was a lack of ethnographic engagement on the part of subculturalists. Indeed, we are some way away from asking questions such as: 'What is life after subculture like for young people in the Arab world?', or 'What is straight-edge culture in the Arab world?'[38]

As Marchart demonstrates, the rethinking of subculture analysis has challenged the assumption that subcultures act counter-hegemonically simply by virtue of their assumed position in relation to the dominant. What Marchart describes as the 'incorporation myth' is based fundamentally on the expression of authentic aesthetic resistance by marginalised and subordinated groups in relation to a dominant and cannibalistic mainstream. Often, the extent of collaboration and interdependence between subcultures and big business – or cultural imperialism – is underestimated.[39] In fact, in places such as Egypt, music and art-based subcultures are extremely reliant on commercial sponsorship, or on funding from international grant-making bodies. There is nothing new about this, as Hall put it: 'Today's rebel folk singer ends up tomorrow on the cover of the *Observer* colour magazine.'[40] Simplistic distinctions between subculture and the mainstream rely on a register of terms such as 'dominant' and 'subordinated', 'underground' and 'mainstream', which potentially say more about the paradigms that we prefer than about the lived experiences that we consider our 'evidence'. As Marchart suggests, a close reading of Hebdige, for example, shows that his account does not easily slip into an idealisation of youth culture. Hebdige recognises that to some extent, subculture groups 'stand on a common ideological ground with the dominant culture: they speak a language commonly available at that time'.[41] Indeed, Hall goes on to advocate a form of neo-Gramscianism, where high and popular culture are mutually constitutive, and not straightforwardly a case of the blunting of authentic working-class popular culture by a hegemonic high culture.[42]

Subcultures, countercultures and the problem of cultural translation

This brings me to a point that I find difficult to resolve. Quite understandably, scholarly interest is often drawn to 'spectacular subcultures', which involve a small number of cultural innovators who produce 'authentic subcultures'. However, Clark argued that focusing on the innovatory moments of subcultural production has produced a teleological, class-based analysis.[43] Of course, we need research on emos, online communities, metalheads, rappers, techno music, breakdancers and the like, as these forms and styles become more discernable and prominent among young people in the region. However, we should be wary that these locally appropriated forms are not locally innovated or authentic, and should consider what implications these might have for the use of schemes such as 'subculture'. In her discussion of rap in France, Huq, for example, argues from a post-subcultures perspective that 'the adoption and adaptation of various prima-facie US musical styles' in other countries, challenges 'the assumed American hegemony in youth culture'.[44] Her formulation is a clear departure from the Marxist and Gramscian formulations that have influenced Youth Culture Studies, on the one hand, and panics around cultural imperialism and monocultures, on the other. However, before we throw the CCCS baby out with the bathwater, perhaps we could consider whether the adoption of these musical styles in the Arab world is in fact the best evidence for consensual hegemony, and that perhaps what these Arabised forms might be are the double-consciousness of hegemony: the evidence of its necessary gaps and incompleteness. In the Arab world, subcultures are not party to exactly the same kinds or intensity of commodification and normalisation, as they may now be in parts of the world where 'deviant styles [have become] safe, suburban, normalised [and where] subcultural presence is now taken for granted [...] a useful function for capitalism [or] positively commercial'.[45] As Brown lucidly argues, punk is not dead: it has been stripped of its stylistic and semiotic powers to stand for anarchy; now, its authenticity is not in hairstyles, clothes or even music, but in ideology and praxis.[46]

Mafessoli has argued that contemporary youth formations are about a particular 'ambience', which he tried to capture by suggesting that they were 'neo-tribes' informed by dispositions, tastes, attitudes and states of mind, and not a rigid or bounded subcultural structure.[47] The concept has been popular among post-subculturalists and those who read youth cultures in the contexts of diaspora, globalisation and post-modernity. Andy Bennett argues that the concept of the neo-tribe allows for 'new understandings of how and why young people are bought together in collective affiliation'.[48] He argues that some youth formations come together on the basis of both local and globally driven aesthetics, orientations towards taste and issues while, at the same time, being engaged in overtly political ways in the process of social critique and change.[49] However, Hesmondhalgh rejects the move to underplay the process of boundary-making in youth culture formations, retorting that even if CCCS subculturalists have overstated the boundedness and integrity of subcultural groups,

> instability and temporariness as alternatives does not get us very far [...] We need to know how boundaries are constituted, not simply that they are fuzzier than various writers have assumed. And confusingly, 'tribes' carries very strong connotations of precisely the kind of fixity and rigidity that Bennett is troubled by in the work of the subculturalists.[50]

In short, the concept of the neo-tribe does *not* assume that youth formations are formed exclusively by structural inequalities. While social axes of power, like class, 'race', gender and religion, may inform how and why young people come together, it does not necessarily define it. What role, if any, do such readings and theoretical reorientations play in the way that Arab youth cultures are analysed?

Maintaining and developing the established subcultures literature is important in light of their persistence, bifurcation, de-territorialisation, appropriation, politicisation and commodification. They may be subject now to different structural processes, but that is a part of their story, not their passing. Thus, the periodisation and theorisation of subcultures and countercultures is fundamental if we are to avoid the flattening of these groups, ideas and forms. Seeing the connections between subcultures and countercultures over time is vital.

We need to ask what connections exist between the Arab youth formations, movements, subcultures, the countercultures of today and the past. For example, a cursory consideration of the Egyptian student movement shows that rebellions and uprisings at campuses and schools have taken place throughout the twentieth century: as part of the 1919 revolution; against British occupation in 1935; through the strikes, hunger strikes and violent clashes of 1946, when Egyptian secondary school and university students protested against British colonialism, in response to the violent repression of student activism on the part of the Nokrashi government, and in sympathy with Palestine and Indonesia. Egyptian students rose up against the Nasser regime in 1968, rebelled against President Anwar Sadat in 1972, and continued their struggles for social equality, freedom and employment throughout the 1970s and 1980s.[51] That long-standing tradition of radicalism and resistance continues to this day, not just passing through January 2011 and June 2013, but continuing in university campuses all over Egypt, where students continue to defy the hypernationalist and militaristic fascism of Egypt's second transitional period.

What about Egypt's blue-collar culture, which has produced thousands of worker actions since 2011, and has a collective cultural and organisational history that dates back to the Port Said strikes of 1894,[52] that has resisted the exploitation of colonial capitalism, authoritarian populism and neoliberal capitalism. There seems nothing more urgent to an Egyptian youth cultures research agenda than a deeper understanding of the interconnections between the cultures of the military, Islamists, state bureaucrats and employees and urban elites; how young people are implicated in these and youth cultures are affected by them. Arguably, we make poor use of the neo-Gramscian turn in Cultural Studies if we overlook these omissions within scholarship.

It is not simply whether what we find in contemporary Arab youth cultures are subcultures, countercultures, neo-tribes, substreams or subchannels and so on, but whether the combination of events and dynamics in which youth formations, expressions and movements are unfolding within the Arab world warrant a new set of terms and approaches that reflect and relate the specificities of those contexts. The subculture literature offers an interpretive paradigm in the making: one that has an established theoretical terrain, a robust corrective critique and, more recently, a post-subcultural turn. The changes that are taking place in the Arab world in its different regional, national, urban and rural contexts offer an opportunity to engage with that literature more forcefully – to rethink subculture, counterculture, aesthetics, politics, resistance and praxis. Importantly, these reformulations need to do more than to aspire to explain social change and social structure in the region; they need to relate that analysis through a lexicon which has local resonance and meaning.

While scholarship on Arab youth is scattered across a broad range of disciplines, it has yet to see itself as Youth Studies. Perhaps it need not – or should not – seek to mirror the same path that Cultural Studies have in Anglophile scholarship. However, much as we try to suppress it or differ from it, the question of cultural time in Arab Cultural Studies will continue to rear its head. Sabry asks: 'To what cultural time is Arab Cultural Studies contributing? Whose time? How does it define its own time? Is it a hybrid-post-modern cultural time? Is it concerned with the present time? The past?'[53] Here, I return to Stuart Hall's reflection on the field that he helped to establish:

> Cultural studies, wherever it exists, reflects the rapidly shifting ground of thought and knowledge, argument and debate, about a society and about its own culture. It is an activity of intellectual self-reflection. It operates both inside and outside the academy. Indeed, it represents something of the weakening of the traditional boundaries among the disciplines, and of the growth of forms of interdisciplinary research that don't easily fit, or can't be contained, within the confines of the existing divisions of knowledge. As such, it inevitably represents a point of disturbance, a place of necessary tension and change in at least two senses. First, cultural studies constitutes one of the points of tension and change at the frontiers of intellectual and academic life, pushing for new questions, new models, and new ways of study, testing the fine lines between intellectual rigour and social relevance. It is the sort of necessary irritant in the shell of academic life that one hopes will, sometime in the future, produce new pearls of wisdom.[54]

In these words, Hall provides interdisciplinary fluidity, but I am haunted equally by the feeling that as it stands, the would-be Arab Youth Studies do not facilitate 'argument and debate about a society and about its own culture' – it does not involve 'intellectual self-reflection', and is far from finding a balance 'between intellectual rigour and social relevance'. Perhaps I am being too unforgiving, perhaps even self-flagellating; but Arab Cultural Studies and a would-be Arab Youth Studies must subject themselves to the same kind of reflexive scrutiny that has created productive debates about the means and methods through which knowledge is generated in other fields.

Today, it is almost beyond dispute that the study of youth cultures and the politics of resistance in the Arab world are fuelled by a fraught mixture of interests. While this is the result of a primary intellectual and pedagogic engagement on the part of diasporic Arab scholars and area specialists of different shades, Arab Youth Studies are driven by careers at universities, institutes, research centres and development agencies that are conjoined with the neoliberal global centre. The fortunes of this area of research are attributable in part to 'Arab Spring fever' (albeit a fickle one) in the West and the thematic priorities of Western philanthropic donors, research councils, grant-making bodies and development agencies, who make much of the research and activism on and in the region possible. It might be 'overdetermined', as Hebdige recalls in his retrospective on writing *Subculture: The Meaning of Style*, 30 years after its publication:

> *Subculture* was thrown together on the run between 1977 and 1978 with events (e.g. UK punk) haphazardly unfolding and the publication deadline ominously descending so that, far from being freely chosen at leisure, the conceptual architecture of the book, such as it is – rickety, ramshackle, heterogeneous – was 'over-determined', as they used to say in the 1970s, at every turn by the context and the circumstances in which it was written.[55]

Accounting for the circumstances in which knowledge is produced is an important reality check. It forces one to ask searching questions of one's own implication in the encroachment of hegemonic structures and means on scholarship, the emic and etic features of representation and, perhaps most troubling of all, the issue of translation and audience.

Conclusion

Beyond diasporic Arab Cultural Studies: towards a double critique

In our own Anglophile, francophone, post-modern and transnational way, a significant proportion of the intellectual cohort that constitutes Arab Cultural Studies and Arab Youth Studies is itself a transnational counterculture with authentic, radical, resistive potential: that is, subject to a hegemonic order, a subaltern status, incorporation, codification and commodification. Our analytic lexicon remains largely untranslatable to our peers in Arabic academia, or to those whose resistance we claim to capture and represent. As Abu Lughod has suggested, there are no easy solutions to the dilemmas of multiple audiences.[56] However, it seems that much contemporary commentary and scholarship on the region is free from any such dilemmatic unease about its audience. Research is simply published in English or French for an overwhelmingly Western academic audience that needs to know, understand, track and trace the changes in the Orient. Whether our research becomes available to our peers at universities in the Arab world, or indeed to the communities, groups and subcultures that give so generously of their time and lives, seems of little concern.

I have no shame in recalling and disclosing the countless moments and clunky conversation at conferences and workshops on Arab Cultural Studies and Youth Studies, where the collective powers of articulation and expression of those present struggles to think of the mainstream, public spheres, subcultures, countercultures, space and time in Arabic. This is not simply an issue of translation, for there are translations of our proceedings and work that are as alienating to their authors as they must be to a more general audience. When I think about what scholarship is being produced, by whom and in relation to what kind of intellectual paradigms, I often feel (and I do not exclude myself) that the field is better described as 'disaporic Arab Cultural Studies'. Those of us trained and employed in Europe and North America or at Western universities in the Arab world, who think and write in English or French, understand each other, but struggle to be understood by the object of our research: 'the Arab world'.

Following Khatibi,[57] Sabry argues for *naqd muzdawa,j* (double-critique), as a way to break out of the prevailing historicist/Marxist, rationalist/structuralist and salafist/*turatheya* (traditional) positions which dominate Arab thought on Arab cultural modernity.[58] The strength of the double critique is its rejection of identity, and the way that it assumes a position of difference in relation to culture and modernity. What I am arguing here is that we must embellish the double-critique with a reflexive moment where we question the consequences of our implication in the political economy of 'Western' scholarship on the Arab world, and ask searching questions about the continuing inaccessibility of, and inability to translate, our literature for the silent Arab apparition that is both our subject and object, our self and other.

In conclusion, I return full circle to the initial problem which I alluded to in the discussion of the smiley face on the Qasr al-Aini wall: what are the terms of reference for a would-be Arab Youth Studies? What kind of analysis and representations can be produced within the current political economy of scholarship on the Arab world? How can a would-be Arab Youth Studies become more grounded in the debates and arguments that are taking place within the Arab world? Sometimes, historical circumstances warrant a radical rethinking of the prevailing epistemologies and modes of representation – an attempt to forge a hermeneutics that would be useful in articulating Arab subcultures. This neither involves a complete break with the past, nor the illusion that a would-be Arab Youth Culture Studies can easily innovate an entirely decolonised, local approach that facilitates the kind of broader social engagement that Cultural Studies and Youth Studies has had in Australia, the UK and the US. That literature is the basis of our current understanding, and it is enormously rich and complex. Engaged and self-conscious Arab Youth Culture Studies have much to offer that literature about the most recent episodes in the broader human experience with cultures of resistance. At the very least, those writing about Arab youth at this time must engage with the challenge of historicising youth movements and subcultures, must look for the connections and parallels that these youth formations have with movements and forms of the past; and must look at – but also around and beyond – spectacular subcultures; must articulate both the resistive and the more ominous practices; and account for how these are implicated in local and global processes. Perhaps most importantly, a would-be Arab Youth Studies must aspire to produce accounts, representations and forms of public engagement that are accessible beyond Anglophile academia.

Notes

1 Jack Shenker (2011), 'Egyptians Return to Tahrir Square to Protect against Military Junta', *Guardian*, 18 November. Available at www.theguardian.com/world/2011/nov/18/egyptians-return-tahrir-square-protest (accessed 11 April 2016).
2 Ahram Online and Ahmed Feteha (2011) 'Egypt Military Attcks Occupy Cabinet Protestors: Updates from the Day', *Ahram Daily*, 16 December. Available at http://english.ahram.org.eg/NewsContent/1/64/29489/Egypt/Politics-/Egypt-military-attacks-Occupy-Cabinet-protesters-U.aspx (accessed 11 April 2016).
3 Mostafa Sheshtawy (2011) 'Two Dead, Over 170 Injured in Bloody Crackdown on Cabinet Sit-in', *Daily News Egypt*, 16 December. Available at http://www.dailynewsegypt.com/2011/12/16/1-dead-over-100-injured-in-bloody-crackdown-on-cabinet-sit-in/ (accessed 11 April 2016).
4 At least that is what it looked like to me – but then again I was on the cusp of teenagehood and living in London when the smiley face burst onto the cultural scene, signalling amphetamine-fuelled youthful abandon, escapism and hedonism.

5 Chris Sullivan (2011) 'Smiley Culture: The Symbiotic Relationship between Acid and the Smiley Face', *Red Bull Music Academy*, 13 December. Available at www.redbullmusicacademy.com/magazine/smiley-culture-rave-feature (accessed 10 September 2014).
6 Stuart Hall (1998) 'Notes on Deconstructing the Popular', in John Storey (ed.) *Cultural Theory and Popular Culture: A Reader* (London: Prentice Hall), pp. 442–53, p. 451.
7 Jacques Derrida (1982) *Margins of Philosophy* (Chicago, IL: University of Chicago Press) pp. 93–103.
8 Mona Abaza (2012) 'Walls, Segregating Downtown Cairo and the Mohammed Mahmud Street Graffiti', *Theory Culture and Society* 30(1): 122–39, p. 125.
9 Jacques Derrida (1998[1967]) *Of Grammatology*, trans. Gayatri Spivak (Baltimore, MD: Johns Hopkins University Press).
10 Stuart Hall (1997) *Representation: Cultural Representations and Signifying Practices* (London: Sage Publications).
11 *Derrida* (dir. Kirby Dick and Amy Ziering, 2003).
12 Janet Afray and Kevin Anderson (2005) *Foucault and the Iranian Revolution* (Urbana, IL: University of Chicago Press).
13 Brent L. Pickett (1996) 'Foucault and the Politics of Resistance', *Polity* 28 (4): 445–66.
14 Michel Foucault (1977) *Language Counter-memory, Practice* (Ithaca, NY: Cornell University Press).
15 Pickett, 'Foucault and the Politics of Resistance', p. 456.
16 Michel Foucault (1978) *The History of Sexuality*, trans. Robert Hurley (New York: Random House), p. 96.
17 George McKay (1996) *Senseless Acts of Beauty: Cultures of Resistance Since the Sixties* (London: Verso).
18 Anthony Esler (1972) *Bombs, Beards and Barricades: 150 Years of Youth in Revolt* (New York: Stein & Day Publishers). p. 7.
19 The first 18 days of the revolution, starting on 25 January 2011 until 11 February, when Vice-President Omar Suleiman announced Mubarak's resignation as president, and handing over power to the Supreme Council of the Armed Forces.
20 David Muggleton and Rupert Weinzierl (2003) *The Post-Subcultures Reader* (New York: Berg), p. 14.
21 Shane Blackman (2005) 'Youth Subcultural Theory: A Critical Engagement with the Concept, its Origins and Politics, from the Chicago School to Postmodernism', *Journal of Youth Studies* 8(1): 1–20, p. 2.
22 Stuart Hall (1992) 'Race, Culture and Communications: Looking Backward and Forward at Cultural Studies', *Rethinking Marxism* 5(1): 10–18, p. 11.
23 Stanley Cohen (1997[1980]) 'Symbols of Trouble', in Ken Gelder (ed.) *The Subcultures Reader* (Hove: Psychology Press), p. 154.
24 Walid El-Hamamsy and Munira Soliman (2013) *Popular Culture in the Middle East and North Africa: A Postcolonial Outlook* (New York: Routledge), p. 7.

25 See Mark LeVine (2008) *Heavy Metal Islam: Rock, Resistance and the Struggle for the Soul of Islam*. New York: Broadway Books); see also Titus Hjelm, Lahn Kahn-Harris and Mark Levine (2012) 'Heavy Metal as Controversy and Counterculture', *Popular Music History* 6(1). DOI: 10.1558/pomh.v6i1/2.5.
26 Dalia Said Mostafa (2013) 'Masculinity and Fatherhood within a Lebanese Muslim Community: Assad Fouladkar's Film *When Maryam Spoke Out*', in Walid El-Hamamsy and Mounira Soliman (eds) *Popular Culture in the Middle East and North Africa: A Postcolonial Outlook* (New York: Routledge).
27 Edmundson (1995), cited in Michael F. Brown (1996) 'On Resisting Resistance', *American Anthropologist* 98(4): 729–35, p. 734.
28 Michael F. Brown (1996) 'On Resisting Resistance', *American Anthropologist* 98(4): 729–35; Susan Seymour (2006) 'Resistance', *Anthropological Theory* 6(3): 303–21.
29 See Aihwa Ong (1987) *Spirits of Resistance and Capitalist Discipline: Factory Women in Malaysia* (Albany, NY: State University of New York Press); (1988) 'The Production of Possession: Spirits and the Multinational Corporation in Malaysia', *American Ethnologist* 15(1): 28–42; Sherry B. Ortner (1984) 'Theory in Anthropology since the Sixties', *Comparative Studies in Society and History* 26(1): 126–66; James C. Scott (1985) *Weapons of the Weak: Everyday Forms of Peasant Resistance* (New Haven, CT: Yale University Press); (1990) *Domination and the Arts of Resistance: Hidden Transcripts* (New Haven, CT: Yale University Press).
30 Seymour, 'Resistance'.
31 Lila Abu-Lughod (1990) 'The Romance of Resistance: Tracing Transformations of Power through Bedouin Women', *American Ethnologist* 17(1): 41–55.
32 Douglas Kellner (1995) *Media Culture: Cultural Studies, Identity and Politics Between the Modern and the Postmodern* (New York: Routledge).
33 Sherry B. Ortner (1995) 'Resistance and the Problem of Ethnographic Refusal', *Comparative Studies in Society and History* 37(1): 173–93.
34 Cohen, 'Symbols of Trouble'.
35 David Hesmondhalgh (2005) 'Subcultures, Scenes or Tribes? None of the Above', *Journal of Youth Studies* 8(1): 21–40.
36 Hall, 'Notes on Deconstructing the Popular', p. 449 (emphasis in original).
37 Dennis L. Dworkin (1997) *Cultural Marxism in Postwar Britain: History, the New Left and the Origins of Cultural Studies* (Durham, NC: Duke University Press).
38 See Cohen, 'Symbols of Trouble'; Gary Clarke (1981) 'Defending the Ski-jumpers: A Critique of Theories of Youth Subcultures', Occasional Paper 71 (Birmingham: Centre for Contemporary Cultural Studies, University of Birmingham); Jason Torkelson (2010) 'Life After (Straightedge) Subculture', *Qualitative Sociology* 33(3): 257–74.
39 Oliver Marchart (2003) 'Bridging the Micro-Macro Gap: Is There Such a Thing as a Post-Subcultural Politics?', in David Muggleton and Rupert Weinzierl (eds) *The Post-Subcultures Reader* (Oxford: Berg).

40 Hall, 'Notes on Deconstructing the Popular', p. 449.
41 Marchart, 'Bridging the Micro-Macro Gap', p. 87.
42 Hall, 'Notes on Deconstructing the Popular'.
43 Clarke, 'Defending the Ski-jumpers', pp.177–8.
44 Rupa Huq (2003) 'Global Youth Cultures in Localized Spaces: The Case of the UK New Asian Dance Music and French Rap', in Muggleton and Weinzierl (eds), *The Post-Subcultures Reader*, p. 218.
45 Andy R. Brown (2003) 'Heavy Metal and Subcultural Theory: A Paradigmatic Case of Neglect?', in Muggleton and Weinzierl, *The Post-Subcultures Reader*, p. 231.
46 Ibid., p. 233.
47 Michel Maffesoli (1996) *The Time of the Tribes: The Decline of Individualism in Mass Society* (London: Sage Publications).
48 Andy Bennett (2011) 'The Post-subcultural Turn: Some Reflections Ten Years On', *Journal of Youth Studies* 14(5), 493–506, p. 495.
49 See Andy Bennett (1999) 'Subcultures or Neo-Tribes? Rethinking the Relationship between Youth, Style and Musical Taste', *Sociology* 33(3): 599–617; (2005) 'In Defence of Neo-tribes: A Response to Blackman and Hesmondhalgh', *Journal of Youth Studies* 8(2): 255–59; (2006) 'Punk's Not Dead: The Significance of Punk Rock for an Older Generation of Fans', *Sociology* 40(1): 219–35; 'The Post-subcultural Turn'.
50 David Hesmondhalgh (2007) 'Some Key Terms in Recent Youth Cultural Studies: Critical Reflections from the Sociology of Music', in Paul Hodkinson and Wolfgang Deicke (eds) *Youth Cultures: Scenes, Subcultures and Tribes* (Abingdon: Routledge), p. 24.
51 Ahmed Abdalla (1985) *The Student Movement and National Politics in Egypt: 1923–1973* (London: Al-Saqi Books).
52 Raof Abbass (1968) *Al-Harakah al-'Ummaliyyah fi Misr 1899–1952* [*The Labour Movement in Egypt 1899–1952*] (Cairo: Dar al-Katib al-'Arabi lil-Taba'ah wal-Nashr).
53 Anastasia Valassopoulos, Tarik Sabry, Caroline Rooney, Mark Westmoreland, Adel Iskandar and Rasha Salti (2013) 'Arab Cultural Studies – Thinking Aloud: Theorizing and Planning for the Future of a Discipline', in Anastasia Valassopoulou (ed.) *Arab Cultural Studies: History, Politics and the Popular* (London: Routledge), pp. 14–15.
54 Hall, 'Race, Culture and Communications', p. 11.
55 Dick Hebdige (2012) 'Contemporizing 'Subculture': 30 Years to Life', *European Journal of Cultural Studies* 15(3): 399–424, p. 399.
56 Lila Abu-Lughod (1991) 'Writing against Culture', in Richard G. Fox (ed.) *Recapturing Anthropology: Working in the Present* (Santa Fe, NM: School of American Research Press).
57 Abdelkabir Khatibi (1980) *Annaqd al-Mujdawij* [*Double Critique*] (Beirut: Dār al-'Awdah).
58 Tarik Sabry (2010) *Cultural Encounters in the Arab World: On Media, the Modern and the Everyday* (London: I.B.Tauris).

Bibliography

Abaza, Mona (2012) 'Walls, Segregating Downtown Cairo and the Mohammed Mahmud Street Graffiti', *Theory Culture and Society* 30(1): 122–39.

Abbass, Raof (1968) *Al-Harakah al-'Ummaliyyah fi Misr 1899–1952* [*The Labour Movement in Egypt 1899–1951*] (Cairo: Dar al-Katib al-'Arabi lil-Taba'ah wal-Nashr).

Abdalla, Ahmed (1985) *The Student Movement and National Politics in Egypt: 1923–1973* (London: Al-Saqi Books).

Abu-Lughod, Lila (1990) 'The Romance of Resistance: Tracing Transformations of Power through Bedouin Women', *American Ethnologist* 17(1): 41–55.

―――― (1991) 'Writing against Culture', in Richard G. Fox (ed.) *Recapturing Anthropology: Working in the Present* (Santa Fe, NM: School of American Research Press).

Afray, Janet and Anderson, Kevin (2005) *Foucault and the Iranian Revolution* (Urbana, IL: University of Chicago Press).

Ahram Online and Feteha, Ahmed (2011) 'Egypt Military Attcks Occupy Cabinet Protestors: Updates from the Day', *Ahram Daily*, 16 December. Available at http://english.ahram.org.eg/NewsContent/1/64/29489/Egypt/Politics-/Egypt-military-attacks-Occupy-Cabinet-protesters-U.aspx (accessed 11 April 2016).

Bennett, Andy (1999) 'Subcultures or Neo-Tribes? Rethinking the Relationship between Youth, Style and Musical Taste', *Sociology* 33(3): 599–617.

―――― (2005) 'In Defence of Neo-tribes: A Response to Blackman and Hesmondhalgh', *Journal of Youth Studies* 8(2): 255–59.

―――― (2006) 'Punk's Not Dead: The Significance of Punk Rock for an Older Generation of Fans', *Sociology* 40(1): 219–35.

―――― (2011) 'The Post-subcultural Turn: Some Reflections Ten Years On', *Journal of Youth Studies* 14(5): 493–506.

Blackman, Shane (2005) 'Youth Subcultural Theory: A Critical Engagement with the Concept, its Origins and Politics, from the Chicago School to Postmodernism', *Journal of Youth Studies* 8(1): 1–20.

Brown, Andy R. (2003) 'Heavy Metal and Subcultural Theory: A Paradigmatic Case of Neglect?', in David Muggleton and Rupert Weinzierl (eds) *The Post-Subcultures Reader* (New York: Berg).

Brown, Michael F. (1996) 'On Resisting Resistance', *American Anthropologist* 98(4): 729–35.

Clarke, Gary (1981) 'Defending the Ski-jumpers: A Critique of Theories of Youth Subcultures', Occasional Paper 71 (Birmingham: Centre for Contemporary Cultural Studies, University of Birmingham).

Clarke, John (1976) 'The Skinheads and the Magical Recovery of Community', in Stuart Hall and Tony Jefferson (eds) *Resistance Through Ritual: Youth Subcultures in Post-War Britain* (London: HarperCollins).

Cohen, Stanley (1997[1980]) 'Symbols of Trouble', in Ken Gelder (ed.) *The Subcultures Reader* (Hove: Psychology Press).

Derrida, Jacques (1982) *Margins of Philosophy* (Chicago, IL: University of Chicago Press).

_____ (1998[1967]) *Of Grammatology*, trans. Gayatri Spivak (Baltimore, MD: Johns Hopkins University Press).

Dworkin, Dennis L. (1997) *Cultural Marxism in Postwar Britain: History, the New Left and the Origins of Cultural Studies* (Durham, NC: Duke University Press).

Edmundson, Mark (1995) *Literature against Philosophy, Plato to Derrida: A Defence of Poetry* (Cambridge: Cambridge University Press).

El-Hamamsy, Walid and Soliman Mounira (eds) (2014) *Popular Culture in the Middle East and North Africa: A Postcolonial Outlook* (New York: Routledge).

Esler, Anthony (1972) *Bombs, Beards and Barricades: 150 Years of Youth in Revolt* (New York: Stein & Day Publishers).

Foucault, Michel (1977) *Language Counter-memory, Practice* (Ithaca, NY: Cornell University Press).

_____ (1978) *The History of Sexuality*, trans. Robert Hurley (New York: Random House).

Hall, Stuart (1992) 'Race, Culture and Communications: Looking Backward and Forward at Cultural Studies', *Rethinking Marxism* 5(1): 10–18.

_____ (1997) *Representation: Cultural Representations and Signifying Practices* (London: Sage Publications).

_____ (1998) 'Notes on Deconstructing the Popular', in John Storey (ed.) *Cultural Theory and Popular Culture: A Reader (London:* Prentice Hall).

Hall, Stuart and Jefferson, Tony (eds) (1976) *Resistance Through Rituals: Youth Subcultures in Post-war* Britain (London: HarperCollins).

Hebdige, Dick (1979) *Subculture: The Meaning of Style* (London: Routledge).

_____ (1988) *Hiding in the Light: On Images and Things* (Hove: Psychology Press).

_____ (2012) 'Contemporizing "Subculture": 30 Years to Life', *European Journal of Cultural Studies* 15 (3): 399–424.

Hesmondhalgh, David (2005) 'Subcultures, Scenes or Tribes? None of the Above', *Journal of Youth Studies* 8(1): 21–40.

_____ (2007) 'Some Key Terms in Recent Youth Cultural Studies: Critical Reflections from the Sociology of Music', in Paul Hodkinson and Wolfgang Deicke (eds) *Youth Cultures: Scenes, Subcultures and Tribes* (Abingdon: Routledge).

Hjelm, Titus, Kahn-Harris, Lahn and Levine, Mark (2012) 'Heavy Metal as Controversy and Counterculture', *Popular Music History* 6(1). DOI: 10.1558/pomh.v6i1/2.5.

Huq, Rupa (2003) 'Global Youth Cultures in Localized Spaces: The Case of the UK New Asian Dance Music and French Rap', in David Muggleton and Rupert Weinzierl (eds) *The Post-Subcultures Reader* (New York: Berg).

Kellner, Douglas (1995) *Media Culture: Cultural Studies, Identity and Politics Between the Modern and the Postmodern* (New York: Routledge).

Khatibi, Abdelkabir (1980) *Annaqd al-Mujdawij* [*Double Critique*] (Beirut: Dār al-'Awdah).

LeVine, Mark (2008) *Heavy Metal Islam: Rock, Resistance and the Struggle for the Soul of Islam*. New York: Broadway Books.

McKay, George (1996) *Senseless Acts of Beauty: Cultures of Resistance Since the Sixties* (London: Verso).

Maffesoli, Michel (1996) *The Time of the Tribes: The Decline of Individualism in Mass Society* (London: Sage Publications).

Marchart, Oliver (2003) 'Bridging the Micro-Macro Gap: Is There Such a Thing as a Post-Subcultural Politics?', in David Muggleton and Rupert Weinzierl (eds) *The Post-Subcultures Reader* (Oxford: Berg).

Muggleton, David and Weinzierl, Rupert (eds) (2003) *The Post-Subcultures Reader* (New York: Berg).

Ong, Aihwa (1987) *Spirits of Resistance and Capitalist Discipline: Factory Women in Malaysia* (Albany, NY: State University of New York Press).

_____ (1988) 'The Production of Possession: Spirits and the Multinational Corporation in Malaysia', *American Ethnologist* 15(1): 28–42.

Ortner, Sherry B. (1984) 'Theory in Anthropology since the Sixties', *Comparative Studies in Society and History* 26(1): 126–66.

_____ (1995) 'Resistance and the Problem of Ethnographic Refusal', *Comparative Studies in Society and History* 37(1): 173–93.

Pickett, Brent L. (1996) 'Foucault and the Politics of Resistance', *Polity* 28 (4): 445–66.

Sabry, Tarik (2010) *Cultural Encounters in the Arab World: On Media, the Modern and the Everyday* (London: I.B.Tauris).

Said Mostafa, Dalia (2013) 'Masculinity and Fatherhood within a Lebanese Muslim Community: Assad Fouladkar's Film *When Maryam Spoke Out*', in Walid El-Hamamsy and Mounira Soliman (eds) *Popular Culture in the Middle East and North Africa: A Postcolonial Outlook* (New York: Routledge).

Scott, James C. (1985) *Weapons of the Weak: Everyday Forms of Peasant Resistance* (New Haven, CT: Yale University Press).

_____ (1990) *Domination and the Arts of Resistance: Hidden Transcripts* (New Haven, CT: Yale University Press).

Seymour, Susan (2006) 'Resistance', *Anthropological Theory* 6(3): 303–21.

Shenker, Jack (2011) 'Egyptians Return to Tahrir Square to Protect against Military Junta', *Guardian*, 18 November. Available at www.theguardian.com/world/2011/nov/18/egyptians-return-tahrir-square-protest (accessed 11 April 2016).

Sheshtawy, Mostafa (2011) 'Two Dead, Over 170 Injured in Bloody Crackdown on Cabinet Sit-in', *Daily News Egypt*, 16 December. Available at http://www.dailynewsegypt.com/2011/12/16/1-dead-over-100-injured-in-bloody-crackdown-on-cabinet-sit-in/ (accessed 11 April 2016).

Sullivan, Chris (2011) 'Smiley Culture: The Symbiotic Relationship between Acid and the Smiley Face', *Red Bull Music Academy*, 13 December. Available at www.redbullmusicacademy.com/magazine/smiley-culture-rave-feature (accessed 10 September 2014).

Torkelson, Jason (2010) 'Life After (Straightedge) Subculture', *Qualitative Sociology* 33(3): 257–74.

Valassopoulos, Anastasia, Sabry, Tarik, Rooney, Caroline, Westmoreland, Mark, Iskandar, Adel and Salti, Rasha (2013) 'Arab Cultural Studies – Thinking Aloud: Theorizing and Planning for the Future of a Discipline', in Anastasia Valassopoulou (ed.) *Arab Cultural Studies: History, Politics and the Popular* (New York: Routledge).

2

Hacking Rites

Recoding the Political in Contemporary Cultural Practices

Tarek El-Ariss[1]

In April 2012, Twitter witnessed a series of hackings targeting outspoken Saudi authors and intellectuals, including Abdo Khal. Khal's novel, *Tarmī bi-Sharar* (*She Spews Sparks*, 2009),[2] which earned him the International Prize for Arabic Fiction (the Arabic equivalent of the Man Booker Prize) in 2010, exposes modes of racial, political and sexual violence and inequality in an unnamed Gulf kingdom. When the hacking occurred, Khal intervened to disown the hijacked account, '@Abdokhal,' which was spewing all kinds of vulgarities and indiscretions aimed at embarrassing him and destroying his reputation. Eliminating his 50,000 followers, the attack knocked down the signifier itself – the award-winning author followed by thousands – and exposed the vulnerability of the public intellectual online. In this case, participatory debate and the critique of power, which imagine a Habermasian public sphere extended to the internet, collapsed in one blow.[3]

In exploring Arab political and cultural practices in the age of social media, this chapter focuses on the interplay of hacking and scandal as a new model of cultural production involving attack and resistance, activism and commitment. Specifically, it examines how contemporary Arabic writing stages the political through acts of hacking emerging from, and leading to, instances of vulnerability, injury and erasure. Focusing on a new generation of authors from Egypt and the Gulf, this chapter explores questions of ethical ambivalence and aesthetic fluctuation, translational politics and canon formation. Contesting formalistic and sociological approaches to literature, it investigates the political dimension of sensationalism and scandal, and examines how literature in particular is reimagined and reaffirmed through hacking rites: practices, attacks and manipulation. The attention to literature in what follows serves to expose the fictions through which power gains legitimacy, as well as revisits Sartrean notions of commitment (*engagement*) in the contemporary Arab context. Commitment has been a key framework but also a posture for Arabic cultural production in the context of struggles for self-determination and economic opportunities from the 1950s onward. Revisiting commitment through contemporary scandal and hacking practices highlights new developments in the Arab world that are both technological, linked to writing practices and communication, and political, tied to upheavals that could no longer be explained, given 1950s Marxist and anti-colonial models which traditionally have informed revolutionary mobilisation and cultural production.

The cultural practitioners examined in this chapter expose and hack political models and literary tradition, only to be hacked and exposed by their own hacking and scandal. I argue that their practices create a space for new forms of intervention, but also run the risk of being engulfed, if not reified, in the process of intervening in and critiquing power. Thus examining the tribulations of these practitioners allows us to identify new connections and associations between activism and cultural production in a rapidly changing technological and political landscape.

Wither commitment?

The notion of *iltizām* (commitment) emerged in the 1950s with pan-Arabism and anti-colonial and class struggles. While it was Taha Hussein who first coined the word in 1947, it was Suhayl Idris, author of *al-Ḥayy al-Latīnī* (*The Latin Quarter*)[4] and reader of Sartre who became its most recognisable advocate. Idris's journal, *al-Ādāb*, founded in Beirut in 1953, was one of the crucibles for *iltizām*'s leftist and nationalist articulations through literary criticism and philosophy from across the Arab world. As Verena Klemm argues, '*Al-Ādāb* became the mouthpiece of a whole generation of committed writers and poets.'[5] Critiquing modernist aesthetics as bourgeois and regressive, *iltizām* called for a literature that socially and ethically engages Arab reality within a larger nationalist narrative of progress and emancipation. *Iltizām* was viewed as vehicle of social and political transformation through writing and cultural production. The intellectual contribution of leftist thinkers and literary critics such as Ghali Shukry in Egypt, and Raif Khoury in Lebanon, was key in this regard.

Consecutive Arab defeats and encroachment of Arab totalitarianism from the 1960s onward has undermined *iltizām* over the years. Political and social transformations eventually doomed any hope for 'a new post-colonial Arab subject: confident, politically involved, independent, self-sufficient and above all liberated'.[6] By the end of the twentieth century, the pan-Arab motifs of anti-colonial struggle that went hand-in-hand with *iltizām* became completely exposed to their demagoguery and co-option by political systems seeking to survive at any cost. This exposure (*faḍḥ*) both signalled an end of a discourse of resistance, while creating the possibility for new experiments to occupy the scene of cultural practices. Stimuli for this change included technological developments such as the advent of satellite TV and the internet, and political development such as 9/11 and the invasion of Iraq, which further eroded the legitimacy of Arab regimes. These new realities, compounded by an increasingly dire economic situation, where inequalities were flaunted and justified with government sanction from Egypt and Tunisia to Syria, catapulted new models of cultural production and confrontation. These models were tied intimately to the brewing political change that would unsettle Arab regimes, with such riots as the Mahalla in 2006,[7] and more fully in 2010 with the events of the 'Arab Spring'.

On the literary scene, Arabic writing has been witnessing a boom since the beginning of the twenty-first century, which has made being an author 'cool' again. From Beirut to Cairo, from the Gulf to the Maghreb, a new generation of Arab authors has emerged, benefiting from the decentralisation of the publishing industry and a new culture of prizes and promotion that is not without its faults. Young writers are finally breaking from their predecessors' trappings in discourses and ideologies that no longer (and in fact, never did) reflect Arab social and political reality. For example, in *An Takūn 'Abbās al-'Abd* (*Being Abbas el Abd*), Ahmed Alaidy stages such a break through a violent and experimental narrative.[8] This new-writing manifesto of sorts incorporates techno-writing to describe a young man ruminating over amorous encounters, politics, philosophy and history in modern-day

Cairo. The narrator hallucinates, picks fights, swears and engages in a scathing indictment of Egypt's cultural and political establishment.

Alaidy's text exposes modes of ideological complicity that tie in the production of an antiquated canon with a project of modernity that has gone awry. Breaking with a previous generation of Arab authors and cultural practitioners – the 'generation of the Defeat',[9] Alaidy identifies (and identifies with) the 'I've got nothing to lose' generation. This new generation has cast out the literary and political heritage of the Naksa: the Arab defeat against Israel in 1967. According to Alaidy, the 'generation of the Defeat' is paralysed and paralysing, unable and unwilling to recover from Arab modernity's alleged dystopian moment in 1967. Thus the break not only requires acts of violence, but also hacking in order to expose and move beyond ideological and cultural decay, complicity and paralysis.

Alaidy discusses hacking in a passing yet important reference to a teenage hacker who infiltrated and uploaded music to the Pentagon website.[10] In exposing the vulnerability of the impenetrable structure – the site of American military power – hacking exposes (*yafḍaḥ*) the weakness in the system, or the system as weak, vulnerable and compromised. The website's weakness reflects the problematic nature of the discourses and practices that underlie it: American interventionist ideology and military operations from Vietnam to Iraq. Thus hacking exposes both a flaw in computer security as well as political legitimacy. Intervening abroad in order to make America secure, as the story goes, means exposure to its own insecurity and weakness.

Having outlined the structure of hacking with the teenager episode, Alaidy extrapolates, claiming that these days everything is hacked: '*ḥatta al-ḥukūma bi-tithāk 'aynī 'aynak*' ('Even the government gets hacked, right before your eyes'[11]). Alaidy stages hacking as a performance of infiltration, targeting both the ideological and historical narrative and the cultural establishment that continues to legitimise it. In this way, Alaidy's text exposes a scene of denial and complicity that holds literature – new writing – hostage. In taking aim at the government, hacking simultaneously delivers the *coup de grâce* to the 'generation of the Defeat', which continues to lament the post-1967 collapse of the Arab project of modernity embodied in political and cultural paralysis, complicity (the Camp David accords) and totalitarianism (Mubarak). Thus, the experience of loss with which Alaidy breaks is a moment of historical misrecognition. The political intervention of new writing through hacking and *faḍḥ* (exposing) takes shape as a dismantling of this structure of loss and its association with nostalgia, melancholia, paralysis and the discourse on ruins.

The *faḍḥ* staged in Alaidy's text, figuratively perpetrated by the Russian teenager and the new author alike, 'makes a scene' of that which is already *mafḍūḥ* (exposed). Thus, hacking as *faḍīḥah* (scandal) does not reveal a secret or something hidden, rather that the economy of secrecy, veiling and loss is already compromised and fractured. The *faḍīḥah* consists in the realisation that decay is not internal or unseen but public, '*aynī 'aynak*' (right before your eyes).[12] Hacking as *faḍḥ* exposes the fact that as a multiplicity of discourses and practices, the *ḥukūmah* (government) is already *mithākah* – hacked, stripped naked and illegitimate. Alaidy's text, among others, unsettles the structure of debt or cross-generational transference in order to create the possibility of movement, play, transformation and confrontation, thereby enacting in the process a new form of *iltizām* that has moved beyond its pan-Arab, 1950s model. Embodied in contemporary literary and cultural practices and constituted through various hacking operations and scandalous revelations, the new political unfolds in Alaidy's text through the deconstruction of historical continuity, and of the fiction of power that sustains it.

Alaidy's work and tactics could be positioned in relation to the 1960s generation of Egyptian modernism that gave us authors such as Sonallah Ibrahim, hailed by Alaidy as a literary inspiration.[13] In her reading of the relation between journalism and literature at the intersection of social and political change in Egypt, Elisabeth Kendall focuses on avant-garde authors writing for the journal, *Gallery 68*. According to Kendall, these innovators evolved from a long tradition of journalism and subversive and marginal literature to produce *al-adab al-jadīd* (new literature).[14] This new literature, she argues, was intimately tied to experiences of shock and disappointment with the political and cultural establishment blamed for the 1967 defeat.[15] Although Alaidy's writing claims to be post-loss (the aforementioned 'I've got nothing to lose' generation), it is tied to a tradition that stages the tension between the literary and the non-literary at the intersection of journalism and literature, activism and art. Thus contemporary acts of hacking and revelation stage both ruptures as well as continuities with literary traditions, thoroughly undermining the author/intellectual model foregrounded by traditional *iltizām* and the *udabā'* (literati), both of which have been co-opted by the state.¹⁶ The interplay of hacking and scandal in this context points to a new scene of negotiation of the relation between the aesthetic and political. This new scene of writing, scandal, infiltration and collapse, shapes and is shaped by the cultural and political practices that are now associated with the 'Arab Spring'.

Hacking rites

The current media landscape abounds in scandals of hacking emails, mobile phones and websites, and tampering with secure structures in order to obtain and spread classified information. Jinn-like, hackers are both good and bad, and thus ambivalent in their social and political aims and constitution.[17] In Britain, the scandal of Rupert Murdoch's (now-defunct) *News of the World* has been making headlines since 2009, highlighting hacking as a way of obtaining and producing news.[18] In May 2010, Iraq-based army intelligence analyst Bradley Manning, 22, copied thousands of classified documents and diplomatic correspondence and leaked them to Julian Assange, Wikileaks' founder.[19] In both cases, the hacking caused scandal for the Murdoch media empire, British and American governments and political groups and organisations the world over. 'Anonymous', an organisation of anarchist hackers (or hacktivists) systematically targets government sites and financial institutions. 'Raise Your Voice', a self-proclaimed offshoot of 'Anonymous', repeatedly hacked the Lebanese government websites in April 2012, protesting against economic policies and inadequate social services.[20] This organisation's video manifesto portrays an individual wearing the mask featured in the film, *V for Vendetta* (dir. James McTeigue, 2005), one of the iconic symbols of the 'Arab Spring' protests.[21]

Associated with infiltration, scandal and leaks, hacking is the instrument of activists, conscientious objectors, disgruntled fans, random saboteurs (*kharābkārī*, in Farsi),[22] and conservative forces seeking to silence dissent. It is a bricolage with wide-ranging aesthetic, social and political repercussions. Andrew Ross argues that Steven Levy's cult novel, *Hackers* (1984),[23] established hacking as 'libertarian and crypto-anarchist in its right-to-know'.[24] Ross argues that hacker activities were presented as a romantic countercultural tendency',[25] only to degenerate into a form of 'techno-delinquency' and then crime. *Jargon File*, an online resource for hacker subculture, defines the 'cracker' (a type of hacker) as someone who stretches the capabilities of programmable system [...] delights in having an intimate understanding of the internal workings of a system [...] programs enthusiastically (even obsessively) [or is a] malicious meddler who tries to discover sensitive information by poking around.[26]

Hacking a website can involve writing a malicious program that infiltrates and infects it. It also can occur by overloading the site with requests that it cannot handle; this process depends on a consorted attack of a group of individuals who all send requests simultaneously in order to crash the site (a 'denial of service' (DOS) attack). In this sense, hacking exposes the *secure* system's inability to handle overwhelming requests, thereby stretching its limits and forcing it to recant its protected status. Thus, hacking consists in writing practices that generate specific affects, centred on the name, signifier and signification as such. Crash, collapse, infiltration and replication expose (*tafḍaḥ*) sites of vulnerability and instability.

With the expansion of the internet and computer culture, hacking as a process of infiltrating systems and exposing vulnerability has moved beyond the digital world into the limelight of cultural debates and political action. Abandoning its subcultural status in the mystified domain of subversive agents with special codes, hacking increasingly characterises knowledge production and learning processes. Hackathons – festivals for computer programming – are becoming tools for both learning and innovation, involving adults and children, further anchoring hacking as an epistemological framework in the cyber age. Tied to acts of knowing and revealing, hacking arises from a set of writing practices that enables the hacker to learn and protest, express desire, love or outrage. Like any learning processes, these practices involve repetition, imitation and infiltration, which characterise the acquisition of skills ranging from computer programming to writing fiction.

In a 2010 article in *Al-Ahram Weekly*, author, blogger and activist Youssef Rakha[27] provided a detailed description of an act of 'literary hacking' that occurred in Cairo. Unlike the saboteurs who hacked Abdo Khal's Twitter account or the Russian teenager in Alaidy's novel, the hackers according to Rakha are wannabe authors, mobbing Cairo's literary scene. As Rakha goes into a bookshop for a creative writing workshop, he notices a strange-looking crowd that seems out of place in the close-knit literary circle with which he is familiar. Rakha then sarcastically points out that the unfamiliar faces are those of 'engineers' aspiring to enter the literary field through mimetic desire and groupie behaviour:

> For a moment it seemed as though a mafia of those lever-wielding un-poets were ambushing the literary sphere, infiltrating writerly circles all across the city, befriending with a view to replacing true writers and eventually, well – eliminating them.[28]

The crescendo in Rakha's text moves from terms such as 'mafia' and 'un-poets' to 'ambushing', 'infiltrating', 'replacing' and 'eliminating'. Thus Rakha describes an attack or an aggressive takeover that threatens to erase 'true writers'. A flash mob, which unexpectedly appears at the event, stuns the author and takes him by surprise. The fear of elimination is the effect of a hacking that seeks to infiltrate the literary scene and reproduce itself in the guise of destroying it. Rakha's anxiety echoes the hacking of Khal's account, which overrides yet replicates the author and his text, redirects his tweets and appropriates his function altogether. The literary workshop, like the author's Twitter account, becomes a site of vulnerability that both empowers and undermines the author – the 'true writer' who gives writing workshops and goes online as a public intellectual engaging a wider audience.

A new literary canon emerges from a liminal space of potential and possibility, which becomes exposed in the act of infiltration. Having distinguished 'un-poets' from 'true writers', Rakha proceeds to name the latter. The threat of elimination at the hand of an insidious and destructive mob leads him to identify the representative figures of a new generation of Egyptian authors, who

> might be called the Twothousanders but not only because they started publishing after 2000. People like Nael El-Toukhy, Ahmad Nagui and (to a lesser extent) Mohammad Kheir and Mohammad Abdelnaby also share something more profound. They are all internet-savvy, down-to-earth agents of subversion as interested in things as they are in people and as closely connected to pop culture, communications technology and the global media as they are to literary history. Kundera is their Balzac, Mahfouz their Greek tragedy. They are cynics and jokers and glorifiers of what they refer to (admittedly often with ignorance) as kitsch. By and large they eschew poetry; and until the Egyptian quasi-literary blogging craze fizzled out, many of them

professed to eschew print publication. They may not always have as much access to non-Arabic culture as they claim or desire, but their position is truly postmodern in the sense that they own and disown many histories at once; they don't have a problem revolving around the commodity as a mode of being; they don't have a problem with commodification. In short, they live mentally in our times – and they try to do it unselfconsciously.[29]

In a Hegelian moment, which is experienced as a fear of death and erasure, Rakha embraces the position of the critic who assesses the literary work, identifies its main protagonists and establishes its aesthetic values. This moment of consciousness calls attention to the vulnerability of the literary work – its compromised position at the workshop for new writers – yet simultaneously asserts its literary worth and significance. This double movement is key for understanding how hacking and infiltration stage moments of *faḍḥ* online, in public forums and in texts. Thus, hacking threatens and consolidates at the same time. The negation, through Foucault this time, is productive of discourse: that is, new writing. In this context, the attribute 'truly post-modern' – as opposed to 'phony' or 'fake' post-modern – that Rakha employs to describe these authors' position does not announce the end of literature *à la* Fukayama, or its depoliticisation. Rather, it carves out a literary space for those authors threatened by mimicry and elimination. This literary space no longer refers to 'literature' as such, but instead heralds a new site of interaction wherein the political and the aesthetic are refigured in a 'truly' post-modern position.

Rakha presents the historical and technological context of new authors as playful hackers and agents of subversion in their own right. He identifies their position vis-à-vis world literature, new media and political participation. Furthermore, he addresses their relation to the canon associated with Mahfouz, which he incorporates as 'Greek tragedy' in a new literary setting. The reference to Mahfouz ties into the 'truly post-modern' framework that Rakha introduces as a direction, motif and orientation in new (and noteworthy) works. As he situates new writing in relation to Mahfouz, he claims a literary trajectory that unsettles yet refigures tradition, instead of breaking with it. The politics of the canon in this context are complex: they operate across philosophical and literary models that position Arabic literature in a larger comparative context. Articulating the new author's relation to blogs and print, Mahfouz and Kundera, Rakha suggests that the new author, operating across media and genre, is by no means a free-floating entity, lost and unhinged. Neither are they simply an innovator in the tradition of Arab and European modernism, as discussed by Elisabeth Kendall or Stefan Meyer in their different studies of Arabic experimental literature.[30] Although the 'true writer' is innovative and complex, they lie at the intersection of a multiplicity of media and literary traditions and practices that are identified, if not produced, in a moment characterised by fear of elimination and mimetic anxiety. This releases new writing in Rakha's characterisation from a fixed and homogeneous literary model that could be clearly identified, in fact, reified. Instead, his characterisation relegates new writing to a series of events, accidents and scandals that shape and produce it. Moreover, it positions new writing as a practice, bricolage and intervention that is aware, political and aesthetic in its own right. In the post-modern setting defined by Rakha, political commitment takes shape in different ways: it is unsubordinated to the will of the author or consistent with a specific model of dissent, ideology and 'politburo' directives. When rethought as a writing and political practice, hacking brings about a deluge, a revelation and a text that cannot be foreclosed or overdetermined politically or aesthetically.

Cultural production as a scandalous act

Framing the notion of hacking with regard to new writers performing systematic infiltration and knocking down of literary spaces brings to mind Rajaa Alsanea's text, *Banat al-Ryadh* (*Girls of Riyadh*).[31] This tell-all novel was published by Saqi Books in 2006 and subsequently translated, not without controversy, by Marilyn Booth for Penguin, in 2009.[32] Booth, along with other critics, identifies the process of 'hacking the literary' in the production and translation of Alsanea's work. While Rakha describes how engineers or 'un-poets'[33] mob the literary scene, Booth engages the celebrity author of the literary hit by examining the way that her work is produced through the manipulation of translation, circulation and media. Whereas the hacking of Abdo Khal's Twitter account knocked down the literary signifier – the author – by eliminating his readership, in Alsanea's context hacking serves to consolidate, if not construct, the position of the author of the bestselling novel.

Girls of Riyadh tells the story of four girlfriends as they flirt, fall in love, get married, divorce, travel and drive around Riyadh in SUVs with tinted glass. The novel weaves in the role of the external narrator, Rajaa herself, who introduces every chapter as a weekly email sent after Friday prayers to Saudi internet subscribers. Alsanea starts her chapters by acknowledging the readers' responses to her emails. She claims that her *faḍīḥah* (scandal) of the previous week angered some readers due to her revelations. She also critiques Saudi authorities' alleged intention to ban her site and prevent her from sending the weekly scandals. Setting itself an imagined origin in cyberspace,[34] the novel takes email – an older technology compared to Twitter – as its narrative model. This techno-fictionalisation transforms the author into a character in her own text, writing herself as a persecuted yet courageous young woman, armed with the power of scandal and confronting political power and disgruntled readers online.

Alsanea's literary narrative about the exposer of the intimate, the social and the political enacts a breakdown of the imagined boundary between private and public. The *faḍḥ* in this context unveils the erasure of the very notion of the private. Alluding to Alsanea's framing of her task as a *faḍḍāḥah* (exposer, scandaliser), Moneera al-Ghadeer suggests that the author's play on the word *fataḥa* ('open') and *faḍaḥa* (expose) is fundamental to the narrative. Specifically, Alsanea appropriates the register of *faḍḥ* from an *Oprah*-like TV show, which airs via satellite on the Lebanese Broadcasting Corporation. Alsanea *hacks* Zaven Kouyoumjian's *sīreh w-infataḥit* (open talk), transforming it into *sīreh w-infaḍaḥit* (scandal talk), thereby accentuating the process of scandal and unveiling. Discussing the translation of Alsanea's phrase, Marilyn Booth notes: 'The literal meaning of this cyber-transliteration is "A life story and it has been exposed"; the verb *infaḍaḥ* implies exposure of something disgraceful or shameful.'[35] In doing so, Alsanea 'provokes the phantasm that ultimately intensifies the interest in gazing at *Girls of Riyadh*',[36] thereby transforming the narrative into 'a peephole into what a young woman sees in her society'.[37] However, this peephole expands in order to expose the author herself in the process of exposing her society and producing a literary hit.

Appropriating Zaven's TV show as *sīreh w-infadaḥit*, Alsanea takes the act of *faḍḥ* on stage, into the studio, in front of the cameras and under the projectors' lights. According to the medieval lexicon, *Lisān al-'Arab*, *faḍaḥ* means 'to expose a misdeed'.[38] Specifically, Ibn Manzur emphasises in his lexicon the visual aspect of *faḍīḥah*, comparing it to the sudden advent of morning light that exposes (as in exposure to light and photography) the true shape, colour and contours of an object. It is also used in the context of awakening the sleeper in the morning (*faḍaḥah al-ṣabāḥ*), catching them off-guard. In this sense, the stage (*scène* in French, as in 'scene of writing') functions as light shed on a topic or social or political practice (*Oprah*-like show), which is simultaneously exposed in the process of *faḍḥ*. Thus the chronicle of *faḍā'iḥ* in Alsanea's text (the weekly emails) is implicated in its process of production, blurring the distinction between subject and object. The desire to be on stage and acquire recognition as a courageous woman author from Arabia, with translations in multiple languages, coincides with the desire to expose the social and political context from which the work arises. Specifically, Alsanea's chronicle of scandals becomes exposed in the process of translation. The true scandal, it turns out, lies in the construction and manipulation of the author-narrator function – a form of hacking that produces the literary hit.

The author's intervention in the process of translating her work into English sought to minimise the role of the translator, if not dismiss it altogether. In a series of articles, Marilyn Booth exposed (*faḍaḥat*) this intervention that aims at 'effacing the translator' and 'dismissing her reading of the text'.[39] This dismissal, argues Booth, produces and consolidates the position of the Arab woman writer as 'celebrity author'.[40] The politics of translation and editing subject the translator to market forces, wherein the publisher sides with the author of the coveted work as she alters – if not neutralises – the expert's translation. The threat to the translator's role and the attempt to eliminate it operate as an attack, infiltration and hacking of the economy of literary production (writing, reading, translating and publishing). Just as Rakha distinguishes between 'un-poets' and 'true writers' when threatened by the hacking mob in Cairo, Booth explains what distinguishes the literary work from the ethnographic account when she experiences erasure herself. In her *faḍḥ* of Alsanea's and Penguin's practices, Booth identifies a genre of orientalist ethnographicism, which packages and transforms the fictional text with an Arab female narrator and author into an authoritative testimony that provides a window into her culture.[41] Both in Rakha's and Booth's cases, the threat of elimination through infiltration and mimesis produces a reclaiming or a new articulation of a literary model that reaffirms the aesthetic. Thus the hacking/*faḍḥ* dialectics operate as a process of anchoring new writing along a trajectory that is new yet recognisable, innovative yet literary – 'truly post-modern', as Rakha would say.

Exposing the structure of editorial and economic power integral to the work's circulation and notoriety, Booth sheds light on the scandalous author herself, the alleged *faḍḍāḥah* (exposer, scandaliser) of Saudi society. In this context, the process of veiling and anonymity associated with the Arab woman *writing* her culture becomes something that exposes its own pretences to, and staging of, this structure of desire. The *faḍīḥah* that the translator enacts is of the literary *faḍḥ* itself as a quest for a stage (TV interviews, fame, limelight) and readership. In this context, *faḍḥ* implicates, exposes and takes over the act of writing, promotion and translation. It also shifts the emphasis from the alleged object of scandal – Saudi society – to the process of cultural production, which engulfs the *faḍḍāḥah* and hacker of the literary hit who initiated it in the first place. Thus *faḍḥ* becomes a kind of dangerous and wild writing and set of practices that unfold beyond the text in order to shape its circulation, reception and translation.

Although the literary text initiates or sets in motion a process of *faḍḥ*, the economy of its cultural production from translation to politics, aesthetics and mediatisation, takes it out of control of the initial literary *faḍḍāḥah*: namely, Alsanea. The Jinn out of the box, *faḍīḥah* moves like fire or a viral infestation that affects all that it touches, from the translation act to the cultural politics involved. The logic of *faḍīḥah* has broken with its initial cause: the desire to expose a misdeed, reveal the truth of a particular condition and expose an injustice. In this context, *faḍīḥah* engulfs all its participants and, in the process, redefines questions of origin, ethics and truth.

Faḍḥ as all-consuming text forces us to rethink political practices and activism, interrogating configurations of rights, justice and ethics. However, when the process of *faḍḥ* takes over completely, Booth returns to the literary text as an act of reclaiming it. This reclaiming is not so much a *faḍḥ* of Alsanea, Penguin and the orientalist and commercial appropriation of Arab women's literature. Rather, it constitutes a moment of resistance to the very act of *faḍḥ*, wherein writing and literature and their association with ethics and aesthetics have been completely compromised. Defining literature *in extremis* by exposing the scandal (*faḍḥ al-faḍīḥah*) seeks to anchor the text in an aesthetic economy from which its translation and publication in English is trying to move it away. Thus, in this context, Booth's *faḍḥ* – the moment of the aesthetic based in a system of respect, rights and exchange – is both aesthetic and political, characterising a new practice of dissent, resistance and shaming.

Conclusion

The new authorial position discussed in these examples – scandalous and scandalised, moving back and forth between the scene of writing and 'making a scene' – challenges our reading of the political in the traditional context of *iltizām*, *adab* and *hazīmah* (the defeat of 1967). It also contests the Habermasian model of the public sphere, which presupposes a rational subject engaging in debate and exchange. In this new setting, the author is compelled to expose themself in the process of exposing the other. However, while Ahmad Alaidy makes a scene at the *faḍīḥah* of 1967, Marilyn Booth exposes the scandal at Penguin. In both cases, the *faḍḥ* as 'making a scene' – which exposes the *faḍḍāḥ/ah* and threatens them with erasure, as in Rakha's case – characterises an act of resistance. Reclaiming the text from the wildfire of *faḍīḥah*, this new kind of political commitment has gone down to the street, taken the gloves off and given up on the utopia of an Arab future invested in the novel as its historical vehicle. However, it is no less political or effective as Sartrean and other similar models of commitment that configure the relation between political action and cultural production.

Like the author, the critic is equally implicated in identifying an elusive model that they associate with new cultural practices unfolding in the Arab world. The ambivalent nature and mitigated political aims of hacking refigure questions of activism, ethics, literature and the law, and shifts the debate from the critique of imperialism and colonialism in the context of loss as *hazīmah* to infiltration, *faḍḥ* and flash mobs. Unsettling the models of ideology and causality ('What caused the Arab Spring?') through which political action, resistance and protest have been traditionally explained, the multiple scenes and scandals of hacking (*faḍā'iḥ*) require an engagement with notions of affect, simultaneity, complementarity and circulation of texts, images and stories, both online and offline. The economy of *faḍḥ*, vulnerability and confrontation identified in these texts breaks with previous conceptions of the literary, the author and the relation between the intellectual and power. Replacing these 'older fictions' are new genres and writing practices that embrace – or are forced to embrace – the street and Twitter. The aesthetic characteristics of these new texts are constituted and recognised in instances of hacking and attack which are unpredictable and threatening. These texts and modes of circulation give rise to new forms of imagined communities, political authority, subjectivity and authorial functions that require further investigation.

Notes

1 This piece has been adapted for the purpose of this anthology from an article entitled 'Fiction of Scandal', *Journal of Arabic Literature* 43(2–3): 510–31.
2 Abdo Khal (2009) *Tarmi bi Sharar* (Beirut: Dar al-Saqi).
3 Egyptian writer and journalist Ibrahim Farghali claims that online interactions often involve a certain tone and mode of expression that break with 'the propriety of bourgeois and middle-class conventions'. See Ibrahim Farghali (2012) '*Al-Internet ka-Fāḍā' lil-Thawrah*' ['The Internet as the Space of Revolution'], 19 March. Available at http://ifarghali.blogspot.co.uk/2012/03/avatar.html(accessed 11 April 2016).
4 Suhayl Idris (1953) *Al-Hayy al-Latini* [*The Latin Quarter*] (Beirut: Dar Al-Ādāb).
5 Verena Klemm (2000) 'Different Notions of commitment (*Iltizam*) and Committed Literature (*al-Adab al-Multazim*) in the Literary Circles of the Mashriq', *Middle Eastern Literature* 3(1): 51–62, p. 54.
6 Yoav Di-Capua (2012) 'Arab Existentialism: An Invisible Chapter in the Intellectual History of Decolonization', *American Historical Review* 117(4): 1061–91, p. 1061.
7 The riots in Mahalla Al Kubra erupted between 2006 and 2008, where workers at Egypt's spinning and weaving company carried out industrial action and protested against the low income and employment conditions to which they were subjected.
8 For a detailed discussion of this work, see Tarek El-Ariss (2013) *Trials of Arab Modernity: Literary Affects and the New Political* (New York: Fordham University Press), chapter 6.
9 'Egypt had its generation of the Defeat. We're the generation that came after it. The "I've-got-nothing-to-lose generation."' Ahmed Alaidy (2003) *An Takūn 'Abbās al-'Abd* (Cairo: Dar Merit), p. 41; (2006) *Being Abbas el Abd*, trans. Humphrey Davis (Cairo: American University in Cairo Press), p. 36.
10 Alaidy, *An Takūn*, p. 98, *Being Abbas el Abd*, p. 96.
11 Ibid. There is a play on the meaning of the words *hāk* [infiltrate] and *nāk* [fuck] in this phrase.
12 See Winfried Menninghaus (2003) *Disgust: The Theory and History of a Strong Sensation*, trans. Howard Eiland and Joel Golb (Albany, NY: State University of New York Press), p. 134.
13 In fact, Alaidy dedicates the book to Sonallah Ibrahim and Chuck Palahniuk, author of the cult novel, *Fight Club* (1996).
14 Elizabeth Kendall (2006) *Literature, Journalism and the Avant-Garde* (New York: Routledge), p. 188.
15 Ibid., p. 85.
16 When the wave of uprisings swept through the Arab world started in autumn 2010, they exposed (*faḍaḥat*) and continue to expose the complicity of many Arab intellectuals and authors with authoritarian regimes.

17 In the hacking world, there are white, black and grey 'hat crackers', thereby characterising various ethics and aims of infiltration. See 'Black Hat' (n.d.) 'Jargon File'. Available at www.catb.org/jargon/html/B/black-hat.html (accessed 11 April 2016).
18 As a result of the scandal, which involved hacking family victims' mobile phones in order for the newspapers to influence events and increase sales, a British parliamentary committee found Murdoch 'unfit' to run his corporation. See John Burns and Ravi Somaiya (2012) 'Panel in Hacking Case Finds Murdoch Unfit as News Titan', *New York Times*, 1 May. Available at www.nytimes.com/2012/05/02/world/europe/murdoch-hacking-scandal-to-be-examined-by-british-parliamentary-panel.html?_r=1&hp (accessed 11 April 2016).
19 Elisabeth Bumiller, 'Army Leak Suspect Is Turned in by Ex-hacker', *New York Times*, 7 June 2010 www.nytimes.com/2010/06/08/world/08leaks.html (accessed 11 April 2016).
20 Oliver Holmes (2012) 'Hackers Take Down 15 Lebanese Government Websites', *Reuters*, 17 April. Available at www.reuters.com/article/2012/04/17/net-us-lebanon-hackers-idUSBRE83G0IQ20120417 (accessed 11 April 2016).
21 Anonymous (2012) '#OpLebanon Announcement', *YouTube*, 3 March. Available at http://youtu.be/3YyWvZP1QcQ (accessed 11 April 2016).
22 I would like to thank my colleague, Professor Faeqah Shirazi, for this reference.
23 Steven Levy (1984) *Hackers* (New York: Doubleday).
24 Andrew Ross (2000) 'Hacking Away at the Counterculture', in Barbara Kennedy and David Bell (eds) *The Cybercultures Reader* (New York: Routledge), p. 256.
25 Ibid.
26 Hacker (n.d.) 'Jargon File'. Available at www.catb.org/jargon/html/H/hacker.html (accessed 11 April 2016).
27 Rakha is the author of (2011) *Kitāb al-Ṭughra* [*The Sultan's Seal*] (Cairo: Dar al-Shourouk). He blogs at *The Arabophile* http://yrakha.wordpress.com/tag/youssef-rakha/.
28 Rakha (2011) 'E-cards for Mohammad Rabie', *Al-Ahram Weekly Online* 1031, 13–19 January http://weekly.ahram.org.eg/Archive/2011/1031/cu2.htm (accessed 11 April 2016).
29 Ibid.
30 While Meyer reads modernist innovation in the 1960s in the works of Sonallah Ibrahim and Edward Kharrat in relation to European authors such as Camus (Stefan G. Meyer (2000) *The Experimental Arabic Novel* (Albany, NY: State University of New York Press), Kendall maintains that the avant-gardist of the 1960s publishing in the journal *Gallery 68* should be 'judged by its distinctiveness and specific concerns rather than its provenance in or ability to match to European or American culture' (Kendall, *Literature*, p. 145).
31 Rajaa Alsanea (2006) *Banat al-Ryadh* [*Girls of Riyadh*] (Beirut: Dar Al-Saqi).
32 This controversy became public when Marilyn Booth first wrote a letter to the editor in the *Times Literary Supplement*, 27 September 2007, which she eventually developed into a series of articles.

33 Alsanea is a dentist by profession.
34 For a recent epistolary novel structured as emails, see Ezzat al-Qamhawi (2009) *Kitāb al-Ghiwāyah* [*Book of Seduction*] (Cairo: Dar al-'Ayn).
35 Marilyn Booth (2008) 'Translator v. Author (2007): Girls of Riyadh go to New York', *Translation Studies* 1(2): 197–211, p. 204.
36 Moneera al-Ghadeer (2006) 'Girls of Riyadh: A New Technology Writing or Chick Lit Defiance', *Journal of Arabic Literature* 37(2): 296–301, p. 299.
37 Ibid.
38 Ibn Manzur (2008) *Lisān al-'Arab* (Beirut: Dar Sader), 11–12, 190–1.
39 Marilyn Booth (2010) 'The Muslim Woman as Celebrity Author and the Politics of Translating Arabic: Girls of Riyadh Go on the Road', *Journal of Middle Eastern Women's Studies* 6(3): 149–182, p. 153.
40 Ibid.
41 Ibid., p. 151.

Bibliography

Alaidy, Ahmed (2003) *An Takūn 'Abbās al-'Abd* [*Being Abbas al-Abd*] (Cairo: Dar Merit, 2003).

_____ (2006) *Being Abbas el Abd*, trans. Humphrey Davis (Cairo: American University in Cairo Press).

Al-Ghadeer, Moneera (2006) 'Girls of Riyadh: A New Technology Writing or Chick Lit Defiance', *Journal of Arabic Literature* 37(2): 296–302.

Al-Qamhawi, Ezzat (2009) *Kitāb al-Ghiwāyah* [*Book of Seduction*] (Cairo: Dar al-'Ayn).

Alsanea, Rajaa (2006) *Banat al-Ryadh* [*Girls of Riyadh*] (Beirut: Dar Al-Saqi).

Anonymous (2012) '#OpLebanon Announcement', *YouTube*, 3 March. Available at http://youtu.be/3YyWvZP1QcQ (accessed 11 April 2016).

Black Hat (n.d.) 'Jargon File'. Available at www.catb.org/jargon/html/B/black-hat.html (accessed 11 April 2016).

Booth, Marilyn (2008) 'Translator v. Author (2007): Girls of Riyadh go to New York', *Translation Studies* 1(2): 197–211.

_____ (2010) "The Muslim Woman as Celebrity Author and the Politics of Translating Arabic: Girls of Riyadh Go on the Road', *Journal of Middle Eastern Women's Studies* 6(3): 149–82.

Bumiller, Elisabeth (2010) 'Army Leak Suspect Is Turned in by Ex-hacker', *New York Times*, 7 June. Available at www.nytimes.com/2010/06/08/world/08leaks.html (accessed 11 April 2016).

Burns, John and Somaiya, Ravi (2012) 'Panel in Hacking Case Finds Murdoch Unfit as News Titan', *New York Times*, 1 May. Available at www.nytimes.com/2012/05/02/world/europe/murdoch-hacking-scandal-to-be-examined-by-british-parliamentary-panel.html?_r=1&hp (accessed 11 April 2016).

Di-Capua, Yoav (2012) 'Arab Existentialism: An Invisible Chapter in the Intellectual History of Decolonization', *American Historical Review* 117(4): 1061–91.

El-Ariss, Tarek (2013) *Trials of Arab Modernity: Literary Affects and the New Political* (New York: Fordham University Press).

Farghali, Ibrahim (2012) '*Al-Internet ka-Fāḍā' lil-Thawrah*" ['The Internet as the Space of Revolution'], 19 March. Available at http://ifarghali.blogspot.co.uk/2012/03/avatar.html (accessed 11 April 2016).

'Hacker' (n.d.) 'Jargon File'. Available at www.catb.org/jargon/html/H/hacker.html (accessed 7 November 2016).

Holmes, Oliver (2012) 'Hackers Take Down 15 Lebanese Government Websites', *Reuters*, 17 April. Available at www.reuters.com/article/2012/04/17/net-us-lebanon-hackers-idUSBRE83G0IQ20120417 (accessed 11 April 2016).

Ibn Manzur (2008) *Lisān al-'Arab* [*The Arab Tongue*] (Beirut: Dar Sader).

Idris, Suhayl (1953) *Al-Hayy al-Latini* [*The Latin Quarter*] (Beirut: Dar Al-Ādāb).

Kendall, Elizabeth (2006) *Literature, Journalism and the Avant-Garde* (New York: Routledge).

Khal, Abdo (2009) *Tarmi bi Sharar* (Beirut: Dar al-Saqi).

Klemm, Verena (2000) 'Different Notions of Commitment (*Iltizam*) and Committed Literature (*al-Adab al-Multazim*) in the Literary Circles of the Mashriq', *Middle Eastern Literature* 3(1): 51–62.

Levy, Steven (1984) *Hackers* (New York: Doubleday).

Menninghaus, Winfried (2003) *Disgust: The Theory and History of a Strong Sensation*, trans. Howarsd Eiland and Joel Golb (Albany, NY: State University of New York Press).

Meyer, Stefan G. (2000) *The Experimental Arabic Novel* (Albany, NY: State University of New York Press).

Rakha (2011) 'E-cards for Mohammad Rabie', *Al-Ahram Weekly Online* 1031, 13–19 January. Available at http://weekly.ahram.org.eg/Archive/2011/1031/cu2.htm (accessed 11 April 2016).

Rakha (2011) *Kitāb al-Ṭughra* [*The Sultan's Seal*] (Cairo: Dar al-Shourouk).

Ross, Andrew (2000) 'Hacking Away at the Counterculture', in Barbara Kennedy and David Bell (eds) *The Cybercultures Reader* (New York: Routledge).

3

Just a Bunch of (Arab) Geeks?

How a 'Techie' Elite Shaped a Digital Culture in the Arab Region and Contributed to the Making of the Arab Uprisings

Donatella Della Ratta and Augusto Valeriani[1]

When debating the so-called 'Arab Spring' – a wave of uprisings that has shaken the Arab world and reshaped its geopolitics since December 2010 – the international media often have emphasised the role that social networks, particularly Facebook and Twitter, have allegedly played in boosting the revolt and ousting ruling regimes, at least in the case of Tunisia and Egypt. Whether because it was deemed 'catchy', or as being 'far easier to document than less virtual kinds of activism',[2] the technology dimension of the uprisings seems to have inspired many to talk about an emerging 'democracy's fourth wave'[3] that has been nurtured by the internet. In this framework, the latter is understood as the 'technology of freedom'[4] *par excellence*; consequently, the participatory culture[5] that it generates is interpreted as being quintessentially political, as if intrinsically acted in the direction of democracy.

This chapter problematises this approach, making it more nuanced by framing the debate on the 'Arab Spring' and, in general, on the relationship between contemporary social movements and new technologies in light of the following considerations.

First, even within tech-savvy and highly skilled communities, participatory culture does not necessarily translate into a fully-fledged political project. As Jenkins, Ford and Green[6] have noted, participation is a complex process that implies production per se, but which also involves evaluation, appraisal, critique and sharing material. Such practices of curation, conversation and sharing could hint at a 'broader political process'[7] in the making, yet this does not automatically turn into direct political actions; neither does it lead, by its own nature, to establishing a framework for democracy. The novel opportunities for self-expression that are enabled by the internet should not be necessarily interpreted as though they were empowerment tools given to the people so that they can exercise more influence (and pressure) on political institutions.

A theoretical possibility exists that this self-expression could turn into political awareness or political engagement. Yet it would be problematic, at the least, to read such practices of creating, sharing and manipulating content as though they quintessentially hinted at a democratic process in the making; or to interpret the internet as the paradigmatic framework that is enabling a democratic political structure. However, participatory culture indeed does unsettle conventional hierarchies, as people have higher expectations about monitoring and debating publicly on the politics of the powers that be – and thanks to Web 2.0-based and cost-effective platforms, they now have more tools with which to engage in those activities. This might be a more appropriate framework with which to reflect on the contribution that participatory culture and internet-based technologies have made to contemporary social movements in general, and to the Arab uprisings in particular.

Second, rather than emphasising the role played by technology, and in particular by social networking websites as a mobilisation tool[8] in protest movements, this chapter draws attention to the culture[9] that this technology generates. Scholarship on Web 2.0, a term popularised by the internet entrepreneur Tim O'Reilly in 2005,[10] has pointed to its relational nature as a system of human interconnections that are supported by a 'collective intelligence'.[11] Social networking websites and platforms which lie at the core of Web 2.0 (also dubbed the 'participatory' or 'social web') make content creation and distribution more accessible and cost-effective; yet rather than it being a purely technological shift, this process has direct implications for the reshaping of social relations, and in reconfiguring the production and circulation of knowledge. When discussing the idea of the cyberculture that is nurtured within cyberspace, Pierre Lévy underlined that:

> [T]he term refers not only to the material infrastructure of digital communication but to the oceanic universe of information it holds, as well as the human beings who navigate and nourish that infrastructure. Cyberculture is the set of technologies (material and intellectual), practices, attitudes, modes of thought and values that developed along with the growth of cyberspace.[12]

This emphasis on the process rather than on the product, and on the social relationships enabled by the technology rather than on the technology itself, is echoed in the description of the 'network society' and its protocols of communication. That is, 'the practices and their supporting organisational platforms'[13] that make sharing cultural patterns possible, as Manuel Castells has put it: 'in our society, the protocols of communication are not based on the sharing of culture but on the culture of sharing.'[14]

Here, Castells refers to a new possibility of content production that is enabled by internet-based technologies: a culture of 'co-production of the content that is consumed, regardless of the specific content'.[15] He places the value of sharing at the core of the network society's emerging culture, underlining how the technologies that characterise Web 2.0 help this new culture to be formed and to emerge. Castells' emphasis on culture rather than technology matches Jenkins' idea of 'convergence'[16] as a cultural phenomenon that takes place 'in the minds of the communicative subjects who integrate various modes and channels of communication in their practice and in their interaction with each other'.[17] The same idea has been put forward by Lawrence Lessig[18] in speaking of 'remix' or 'read/write culture' as the possibility for users to produce, reproduce and manipulate content as well as consume it.

Introducing the 'Arab Techies'

In light of these considerations, which prove useful in moving the debate away from the far too simplistic 'Twitter and Facebook revolutions' approach, the aim of this chapter is to focus on a specific group of people who helped shape digital culture in the Arab world and who, to some extent, gave an active contribution to the successful outcome of the uprisings in ousting the ruling regimes – at least in the case of Tunisia and Egypt. By adopting a micro-sociological approach,[19] the chapter aims to outline a sort of ethnography of this group of people, their activities and mutual interconnections prior to the uprisings.

Borrowing the name of one of the regional gatherings held in Cairo in 2008, we will define this community as the 'Arab Techies'. This group of 100 people, coming from different Arab countries, cannot possibly include all of the tech-savvy individuals and communities who were active in the Arab region prior to the uprisings. Moreover, it definitively would not be the sole online community using Web 2.0-based tools and platforms to confront the Arab regimes or to express defiance. However, as this chapter will try to underline, this very group of Arab Techies has played an important role in the context of the social movements that erupted in late 2010, and resulted in the ousting of Zine El Abidine Ben Ali and Hosni Mubarak's regimes in Tunisia and Egypt, respectively.

During the past decade and long before December 2010, this regional but small community had developed a common ground where technology was meant to embody both the symbol of freedom of expression, and the tool with which to seize it. Individual Arab Techies, people such as Slim Amamou in Tunisia, or Alaa Abdel Fattah in Egypt, were arrested prior or during the uprisings and have later become popular icons of political dissent in their countries. Others, such as the Tunisian activist Sami Ben Gharbia, or the Egyptian blogger Wael Abbas, gained international visibility and credibility as sources of information while events unfolded. Yet the role played by the community of Arab Techies as a whole, particularly when exercising what this chapter will describe as a connective function between anti-regime movements of a different nature – whether online or offline, or traditional agencies such as trade unions or novel forms of grass roots movements, such as the 'smart mobs'[20] nurtured by the internet – was even more significant.

In light of the broader debate revolving around the role that the internet as a social infrastructure played in shaping and reshaping social movements in the context of the Arab uprisings, the focus on a handful of people might appear inappropriate or too narrow, at first glance. However, this chapter argues that a micro-ethnography is useful in understanding how the application of a cultural framework derived from technology – practices such as curation, framing, tagging and the like, in the context of contemporary social movements – can help to link and reconnect the online and the offline, the virtual and more traditional types of activism, in some cases even leading to a successful outcome for the movement's demands.

There are two background considerations to be made before describing the Arab Techies. First, many different and nuanced ways exist through which to express activism and participatory culture, as well as resistance to a social and political status quo. They are not necessarily manifested in strictly political terms or the generation of political action, yet they can take the shape of novel and unexpected possibilities for undoing previously existing hierarchies, manifesting dissent and channelling defiance. Such action might include forms of 'semiotic guerrilla warfare',[21] where expression of creativity or alternative lifestyles suggest an implicit or explicit counter-hegemonic meaning and function. People and communities also understand and use technology differently: the Arab Techies are just one of the many groups of individuals that have aimed to use the internet and new technologies to achieve change. This is something which in their case (but not in all cases) came with political awareness. Second, the ethnography on the Arab Techies should be read in light of a set of cultural patterns generated by technology, not within the frame of technological determinism.

This chapter argues that, having largely familiarised themselves with Web 2.0-based tools and platforms prior to the uprisings, the Arab Techies had become acquainted with the broader cultural ecosystem that these technologies define and help to nurture. In order to use technology, one not only needs to have technological skills and to master the tools, but also to master a culture. As Stuart Hall[22] emphasised, culture results from a combination of 'ideas' and 'practices', the latter generating social relationships which, in turn, contribute to the reshaping of culture.

Thus, by *practising* technology for a decade, the Arab Techies have generated a culture. This culture was first developed on a common ground provided by a shared tech language defined around free and open source software (FOSS), open licensing (Creative Commons), the distribution of rights-free content (copyleft) and so forth, that hints at symbolic values such as freedom of expression, freedom to manipulate and share content, and the right to privacy and anonymity. More generally, this suggests an understanding of the internet and new technologies as being basic human rights. It is thanks to this shared language that such a diverse group of individuals, from those who were strictly techies (such as developers, geeks, hackers and hacktivists), to bloggers, citizen journalists, artists, human right activists, with different degrees of political awareness and affiliation[23] could develop their own version of Arab digital culture and shape its identity as a community; and where the latter, according to McMillan and Chavis,[24] is defined by membership, reciprocal influence, reinforcement and shared emotional connection.

Here, our aim is to understand how, in the context of the Arab region, a diverse group of youth has come together and created a network of relationships, developing projects to promote freedom of expression, information sharing, open source awareness and, ultimately, social and political change. Our argument is that while sharing ideas and socialising practices around the use of technology, the Arab Techies also socialised values and shaped and negotiated a specific culture: that is,. their own version of digital culture.

Reorienting the nexus between subcultures, class and globalisation

Our micro-ethnography of Arab Techies is situated in the wider framework of subcultural studies theories. It aims to contribute to the theoretical debate by suggesting that there is a shift from a class-oriented to a more medium-oriented approach in the study of contemporary social movements and political change.

As outlined earlier, it is not the medium or the technology per se which defines a subculture, but the *culture* that this technology generates and the ways in which the medium is reconfigured, and even displaced, through the creative practices of bricolage and remixing. This rearticulation of the relationship between subculture and social class could contribute to a readjustment of the focus of subcultural studies towards a more nuanced, less class-oriented direction, where technology as a social and cultural milieu can function as an important driver for the redefinition of (sub)cultural practices and identities.

The strong class emphasis that scholarship traditionally has placed on the study of subcultures[25] was nurtured by a theoretical opposition to the idea that class was no longer a pivotal dimension in the analysis of social structures. As shown by the work of Christine Griffin,[26] several of the seminal studies on subcultures that were conducted at the Birmingham School focused heavily on class, and were inspired by the objective of understanding how working-class youth negotiate and transform their material conditions of living through cultural practices of everyday life. The prominent position occupied by class in these studies has been questioned from different perspectives and by different authors; such as Sarah Thornton[27] who, in her study of techno and club cultures in the 1990s, has emphasised the common desire for classlessness within these subcultures.[28] However, as Griffin contends, this 'will to classlessness'[29] did not suggest that class, as an explanatory category, was no longer relevant to the analysis of subcultures. Actually, this attitude came to signal quite the opposite, and should be historically framed and understood within a specific sociopolitical context: that of Europe in the 1990s.

Far from portraying class as the pivotal factor in driving cultural practices and identities, or from completely dismissing its role, our ethnography of these Arab Techies suggests that a less class-centred approach could be adopted in the study of contemporary subcultures and social movements. It also shows that in the latter case, a medium-oriented approach could prove to be useful, provided that it does not overplay the technological dimension at the expense of the cultural one.

The Arab Techies are indeed an elite of tech-savvy youth, mostly English-speakers, who come from a middle-class, socio-economic background, with a liberal orientation in terms of religious beliefs. They are familiar with international online movements that fight for free and open software (such as FOSS), copyright reform and legal sharing (such as Creative Commons), or advocacy groups (such as Global Voices). Yet instead of reading this exclusively in class-oriented terms, we propose here to shift the focus to the medium that defines the identity of this community and shapes its culture: the internet.

Discussing the cultural patterns enabled by different forms of communication, the sociologist Manuel Castells identifies 'networked individualism'[30] as the quintessential expression of the network society.[31] While cosmopolitanism would be the cultural pattern attached to a more traditional form of communication relating to global news networks, the internet encourages a 'multicultural global culture characterised by the hybridisation and remix of cultures from different origins'.[32] Although being intrinsically global and networked, this culture is characterised by a high degree of individualism. In Castells' view, 'networked individualism' is the cultural pattern which better expresses the attitude of individuals who expand their sociability by using the 'wealth of networks'[33] selectively, and to the advantage of their own values and interests. By being infra-structurally based on 'autonomy, horizontal networking, interactivity and the recombination of content under the initiative of the individual',[34] the internet becomes the technology that better embodies the multicultural global culture framed within the pattern of networked individualism.

Our micro-ethnography of Arab Techies will show how, within the multicultural global culture rooted in networked individualism, this group of individuals was able to build a community and its own personal approach to digital culture.

How the Arab Techies developed their community and culture before 2011

The Arab digital culture developed by the Arab Techies during the years in which their community was formed exhibits two main features: a 'coder' aspect, tech-oriented and geeky, focused on technology and computer programming; and a 'blogger' aspect, content-oriented, revolving around user-generated media production. The core members of the Arab Techies have backgrounds either in web development, programming, engineering, or in blogging and content creation. This intertwining of technology and content is one of the most peculiar features of the Arab digital culture that we studied. In other digital cultures, either the 'coder' or 'blogger' identity is usually privileged at the expense of the other. The other feature to be underlined here is the regional or pan-Arab dimension of these techies: that is, the transborder interconnections between people who speak the same language and share cultural similarities. Thanks to the internet and new technologies, a sort of 'grassroots Pan Arabism'[35] was shaped, reconnecting Arabs from different countries and professional backgrounds around the idea of, and passion for, technology for social change.

These two features that identify the particularity of Arab digital culture, as defined by the Arab Techies, were shaped in the early 2000s but only became apparent towards the end of the past decade. Although technology-themed meetings and gatherings were held in the Arab region through the first decade of the 2000s – for example, the Linux Install Fest (Egypt, 2004), software freedom days (Tunisia, 2007), youth tech camps (Egypt, 2007), the first truly regional platform to bring together Arab activists, bloggers and tech-savvies was the Arab Techies Workshop (Egypt, 2008), where around

80 people from almost the entire region gathered; and the first Arab Bloggers Conference (Lebanon, 2008), with a total of 29 participants from ten Arab countries.

Both gatherings were inspired by a shared feeling that a regional framework was needed in order to create new relationships, or to consolidate existing ones, between activists from different Arab countries. Also, that technology could work as a common ground from which to link people coming from a strictly tech background and those bloggers or citizen journalists who made a daily, although basic, use of Web 2.0-based applications and tools to produce and distribute their own content. Hence, these gatherings had the objective of creating more synergy and solidarity, both at a regional level and across different skills, backgrounds and professional experiences. As emphasised by the official website of the Arab Techies' meeting:

> Despite the emergence of such highly connected communities of citizen journalists, cyber artists and digital activists, the techies who provide support and infrastructure to these communities, are still working in isolation [...] Hence the need for an event to bring those isolated techies together and build a regional community, to share experiences and knowledge, learn from each other and collaborate on solving common problems.[36]

The need to hook up with other groups that shared a similar interest in technology was also reaffirmed by the Arab Bloggers Conference, which stressed the importance for content creators and digital activists to learn about the 'means and tools available for creative use of the internet in the Arab region'.[37]

Two techies, Sami Ben Gharbia and Alaa Abdel Fattah, from Tunisia and Egypt, respectively (the two countries at the forefront of digital activism in the Arab world), were among the most active individuals behind the idea to turn a savvy but loose community of geeks into a regionally organised network of activists, and to link this up to bloggers and citizen journalists. Here, we do not aim to overplay the role of a few individuals in forming the Arab Techies' community and in shaping an Arab digital culture. However, we want to underline how these people have played the key role of community organisers to connect people, and facilitate dialogue and the coming together of those both with a tech background and who were mostly working in content creation.

Ben Gharbia is a Tunisian blogger and activist who, in 1998, was forced into exile in the Netherlands, where he remained until the fall of Ben Ali's regime. During his years in exile, Ben Gharbia never stopped writing about censorship and freedom of expression-related issues, denouncing the repressive (yet in the eyes of Western countries, apparently mild) apparatus of the Tunisian government. In 2004, he co-founded the award-winning collective blog *Nawaat*,[38] an aggregator of news, videos and other information sources which, over the years, has acted as a catalyst for many dissident voices against the Tunisian regime, and which has hosted debates and campaigns to raise awareness on cyber-surveillance, online censorship and government abuse of personal freedoms. During the outbreak of the Tunisian revolution, *Nawaat* played a pivotal role in aggregating, translating and disseminating information by performing a content curation function, which proved key in reaching out to Arab and international media outlets, many of which either were based abroad or barred from entering the country – as in the case of Al Jazeera, winning them over to the cause of the anti-regime uprising.[39]

Ben Gharbia was also the founder and acting director, until 2012, of the advocacy initiative supported by Global Voices Online,[40] with the goal of seeking to build a 'global anti-censorship network of bloggers and online activists throughout the developing world that is dedicated to protecting freedom of expression and free access to information online'.[41] Global Voices Advocacy has organised and supported several anti-censorship initiatives and action that aimed to free digital activists and bloggers in the Arab world. These campaigns, as we will see, have contributed strongly to bringing activists together around common battles, and have helped shape their awareness of being a fully-fledged community.

Fattah is an Egyptian blogger and software developer who grew up in a family of political and human rights activists. In 2005, together with his wife Manal Hassan, also a techie and activist, he founded the first Egyptian blog aggregator, *Manaala*, which was awarded the special Reporters Without Borders prize in Deutsche Welle's 'Best Blog' competition. Fattah was also among the founders of the Egyptian Linux Users Group, which organised the aforementioned Install Fest in Cairo back in 2004, with the aim of familiarising people with the use of FOSS not only as an alternative to proprietary systems, but also as a viable solution to circumventing online surveillance and to protect anonymity and privacy. On 7 May 2006, Fattah was imprisoned for calling for an independent judiciary during a peaceful sit-in. Three days after his arrest, the Global Voices community, to which the Egyptian activist was already connected, launched 'Google bomb for Alaa', a global campaign that aimed to draw international attention to the Fattah's case. Not only was Fattah released, but the initiative was so successful that, as Jillian York from the Electronic Frontier Foundation (EFF) has underlined, it also had 'the unintentional effect of creating a meme'[42] which has spread across several Arab countries, inspiring similar campaigns from Morocco to Syria that call for the release of other activists and bloggers.

The importance of sharing a cause to advocate and fight for is crucial in building and strengthening those elements of membership, influence, reinforcement and emotional connection that have been identified as key constituents of a community. To this extent, campaigns such as the 'Google bomb for Alaa' have helped Arab Techies, bloggers and digital activists to get together and build a solid transnational network of interests and action. Actually, this process had already started a year before Fattah's imprisonment, when the Ali Abdulemam case occurred. Abdulemam is a Bahraini blogger who anonymously founded the Bahrain Online portal in 1998. In 2002 he revealed his identity and the website, which had gained popularity among the Bahraini opposition, was blocked in the country. Eventually, savvy users circumvented the ban and were able to access Bahrain Online by using online anti-censorship tools. Three years later in February 2005, Abdulemam, together with the Bahrain Online team, was arrested on the charge of inciting hatred of the government. The arbitrary arrest of the Bahrain Online team and their refusal to be bailed out, in a further act of defiance and de-legitimisation of the government, encouraged several Bahraini bloggers and international activists to establish the 'Free Ali' web page and start a global mobilisation campaign. Not only was the 'Free Ali' campaign 'Bahrain's first blogging-led mass protest',[43] but it was also successful in mobilising the country's liberal press, resulting in further international attention. Suddenly, pictures of pro-'Free Ali' demonstrations went viral on the internet, and were shared and republished on international and Arabic blogs and media outlets. Finally, thanks to international pressure on the Bahraini authorities, the web-led 'Free Ali' movement succeeded in achieving Abdulemam's release.

The 'Free Ali' campaign was probably the first example of a cross-country initiative to gather a regional community of bloggers, activists, techies and geeks around a common issue which, for the first time, conceived of technology as being something closely intertwined with freedom of expression and human rights. Finally, 'Free Ali', 'Google bomb for Alaa' and other campaigns and online protests that were launched to protect activists' rights, as well as outreach initiatives to keep the internet free and uncontrolled by using circumvention tools – a tech issue that quickly turned into a human rights issue – resulted in the catalysing and consolidating of a regional community of activists and techies. These initiatives provided them with membership and a deep feeling of belonging; influence and a sense that their efforts would make a difference; reinforcement and integration; and above all, a shared sense of having a common history. Briefly, these campaigns triggered the formation of a community, as described above, following the definition proposed by McMillan and Chavis.

It is interesting to note that all the activists mentioned above – Ben Gharbia, Fattah and Abdulemam – played a prominent role both in the Arab Techies' meeting and the Arab Bloggers' conference in 2008. Ben Gharbia and Fattah co-founded and organised the techies' meeting, and were consultants to the participants' selection process; they were also session leaders at the bloggers' conference. Abdulemam was one of the most prominent guests of the tech-themed gathering, welcomed as an icon of free speech (which he effectively was), while another member of Bahrain Online, Ali Abdel Imam, joined the Beirut, Lebanon gathering in 2008. Moreover, they all actively contributed to the Global Voices network, either by writing and translating articles or by planning outreach campaigns and advocacy efforts. This international network of bloggers, contributors and human rights activists who gathered around the online portal – which was incubated by the Berkman Center for Internet and Society at Harvard University, and later became a non-profit organisation registered in the Netherlands – resulted in the Arab activists being provided with quality contacts and crucial connections. The international links with people such as the former Harvard scholar Ethan Zuckerman, co-founder of Global Voices, Jillian York, EFF director for International Freedom of Expression, as well as international journalists and other techies, proved invaluable when the already promising Arab community needed training and advice on specific issues. Furthermore, during the unfolding of the Arab uprisings, the strong connection with Global Voices' highly qualified network of supporters helped Arab activists, especially those from Tunisia and Egypt, to reach out to international media outlets and to frame their content and information sources within a narrative of non-violent, pro-democracy uprisings that was very appealing to Western audiences.

Hence, the first Arab regional meetings held in 2008 were successful in two ways. First, they managed to catalyse a community of techies, activists and content creators that had existed in the Arab world since the early 2000s, but which was scattered and only loosely joined. Previous online initiatives such as the 2005 and 2006 campaigns to free Abdulemam and Fattah had boosted the community – yet a common framework was needed, and technology offered it. A culture of technology, derived from practices of sharing, curating and framing that are embedded in Web 2.0 platforms, helped to gather and cohere disparate groups with different approaches to political activism. In this way, a common ground was formed between computer engineers, content producers, educators and non-governmental organisation employees, and a rhetoric was shaped around the culture of sharing that would be enabled and boosted by technology, particularly the internet.

As noted by our previous research,[44] even though these techies come from such different backgrounds, they have contributed to forging a vision for technology being the main driver for social change. Here, technology is not understood as a set of tools and applications, but rather as being primarily a *culture*. 'We used technology because technology is intrinsically part of our life,' as Fattah stated.[45]

Second, a further achievement of these meetings was that they were able to consolidate links and connections between the Arab community of activists, bloggers and techies and the international one. Prominent international activists in the domain of technology and freedom of expression – such as EFF's Jillian York, Jacob Applebaum, the activist and computer programmer behind the Tor circumvention software that is widely used to avoid surveillance and identity tracking, and Marek Tuszynski, co-founder and creative director of the Tactical Technology Collective[46] – have been invited to attend several regional tech-themed meetings in the Arab world with the aim of giving workshops, talks or training sessions there. This ongoing interchange between Arab and international activists, which has developed and strengthened over the past decade, has proved key in crisis situations such as the Arab uprisings and, at least in the case of Tunisia and Egypt, has contributed to framing events in a way that an international audience could relate to easily, and with which they could sympathise.

The Arab Techies and Arab bloggers' communities have gathered regularly in recent years,[47] and become a solid platform for regional cooperation between techies and activists, boosted by the achievements of digital activism in Tunisia and Egypt. In addition, they have generated several spin-offs, such as the 'Arabisation' Code Sprint (Cairo, 2009), a marathon for computer programmers that aimed to 'localise' software in the Arabic language; or Arab Techies Women (Beirut, 2010)[48] led by Fattah's wife, Manal Hassan. Moreover, sister communities such as Creative Commons[49] have adopted both the regional cooperation approach, by holding annual Arab world meetings and the localisation model, by hosting locally organised, grass roots events that aim to combine the global internet culture with local cultures – as in the case of Creative Commons Iftars, community gatherings held during *iftar* (the meal which breaks the Ramadan fast) to discuss technology and brainstorm about collaborative ideas and projects.

In this way, a local version of digital culture, whose main features were the integration of diverse communities, coders and content creators into a regional, pan-Arab network, was shaped by the Arab Techies. When the Arab uprisings unfolded in late 2010, this community finally was able to put its regional and international connections to work and to prove its technical and curational skills in gathering, spreading and distributing information about the events. Eventually, a patient and out-of-the-spotlight 'work of at least a decade'[50] became the much trumpeted Facebook and Twitter revolutions of the media headlines.

Did the Arab Techies boost the 2011 uprisings?

Before discussing the role played by the Arab Techies in the uprisings, particularly in the cases of Tunisia and Egypt, it is useful to look briefly at the scholarship on contemporary social movements and their contribution to social change. Social movements, in Della Porta and Diani's view, are 'networks of interaction between different actors which may either include formal organisations or not, depending on shifting circumstances'.[51] Yet the loose nature of these networks requires steady work from individuals who should act as 'brokers':[52] connectors between the different nodes of the network. According to the scholarship,[53] these brokers should perform three main tasks within the network:

- develop and expand the movement's web of relationships and its connections at the local, regional and global levels;
- disseminate information concerning the movement, after having framed it in ways that might generate internal and external support for its cause;
- plan tactics and strategies that are based on bricolage – that is, reinventing opposition practices by remixing and re-manipulating the existing ones.

We argue that by the time the uprisings had erupted in the region, the Arab Techies already had acquired the cultural tools to perform these three tasks, and that their brokering role had been nurtured long before by a common ground developed around technology, and the sense of sharing a common (Arab digital) culture (as described earlier).

Concerning the first task, which should be performed by a broker within social movements – that is, to connect people[54] – the Arab Techies were successful in establishing local and regional connections between Arabs from different countries and professional backgrounds. Moreover, they were able to act at an international level by building a solid network of techies, journalists, scholars and activists who helped to frame information and news sources during the outbreak of the uprisings. Andrew Carvin probably represents the best example in this respect. Although never having been on the ground during the unfolding of the Arab uprisings, the former senior strategist for social media at the US public broadcaster NPR produced an up-to-date account of the events in Tunisia, Egypt and Libya by profiting from an online network of contacts that he had developed previously in the region. Both Ben Gharbia and Fattah, together with many others from the Arab Techies' community, were in Carvin's selected network of sources. Thus, they were able to reach out to the American audience, feeding it with up-to-date information from the ground.

The second task to be performed by social movements' brokers is connecting the information. The scholarship in the area has described this function as 'information politics',[55] meaning the process of producing and sharing information (text, pictures, videos), creating slogans and engaging in an ongoing dialogue with the media in order to inspire sympathy with the cause of the movement and discredit its opponents. Meikle has argued that in a participative framework such as Web 2.0, content production can be generated anywhere and everywhere in the network.[56] However, since this process might result in chaos and an abundance of information, this content has more chances of being circulated and shared if it is properly framed and curated. The practice of curation requires framing content into context: an operation that should be performed by individuals with a reputation (both online and offline) and personal connections outside the network. The Tunisian blogging platform *Nawaat* illustrates this process of content curation well. During the Tunisian uprising, this web portal performed a central role in framing information about the unfolding of events into a context: it selected newsworthy material from Facebook, translated it from Tunisian dialect into formal Arabic or French, tagged and distributed it to mainstream media networks. As Ben Gharbia has noted,[57] the information cascade generated by this process worked perfectly in the Tunisian case, since the grass roots activism generated within social networks (the only sources of information on the ground) was finally put in touch with the mainstream media (those who delivered official news and updates to Arab and international audiences). Curation platforms such as *Nawaat* made this connection between the grass roots and the mainstream possible – and eventually successful.

Finally, the third task that a connective leadership should be able to perform is remixing information in order to rearrange existing repertoires of actions and tactics. In this respect, Campbell has argued that:

> Change in practices generally results from a blending of bits and pieces from a repertoire of elements. This may entail the rearrangement of elements that are already at hand, but it may also entail the blending in of new elements that have diffused from elsewhere.[58]

The idea of bricolage and remixing lies at the heart of the 'do it yourself' (DIY) philosophy that is shared by several subcultural groups which have developed around (and within) the internet[59] since the cyberpunk movements of the early 1980s.[60] This approach also resonates with Deleuze and Guattari's[61] 'rhizomatic' notion of culture, which puts an emphasis on producing meaning instead of consuming it, and suggests a non-hierarchical scheme of knowledge circulation.

Probably the best example of how remixing and DIY ideas have penetrated Arab digital culture is the video *Dans la tête de Aziza* (*In Aziza's Head*), produced in 2005 by Riadh Guerfali,[62] a Tunisian lawyer, computer programmer and a co-founder of *Nawaat*. *Dans la tête de Aziza* is a remix of a well-known Macintosh commercial inspired by *1984*, the novel by George Orwell. By using the same visual language and Orwellian atmosphere of the original video, the remix features an overt critique of Ben Ali's regime, openly suggesting that citizens should wake up from their decade-long sleep and overthrow it. This work clearly shows the fluency of Tunisian activists in the practice of remixing messages, both text and visuals, and in their mastery of genres such as satire and parody to undo the regime's rhetoric.

As these examples have shown, Tunisian and Egyptian activists are proven to have mastered technology not only as a set of applications and platforms, but also as a cultural tool. Undoubtedly, the Arab Techies were among those privileged ones who had access to technological tools and were skilled enough to be able to use them in crisis circumstances by employing advanced techniques such as circumvention, anonymity and the like. However, most importantly, this community developed around a read and write culture, and was deeply nurtured by the belief that on the web, each individual was potentially an active content producer rather than just a consumer. As both Manovich[63] and Lessig[64] have noted, this cultural attitude is far from being an internet-generated phenomenon. Manovich[65] underlines that 'most human cultures developed by borrowing and reworking forms and styles from other cultures; the resulting "remixes" were to be incorporated into other cultures'.

Thus, the internet has just brought back and diffused on a mass scale a way of producing and understanding culture that had existed throughout the centuries. This approach to framing the internet in terms of culture, rather than as a set of technologies, helps us to understand how ideas and practices expressed through the digital could have both high-tech (e.g. the case of memes[66] created and virally circulated through online social networks) and low-tech (e.g. graffiti sprayed on city walls and reproduced virally) manifestations. Similarly, they can develop and spread either in online and/or offline contexts. This explains how someone such as Ali Bouazizi, the first activist to film Mohammed Bouazizi's self-immolation in Sidi Bouzid Square in late December 2010, could use the video, after it was properly edited, tagged and framed in the right context, to distribute virally on social networks and generate a wave of outrage among Tunisians which eventually led to the fall of Ben Ali's regime. At the time of the video, Bouazizi, who has a solid background in traditional offline activism (he is an active member of a trade union and a militant for workers' rights), had very few contacts on Facebook and limited access to the internet.[67] However, low access to technological tools did not prevent him from making use of cultural tools such as remixing and bricolage, tagging, framing and content curation. Here, we do not want to argue that Ali Bouazizi, or other individuals, whether from the Arab Techies or other communities, sparked the uprising through their savvy use of the media. What we want to emphasise is that the 'creative audience' at the 'source of the remix culture'[68] has the potential and capacity to challenge existing power relationships by creating holes within the communication system, which is also a power system. In some cases, such as Tunisia and Egypt, and with the presence of several other processes at work on the ground in the more traditional domains of politics, communities such as the Arab Techies and even non-tech-skilled individuals such as Bouazizi, were able to contribute to the making of social movements and, eventually, to ousting the regimes.

Conclusion

This chapter has reflected on the roles played by the internet and new technologies in reshaping contemporary social movements in the context of the Arab uprisings, particularly in Tunisia and Egypt. A micro-ethnography of a restricted group of people, whom we have identified as the Arab Techies, and who have been active in the region for a decade (in a loose rather than organised way), has inspired our thinking about technology, social movements and political change. The Arab Techies analysed here perfectly fit the description offered by Castells of a society that is defined by networked individualism. It is in light of these considerations that this chapter proposes to add a new element to the theoretical reflection on subcultures and political movements. If, as stated here, technology is defined not only by a set of tools, but also by the cultural milieu resulting from the use and appropriation of those tools, then we should not dissociate the study of subcultures and social movements that are nurtured by networked technologies of communication from their cultural dimension.

Castells' idea of a networked individualism expressing a multicultural global culture has proved to be a useful conceptual frame when approaching study of the Arab Techies and their contribution to the uprisings. It has helped us to understand how a community such as the Arab Techies, who were considered 'just a bunch of geeks', could possibly imagine social and political change in the region – while at the same time acting as one of the many (albeit not necessarily the most significant) driving forces that pushed towards this change, in some cases achieving positive outcomes.

Notes

1. This chapter is the result of joint research work and an ongoing dialogue between the two authors which started with previous joint publications on the topic of Arab tech elites. However, in accordance with the conventions of Italian academia, we specify that Donatella Della Ratta has authored the paragraphs: 'A cultural approach to the study of tech communities in the Arab world' and 'Geeks with a cause: How the Arab techies developed their community and culture prior to the 2011 uprisings'; while Augusto Valeriani has authored the paragraphs: 'Reorienting the nexus between subcultures, class and globalisation' and 'Have the Arab Techies boosted the 2011 uprisings?' 'Introducing the Arab Techies' and 'Conclusion' were jointly compiled by the two authors.
2. Jean-Pierre Filiu, in Paul Hockenos and Jean-Pierre Filiu (2011) 'The Arab Revolution: "We Have a Lot to Learn from Them"', *Open Democracy*, 24 November. Available at www.opendemocracy.net/paul-hockenos-jean-pierre-filiu/arab-revolution-%E2%80%9Cwe-have-lot-to-learn-from-them%E2%80%9D (accessed 25 April 2016)
3. Philip N. Howard and Muzammil M. Hussain (2013) *Democracy's Fourth Wave? Digital Media and the Arab Spring* (New York: Oxford University Press).
4. Ithiel de Sola Pool (1983) *Technologies of Freedom: On Free Speech in an Electronic Age* (Cambridge, MA: Harvard University Press)
5. Bart Decrem, founder and former CEO of online venture Flock, defines Web 2.0 as a participatory web, in contrast with Web 1.0, which is described as source of information. Web 2.0 is all about social networking and interactivity between the creator and the user.
6. Henry Jenkins, Sam Ford and Joshua Green (2013) *Spreadable Media: Creating Value and Meaning in a Networked Culture* (New York: New York University Press)
7. Ibid., p.171.
8. Marc Lynch (2013) 'Twitter Devolutions. How Social Media Is Hurting the Arab Spring', *Foreign Policy*, 7 February. Available at www.foreignpolicy.com/articles/2013/02/07/twitter_devolutions_arab_spring_social_media (accessed 25 July 2013).
9. On the Internet as a culture, see Pierre Lévy (2001) *Cyberculture* (Minneapolis, MN: University of Minnesota Press); Lev Manovich (2001) *The Language of New Media* (Cambridge MA:: MIT Press); Manuel Castells (2001) *The Internet Galaxy* (Oxford: Oxford University Press).
10. Tim O'Reilly (2005) 'What is Web 2.0: Design Patterns and Business Models for the Next Generation of Software', *O'Reilly*, 30 September. Available at http://oreilly.com/web2/archive/what-is-web-20.html (accessed 22 July 2013).

11 See Pierre Lévy (1994) *L'Intelligence collective: Pour une anthropologie du cyberespace* (Paris: Edition La Découverte).
12 Lévy, *Cyberculture*, p. xvi.
13 Manuel Castells (2013) *Communication Power*, 2nd edn (Oxford: Oxford University Press), p. 126.
14 Ibid., p. 126.
15 Ibid., p. 126.
16 Henry Jenkins (2006) *Convergence Culture: Where Old and New Media Collide* (New York: New York University Press).
17 Castells, *Communication Power*, p. 135.
18 Lawrence Lessig (2008) *Remix, Making Art and Commerce Thrive in the Hybrid Economy* (New York: Penguin Books).
19 See Michel de Certeau (1980) *L'invention du quotidien. 1: Arts de faire* (Paris: Gallimard).
20 Howard Rheingold (2002) *Smart Mobs: The Next Social Revolution* (Cambridge, MA: Perseus Books).
21 See Dick Hebdige (1979) *Subculture: The Meaning of Style* (London: Routledge).
22 Stuart Hall (1980) 'Cultural Studies: Two Paradigms', *Media, Culture and Society* 2(1): 57–72.
23 See Donatella Della Ratta and Augusto Valeriani (2012) 'Remixing the Spring! Connective leadership and read-write practices in the 2011 Arab uprisings', *CyberOrient* 6(1). Available at www.cyberorient.net/article.do?articleId=7763 (accessed 22 July 2013).
24 According to David W. McMillan and David M. Chavis in defining communities: 'The first element is membership. Membership is the feeling of belonging or of sharing a sense of personal relatedness. The second element is influence, a sense of mattering, of making a difference to a group and of the group mattering to its members. The third element is reinforcement: integration and fulfillment of needs [...] The last element is shared emotional connection, the commitment and belief that members have shared and will share history, common places, time together and similar experiences.' David W. McMillan and David M. Chavis, 'Sense of Community: A Definition and Theory', *Journal of Community Psychology* 14(1): 6–23, p. 9.
25 John Clarke, Stuart Hall, Tony Jefferson and Brian Roberts (1976) 'Subcultures, Cultures and Class', in Stuart Hall and Tony Jefferson (eds) *Resistance Through Rituals* (London: Routledge).
26 Christine E. Griffin (2011) 'The Trouble with Class: Researching Youth, Class and Culture beyond the '"Birmingham School"', *Journal of Youth Studies* 14(3): 245–59.
27 Sarah Thornton (1995) *Club Culture: Music, Media and Subcultural Capital* (Cambridge: Polity Press).
28 Thornton, quoted in Griffin, 'The Trouble with Class'.

29 Ibid., p. 251.
30 Castells, *Communication Power*.
31 Manuel Castells (2010) *The Rise of the Network Society. The Information Age: Economy, Society and Culture*, Vol. 1, 2nd edn (Oxford: Blackwell).
32 Castells, *Communication Power*, p. 118.
33 Yochai Benkler (2006) *The Wealth of Networks: How Social Production Transforms Markets and Freedom* (New Haven, CT: Yale University Press).
34 Castells, *Communication Power*, p. 125.
35 Donatella Della Ratta (2009) 'Second Arab Bloggers' Meeting Over', *Mediaoriente*, 15 December. Available at http://mediaoriente.com/2009/12/15/second-arab-bloggers-meeting-over/ (accessed 25 April 2016)
36 The Arab Techies (n.d.) 'The Arab Techies Gathering'. Available at http://arabtechies.net/?q=gathering_2008 (accessed 4 August 2013).
37 www.ps.boell.org/web/117–280.html (accessed 4 August 2013; source no longer available).
38 See http://nawaat.org/portail/. In 2011 Nawaat was awarded the Index on Censorship Prize, the Reporters Without Borders Prize and the Electronic Frontier Foundation Pioneer Award.
39 See Della Ratta and Valeriani, 'Remixing the Spring!'.
40 'Global Voices is a community of more than 700 authors and 600 translators around the world who work together to bring you reports from blogs and citizen media everywhere, with emphasis on voices that are not ordinarily heard in international mainstream media', from Global Voices' official website: http://globalvoicesonline.org/about/ (accessed 4 August 2013).
41 From the Global Voices Advocacy official website http://advocacy.globalvoicesonline.org/about/ (accessed 4 August 2013).
42 In Jillian York (2012) 'The Arab Digital Vanguard: How a Decade of Blogging Contributed to a Year of Revolution', *Georgetown Journal of International Affairs* (Winter/Spring). Available at http://jilliancyork.com/wp-content/uploads/2012/02/33-42-FORUM-York.pdf (last accessed 4 August 2013).
43 In Luke Schleusener (2007) 'From Blog to Street: The Bahraini Public Sphere in Transition', *Arab Media and Society* 1. Available at www.arabmediasociety.com/?article=15 (accessed 4 August 2013).
44 See Della Ratta and Valeriani, 'Remixing the Spring!'.
45 In Augusto Valeriani (2011) 'Bridges of the Revolution: Linking People, Sharing Information and Remixing Practices', *Sociologica* 3: 1–28.
46 'We are a diverse team of information specialists, technologists, designers, human rights advocates and environmental justice activists from Europe, Asia, the Middle East and Africa. We are united by a passion for social change and the potential of technology and effective information processes to contribute to it.' From the official website of the Tactical Technology Collective: https://tacticaltech.org/team (accessed 4 August 2013).

47 The last gathering of both the Arab Techies workshop and the Arab bloggers conference was held in 2011, respectively in Cairo and Tunis.
48 'As part of the Arab Techies initiative, the Arab Techies women gathering's crux is to promote the contribution of female techies to communities concerned with social change and who are in dire need of technical support. This contribution is believed to be significant in strengthening the role of ICT in social and political change and cannot be sidelined for trivial reasons, such as the lack of assertiveness among female techies in male-dominated communities.' From the official website www.arabtechies.net/node/5 (accessed 4 August 2013).
49 Creative Commons is a non-profit organisation that enables sharing and use of creativity and knowlege through free, legal tools. It was founded in 2001 by Lawrence Lessig, who was Professor of Law at Stanford University at the time. Creative Commons has communities of volunteers in more than 70 countries in the world, including the Arab region.
50 Ibid.
51 In Donatella Della Porta and Mario Diani (1999) *Social Movements: An Introduction* (Oxford: Blackwell), p. 16.
52 See Mario Diani (2003) '"Leaders" or "brokers"? Positions and Influence in Social Movement Networks', in Mario Diani and Doug McAdam (eds) *Social Movements and Networks* (Oxford: Oxford University Press).
53 See, for example, Alberto Melucci (1996) *Challenging Codes: Collective Action in the Information Age* (Cambridge: Cambridge University Press), or David A. Snow, Sarah A. Soule and Hanspeter Kriesi (eds) (2004) *The Blackwell Companion to Social Movements* (Oxford: Blackwell).
54 See Aldon D. Morris and Suzanne Staggenborg (2004) 'Leadership in Social Movements', in David A. Snow, Sarah A. Soule and Hanspeter Kriesi (eds) *The Blackwell Companion to Social Movements* (Oxford: Blackwell).
55 See Margareth E. Keck and Kathryn Sikkink (1998) *Activists Beyond Borders* (Ithaca, NY: Cornell University Press).
56 Graham Meikle (2002) *Future Active: Media Activism and the Internet* (New York: Routledge).
57 See Della Ratta and Valeriani, 'Remixing the Spring!'.
58 John L. Campbell (2005) 'Where Do We Stand? Common Mechanisms in Organizations and Social Movements' Research', in Gerald F. Davis (ed.) *Social Movements and Organization Theory* (Cambridge: Cambridge University Press), p. 56.
59 Also Mark Deuze – despite his analysis being mostly focused on journalism and news production-identifies in participation, remediation and bricolage as the features that most qualify digital cultures. See Mark Deuze (2006) 'Participation, Remediation, Bricolage: Considering Principal Components of a Digital Culture', *The Information Society* 22(2): 63–75.
60 See Tatiana Bazzichelli (2008) *Networking: The Net as Artwork* (Aarhus: Digital Aesthetics Research Center, Aarhus University).

61 Gilles Deleuze and Félix Guattari (1980) *Mille plateaux* (Paris: Editions de Minuit).
62 At the time, the video was uploaded anonymously. Only later did Guerfali reveal his identity as the creator of the work.
63 Manovich, *The Language of New Media*.
64 Lessig, *Remix, Making Art and Commerce Thrive in the Hybrid Economy*.
65 Manovich, *The Language of New Media*.
66 According to Knobel and Lankshear's definition, memes are 'contagious patterns of cultural information that get passed from mind to mind and directly generate and shape the mindsets and significant forms of behaviour and actions of a social group. Memes include such things as popular tunes, catchphrases, clothing fashions, architectural styles, ways of doing things, icons, jingles and the like'. Michele Knobel and Colin Lankshear (2007) 'Online Memes, Affinities and Cultural Production', in Colin Lankshear and Michele Knobel (eds) *A New Literacies Sampler* (New York: Peter Lang), p. 199,
67 Personal interview with Donatella Della Ratta, Sidi Bouzid, January 2012. Also see Donatella Della Ratta (2012) 'La generazione della net revolution', *East* 42: pp. 40–3.
68 Castells, *Communication Power*, p. 132.

Bibliography

Arab Techies (n.d.) 'The Arab Techies Gathering'. Available at http://arabtechies.net/?q=gathering_2008 (accessed 4 August 2013).

Attalah, Lina (2009) 'Arab Techies Collaborate for Social and Political Change', *Egypt Independent*, 5 August. Available at www.egyptindependent.com/news/arab-techies-collaborate-social-and-political-change (accessed 25 April 2016).

Bazzichelli, Tatiana (2008) *Networking: The Net as Artwork* (Aarhus: Digital Aesthetics Research Center, Aarhus University).

Benkler, Yochai (2006) *The Wealth of Networks: How Social Production Transforms Markets and Freedom* (New Haven, CT: Yale University Press).

Campbell, John L. (2005) 'Where Do We Stand? Common Mechanisms in Organizations and Social Movements' Research', in Gerald F. Davis (ed.) *Social Movements and Organization Theory* (Cambridge: Cambridge University Press).

Castells, Manuel (2001) *The Internet Galaxy* (Oxford: Oxford University Press).

―――― (2010) *The Rise of the Network Society. The Information Age: Economy, Society and Culture*, Vol. 1, 2nd edn. (Oxford: Blackwell).

―――― (2013) *Communication Power*, 2nd edn. (Oxford, Oxford University Press).

de Certeau, Michel (1980) *L'invention du quotidien. Paris:1: Arts de faire* (Paris: Gallimard).

Clarke, John, Hall, Stuart, Jefferson, Tony and Roberts, Brian (1976) 'Subcultures, cultures and class', in Stuart Hall and Tony Jefferson (eds) *Resistance Through Rituals* (London: Routledge).

Deleuze, Gilles and Guattari, Félix (1980) *Mille plateaux* (Paris: Editions de Minuit).
Della Porta, Donatella and Diani, Mario (1999) *Social Movements: An Introduction* (Oxford: Blackwell).
Della Ratta, Donatella (2009) 'Second Arab Bloggers' Meeting Over', *Mediaoriente*, 15 December. Available at http://mediaoriente.com/2009/12/15/second-arab-bloggers-meeting-over/ (accessed 25 April 2016).
——— (2012) 'La generazione della net revolution', *East* 42: 40–3.
Della Ratta, Donatella and Valeriani, Augusto (2012) 'Remixing the Spring! Connective Leadership and Read–Write Practices in the 2011 Arab Uprisings', *CyberOrient* 6(1). Available at www.cyberorient.net/article.do?articleId=7763 (accessed 22 July 2013).
Deuze, Mark (2006) 'Participation, Remediation, Bricolage: Considering Principal Components of a Digital Culture', *The Information Society* 22(2): 63–75.
Diani, Mario (2003) '"Leaders" or "brokers"? Positions and Influence in Social Movement Networks', in Mario Diani and Doug McAdam (eds) *Social Movements and Networks* (Oxford: Oxford University Press).
Griffin, Christine E. (2011) 'The Trouble with Class: Researching Youth, Class and Culture Beyond the "Birmingham School"', *Journal of Youth Studies* 14(3): 245–59.
Hall, Stuart (1980) 'Cultural Studies: Two Paradigms', *Media, Culture and Society* 2(1): 57–72.
Hebdige, Dick (1979) *Subculture: The Meaning of Style* (London: Routledge).
Hockenos, Paul and Filiu, Jean-Pierre (2011) 'The Arab Revolution: "We Have a Lot to Learn from Them"', *Open Democracy*, 24 November. Available at www.opendemocracy.net/paul-hockenos-jean-pierre-filiu/arab-revolution-%E2%80%9Cwe-have-lot-to-learn-from-them%E2%80%9D (accessed 25 April 2016).
Howard, Philip N. and Hussain, Muzammil M. (2013) *Democracy's Fourth Wave? Digital Media and the Arab Spring* (New York: Oxford University Press).
Jenkins, Henry (2006) *Convergence Culture:. Where Old and New Media Collide* (New York: New York University Press).
Jenkis, Henry, Ford, Sam and Green, Joshua (2013) *Spreadable Media: Creating Value and Meaning in a Networked Culture* (New York: New York University Press).
Keck, Margareth E. and Sikkink, Kathryn (1998) *Activists Beyond Borders* (Ithaca, NY: Cornell University Press).
Knobel, Michele and Lankshear Colin (2007) 'Online Memes, Affinities and Cultural Production', in Colin Lankshear and Michele Knobel (eds) *A New Literacies Sampler* (New York: Peter Lang).
Lessig, Lawrence (2008) *Remix, Making Art and Commerce Thrive in the Hybrid Economy* (New York: Penguin Books).
Lévy, Pierre (1994) *L'Intelligence collective: Pour une anthropologie du cyberespace* (Paris: Edition La Découverte).
——— (2001) *Cyberculture* (Minneapolis, MN: University of Minnesota Press).

Lynch, Marc (2013) 'Twitter Devolutions: How Social Media Is Hurting the Arab Spring', *Foreign Policy*, 7 February. Available at www.foreignpolicy.com/articles/2013/02/07/twitter_devolutions_arab_spring_social_media (accessed 25 July 2013).

McMillan, David W. and Chavis, David M. (1996) 'Sense of Community: A Definition and Theory', *Journal of Community Psychology* 14(1): 6–23.

Manovich, Lev (2001) *The Language of New Media* (Cambridge, MA: MIT Press).

Meikle, Graham (2002) *Future Active: Media Activism and the Internet* (New York: Routledge).

Melucci, Alberto (1996) *Challenging Codes: Collective Action in the Information Age* (Cambridge: Cambridge University Press).

Morris, Aldon D. and Staggenborg, Suzanne (2004) 'Leadership in Social Movements', in David A. Snow, Sarah A. Soule and Hanspeter Kriesi (eds) *The Blackwell Companion to Social Movements* (Oxford/Malden MA: Blackwell).

O'Reilly, Tim (2005) 'What is Web 2.0: Design Patterns and Business Models for the Next Generation of Software', *O'Reilly*, 30 September. Available at http://oreilly.com/web2/archive/what-is-web-20.html (accessed 22 July 2013).

Rheingold, Howard (2002) *Smart Mobs: The Next Social Revolution* (Cambridge, MA: Perseus Books).

Schleusener, Luke (2007) 'From Blog to Street: The Bahraini Public Sphere in Transition', *Arab Media and Society* 1. Available at www.arabmediasociety.com/?article=15 (accessed 25 April 2016).

Snow, David A., Soule, Sarah A. and Kriesi, Hanspeter (eds) (2004) *The Blackwell Companion to Social Movements* (Oxford: Blackwell).

de Sola Pool, Ithiel (1983) *Technologies of Freedom: On Free Speech in an Electronic Age* (Cambridge, MA: Harvard University Press).

Thornton, Sarah (1995) *Club Culture: Music, Media and Subcultural Capital* (Cambridge: Polity Press).

Valeriani, Augusto (2011) 'Bridges of the Revolution: Linking People, Sharing Information and Remixing Practices', *Sociologica* 3: 1–28.

Williams, Patrick J. (2006) 'Authentic Identities: Straightedge Subculture, Music and the Internet', *Journal of Contemporary Ethnography* 35(2): 173–200.

York, Jillian (2012) 'The Arab Digital Vanguard: How a Decade of Blogging Contributed to a Year of Revolution', *Georgetown Journal of International Affairs* (Winter/Spring). Available at http://jilliancyork.com/wp-content/uploads/2012/02/33-42-FORUM-York.pdf (4 August 25 April 2016).

4

Resisting 'Resistance'

On Political Feeling in Arabic Rap Concerts

Rayya El Zein

In the months that followed the spectacular uprisings that overthrew, challenged and reshaped the political map of the contemporary Middle East, enthusiasm for the captivating and exciting forms of creative resistance that have been expressed in the streets of Arab cities can be found across the academy. From studies of memes and graffiti to music, theatre and performance, the urge to affirm the centrality of cultural production in political change has been widespread. However, the challenge for those who think about and practise radical politics in rapidly changing Arab cities continues to be how to imagine and implement effective resistance.

Meanwhile, across the humanities, theorisations of what signals 'resistance' continue to reflect normative subject-based agency, and with it a restrictive definition of political engagement. This is so despite the exciting events of 2010–13. The problem for Arab Cultural Studies and for subcultural studies is not, as some subaltern studies and post-colonial theory have suggested, that this literature relies on Western or European philosophy. Rather, the problem is the continued assumption of a very normative understanding of 'politics' – even when searching for or inventing non-Western models. This oft-assumed political framework is steeped almost exclusively in a search for the emergence of agency, and the birth of political subjects.

It is my hypothesis that this model, which I sketch out in the first section of this chapter, threatens to continue to produce ignorable subjects against whose backdrop only some activity can be recognised as resistant. Moreover, it does not account for the significant processes whereby individuals come to take certain actions or positions. Furthermore, a verifiable discourse of resistance within academia and international art circles reflects one of the particular ways in which capitalism today incorporates dissent into its own fabric.

In the second section of this chapter, I identify that this discourse in fact depoliticises art practice and cultural production, operating alongside and through the ways in which Wendy Brown has understood the work of 'tolerance' in multicultural societies. Recognising the limits of theorising resistance in one genre of subcultural production in the Arab world, I abandon it. Instead, I propose a political ethnography of subcultural production based in the documentation of political feeling.

In the third and final section of the chapter, I suggest that paying attention to, trying to understand and often simply testifying to the presence of political feelings can be a way to circumvent the feedback loops generated by the study of, and search for, resistance. I illustrate how some of this theory might work vis-à-vis examples from research on Arabic hip hop concerts in Beirut, Lebanon and New York.

Political activity: subjects and agency

In *The Human Condition* (1958), Hannah Arendt relegates politics to a space she calls the 'polis', which she describes as 'the space of appearance'.[1] Arendt's conceptualisation of political activity in the polis is the seed both of her original contribution to political thought, and the source of the most compelling rebukes of it. Her formulation of what constitutes political activity and with it, political life, has been thoroughly critiqued. In exploring Arendt's definition of political activity in this section, I am not endorsing all the possible implications of her theory, but I am suggesting that Arendt's theorisations of politics (political activity in the polis) can be used to illuminate the tendency to speak of resistance as representative of agency, if not incumbent on it.

In *The Human Condition*, 'political' describes the realm of the human behaviour that Arendt labels 'activity'. For Arendt, activity is one of the three categories of human life, following labour and work. While labour corresponds to the 'biological processes of the human body', and work pertains to the energy required to sustain labour, activity describes that uniquely human behaviour that is necessitated by mankind's social reality – what Arendt calls the 'human condition of plurality'.[2] In this formulation, political activity – or 'speech and action' – are understood as the ways in which human beings recognise their similarity to others and, at the same time, distinguish themselves as individuals.[3] This tension between difference and sameness is what Arendt means by plurality. She writes: 'Through [speech and action] men *distinguish themselves* instead of being *merely distinct*; they are the modes in which human beings appear to each other, not indeed as physical objects, but *qua* men.'[4] Activity renders individuals political subjects. Without it, life is nakedly biological or purely functional: 'A life without speech and without action [...] is literally *dead to the world*; it has ceased to be a human life because it is no longer lived among men.'[5]

For Arendt, then, activity and politics are intertwined: the presence of one indicates the arrival of the other. The formulation of the politics she describes is based in an understanding of public life in the polis, consistent with what Agamben calls 'bios'.[6] Critically, for Arendt, there is no political action without being seen and heard by others. When she says individuals are 'born' via political action, she means it is that she *is recognised by others*: that is, when political life begins: 'With word and deed we insert ourselves into the human world and this insertion is like a second birth.'[7] So, in her formulation, speech and action come to represent the presence of politics. There cannot be political space (i.e. the polis) without individuals speaking and acting; correspondingly, individuals are not participating politically without others recognising their speech or action.

It is this gesture of separating types of behaviour as political that led Jacques Rancière to accuse Arendt of expressing 'the will to preserve the realm of pure politics'.[8] He was concerned that Arendt perpetuates as apolitical – incapable of politics – those whose lives are consumed with the labour of living, whose efforts are largely consumed by the sphere of activity she defines as labour. For Rancière, these categories of behaviour endorse unequal categorisation of political actors. Indeed, Rancière's critiques prove salient when we follow Arendt's idea of activity to its corollary, agency.

The implications of the limitations of Arendt's framework of political activity are made clearer when we interrogate the relationship between it and those subjects who are capable of its execution. For Arendt, it is not political activity alone that has political meaning: 'Action without a name, a "who" attached to it is meaningless.'[9] When an individual performs a recognisable action (activity that is seen and heard by others), they enter the public sphere, proving that they have agency: the ability to act. Speech and action have an 'agent-revealing capacity'.[10] In other words, when we speak of agency, we have attached the dimension of a subject to (political) activity.

This formulation is integral to the larger part of subcultural theory, which has long taken agency as a central concern. Traditionally, subjects of subcultural study have been manifestly unproductive populations. Ken Gelder suggests that the first of six identifying characteristics of subcultures is 'their negative relation to work: as "idle", "parasitical," hedonistic, criminal, etc.'.[11] However, the moral panic accompanying the emergence of marginalised populations and their behaviour is not only spurred by participants' absence from the field of Arendt's 'work'. When prostitutes, skinheads or hippies are castigated as being 'unproductive' or 'delinquent', they are being accused of not being active in Arendt's sense of political activity. In rendering subcultural participants' choices active, sociologists have effectively worked to correct mainstream misunderstandings of subcultural behaviour. These studies render the choices of 'delinquents' active and, frequently, as environmentally motivated political gestures.

This framework has become especially pronounced in subcultural studies of recent decades, under the profound influence of the early work of Stuart Hall and Dick Hebdige. In this literature, the trend has been to frame subcultural activity more explicitly as resistance. Here, the work of the sociologist is frequently one of a decoder who translates the seemingly unproductive into active choices that are symbolically resistant.[12] In studies of the tradition of the Birmingham Centre for Contemporary Cultural Studies (CCCS), the emphasis on the symbolic persists, even as individuals' choices to participate in subcultures are recast in a robust Marxist analysis. Skinheads, punks and others are not communities of degenerates; rather, they are specifically working-class youth who ultimately are articulating powerful critiques of the social and economic order.

Crucially in this literature, visible, recognisable actions (here, manifest almost exclusively in sartorial choices, hairstyles, piercings, tattoos) render working-class youth as a subcultural participant, and thus someone rallying against late twentieth-century capitalism, nostalgic for the working-class *communitas* of his parents' and grandparents' generations.[13] Indeed, Stanley

Cohen has argued that the 'constant impulse [in sociological studies following the Birmingham tradition] is to decode the style in terms *only* of opposition and resistance'.[14] That is to say, the activities that readers of this literature are encouraged to notice are (exclusively) the ones that can be seen to indicate resistance. Gang fights mean that an alternative community is formed that resists the normative order; spiked hair means identification with that community, and a critique of parent, work and schooling expectations. Even the seemingly banal is still spectacular in its distinction from normative behaviour. The best example of this is perhaps Paul Corrigan's 'Doing Nothing', in which he explores the *'intense activity* which is found' in Sunderland street-corner culture.[15] Corrigan argues that activity seen by parents and teachers as being a waste of time is actually teaming with life. He suggests that in fact, the major elements of 'doing nothing' are talking and fighting – Arendt's markers of political activity par excellence (speech and action seen and heard by others).

The recognition in critical theory that different subjects with different kinds of agency may exist has less frequently propelled a search for a different kind of politics, as it has reinforced the urge to find the same kinds of resistance but in heretofore unnoticed activities. Lila Abu-Lughod calls this the 'romance of resistance', which she warns against:

> [T]here is perhaps a tendency to romanticize resistance, to read all forms of resistance as signs of the ineffectiveness of systems of power and of the resilience and creativity of the human spirit in its refusal to be dominated. By reading resistance in this way we collapse distinctions between forms of resistance and foreclose certain questions about the workings of power.[16]

This romance, found across a range of humanistic literature from the subaltern to the subcultural, can be seen to exhibit a shared set of assumptions regarding political activity and agency. We might say that the framework they share begins from a zero-state of no agency. Delinquents or other marginalised populations start as nondescript groups of people, understood as being devoid of the potential for political activity, that then are scripted by the theorist or sociologist as entering and performing on a political stage. The researcher is tasked with interpreting the recognisable activity that renders the demographic in question active: that is, political. These conceptualisations of agency, contingent on certain kinds of action, promise to continue producing ignorable subjects. In fact, tying agency to specific action necessitates the continuing presence of people without agency, in order for some spectacular individuals to assert or declare their difference as agency, or to enact other spectacular behaviour – chaos, solidarity, violence, style – as agency.

Furthermore, the privileging of action as politics, and of activity as resistance, tends to ignore the processes of coming to political engagement, which necessarily informs all such activity. The validating encounters that lead a teenager to shave their head or pierce their nose, or the irritation that pushes an audience to the point of a riot, or the heated arguments that organise a group to stop a performance, are all ignored in favour of the spectacular result (the piercing, the chaos, the strike): the deliberations that foment political actions and resistant choices are invisible.

These considerations lead me to ask: is the framework of resistance the best discursive framework through which to understand how Arab cultural production functions politically today? It is important to be clear about what I am considering. It is not that I believe that resistance – to colonial presences, misogyny, the expansion of capital or other oppressive practices – is not possible. I do not share Foucault's blanketing understanding of power, or his assertion about the nature of resistance and its inability to be 'in a position of exteriority in relation to power'.[17] However, there is a way of talking about resistance that is itself a manifestation and expression of neoliberal power. In order to be able to understand or seriously consider a politics or resistance that is not a part of this framework, it may be necessary to set aside resistance as the central lynchpin in discussions of politics in cultural production.

The discourse of depoliticisation: resistance and neoliberalism

In their study *The Making of Global Capitalism*, Sam Gindin and Leo Panitch point to a collusion between labour and capital that has helped structure the dimensions of capitalism that we see operating on a global scale today. Gindin and Panitch illustrate that today's capitalism must be understood as representing a symbiotic relationship between labour and capital.[18] For his part, Giovanni Arrighi has catalogued how organised protest against capital has been consistently incorporated into the way that capitalism has functioned for at least the past 700 years.[19] His *The Long Twentieth Century* is a humbling look at how centuries of protest against precisely the problems that we critique when we talk about neoliberalism today, have been instrumental in abetting capital to adapt and prolong its domination.

Pre-dating these studies, Joseph Schumpeter argued that an essential feature of capitalism is its 'evolutionary character'. Its drive for 'creative destruction' means that power in capitalism is never constant. It is always 'revolutionising itself from within', adapting so as to be able to maximise profit from changing modes of production and new markets.[20] One of the ways it does this is by incorporating and co-opting dissent – but if protest is an integral part of capitalism and the way it grows and transforms, the discourse of resistance under neoliberalism is, nevertheless, distinct.

Wendy Brown has identified a discourse of tolerance in neoliberal societies that works alongside a state power that is aware of the new limits to the reach of its own power. In expanding on Foucault's ideas of neoliberal governmentality, she offers that 'modern political power not only manages populations and produces certain sorts of subjects, it also reproduces and enlarges itself'.[21] It is here that the discourse of tolerance that Brown identifies has a political function. She argues that through the dissemination of tolerance talk in schools and state institutions, neoliberal power produces itself and enforces its reach. That is, power marks itself as being secular, gentle, universal, understanding and non-threatening – the salve to irrational extremism, inequality and racism. It is extremely successful in masking the institutionalised inequalities that structure neoliberal power. Moreover, tolerance discourse depoliticises by stripping the analysis of difference caused by the real forces of oppression, through a mandate for everyone to 'get along'.

Brown is keen to identify that the discourse of tolerance is separate from the individual practice of tolerating difference on a person-to-person level: surely it is better in one's daily life to practise tolerance rather than intolerance towards others. Rather, her critique is levelled at the way that power uses talk about tolerance, and what that discourse does. In making a case for the existence of a neoliberal discourse of resistance, I am borrowing much from the way that Brown understands this power to operate. I am not suggesting that subversion, critique or other interruption of power is not possible. However, if we are interested in how art practice or cultural production may achieve these things, I think it behoves us to consider how power uses resistance – that is, the ways in which we are taught to talk about, think about and identify political activity – and what that discourse does.

The discourse of resistance, concurrent with that of tolerance 'sneak[s] liberalism into a civilisational discourse that claims to be respectful of all cultures and religions'.[22] That is, it relies on the liberal conceit of the sacred rights of the individual to expression, bemoans the censorship of this expression by other powers, and celebrates the creative power of individual dissent. More than actually exploring alternative politics, the discourse of resistance reflects back on itself and the institutions that promote it as being the protectors of creativity, dissent and freedom. Moreover, resistance implies an enemy that is uniformly deplorable – usually manifest in some form of conservatism, censorship or in its outrageous use of authority. Against this enemy, the discourse of resistance abstracts grievances into a call for 'universal' freedom, or 'universally understood' freedom. Most importantly, it privileges certain kinds of activity as being ideally resistant. Almost all activity discussed in this way is non-violent, secular, colourful, creative. It is frequently drawn from the unique expression of one individual or a designated group of mixed gender.

Showcasing resistant art allows art institutions to trade in expensive, if not downright exclusive, cultural capital that brings in exchange a certain hipness, a street orientation. This aestheticised urban chic affirms the status of their patrons as consumers and savants of the avant-garde. Importantly, this phenomenon is not unique to the art scenes of New York, Paris or Berlin, and can be found in programming in Beirut, Cairo and Ramallah.

One might consider, for example, that for all the academe's celebration of myriad kinds of resistance in literature about music, poetry, social media and activism in the Middle East, it is still difficult to approach cultural practices or political affiliations that position themselves radically against the status quo. There is a growing literature in English and French about the colourful, creative expression in graffiti created by individual Arab youth in Beirut and Cairo, for example, but very little about the subcultural practices among youth affiliated with the Islamist political group Hamas.[23] Surely this is not because the behaviours of these latter youths are less political or less capable of subversion than their more cosmopolitan counterparts. Rather, it reflects how these youths do not fit into the neoliberal model of resistant subjects performing their resistance in a presentable way: oppressive, as religious, gendered and/or militarised practices are understood in this discourse.

Looking for, identifying and explaining resistance can effectively close instead of opening up ways to theorise radical politics. When I consider examples from ongoing dissertation research in the next section, I have abandoned accordingly a search for and theorisation of resistance. Abandoning the search for and explanation of resistance in Arab cultural production means two things. It does not mean that I consider political critique and radical refusal via creative or artistic expression impossible. It specifically means, first, on a philosophical front, abandoning the model of subject-based agency; and second, on a material or geopolitical front, refusing the depoliticising neoliberal discourse of tolerance and dissent.

Political feeling

In this section, my task is to make a case for a catalogue of affective exchanges as an alternative to readings of subject-based agency and, within them, politics or resistance in subcultural production. Considering political feeling allows me to pay attention to the processes of political engagement that are sidelined when we are required to recognise spectacle as evidence of the efficacy or presence of political behaviour. The game of political activity, as theorised by Arendt and discussed above, relies on representational logic. Speech and activity signal the birth of political subjects with agency. However, this logic cannot fully explain a mood, feeling or event as it unfolds. It cannot account for possibility or for chance. It cannot read imminence. It does not perceive hesitation, except as failure. Nonetheless, these processes are central to the unfolding of political experiences, interactions and behaviours. Writing a contemporary subcultural ethnography that is sensitive to political change necessitates a theory that is able to perceive these deliberations; otherwise our theory and critiques run the risk of completely misrepresenting the processes underway, clearly discernible only via hindsight, at some point in the future.

One thing that is tricky about documenting feeling in political demonstrations, concerts and other performances is that, having identified the feeling in question, it is very easy to fall into the trap of asking who was able to successfully create it, and how. This is the widespread disposition to agency returning. To fall into this trap is to circle back to the bind of identifying capable subjects who perform political activity. Instead, theorising politics in subcultural interactions through the affective must – and can – seek to recognise accident, possibility, imminence, not individual credit or aesthetic genius. Of course, it also requires recognising the observer's subjectivity.

Objection

In late August 2013, the forces of the Syrian president Bashar al-Assad used chemical weapons in an attack on a largely residential neighbourhood in the Damascene suburb of Ghouta. The response of the Obama administration and, in particular, of Secretary of State John Kerry's announcement of the US's intention to pursue military options in Syria a week later, came as Beirutis reeled from suicide bombings in the southern suburb of Dahieh.[24] The situation was serious and the mood tense, as people wondered – not for the first time – whether Syria's civil war was at last developing into a regional theatre into which Lebanon would be drawn.[25]

The negative effects of regional violence, government corruption and unequal economic growth have never been borne evenly across Lebanon. The Bekaa Valley in particular, one of the poorest regions in Lebanon with the least access to state support, has absorbed the largest numbers of Syrian (and Iraqi) refugees. The differences between life in the Bekaa and cosmopolitan Beirut are pronounced. The rap duo Touffar (Rebels) address this dynamic through their own experiences of growing up and living in Hermel. Their lyrics are articulated in the pronounced accent of the Bekaa. The duo, Ja'far and Nasseredine, split up publicly in 2013 and each now works on his own pieces. On the day of Kerry's announcement, Ja'far played a short (approximately 40-minute) concert in Hamra Street, a central, bustling road near the American University of Beirut. The neighbourhood of Hamra is the historical home of the Beiruti Left. The concert venue which hosted Ja'far, Metro al Medina, is located in the middle of Hamra Street and opened during a period of recent and rapid genrtrification in the city. Property prices on Hamra rose markedly from 2007 to 2012, accompanied by the opening of dozens of new pubs and coffee shops.[26]

> At around 10pm there are maybe 45 people in the Metro al Medina theatre, some seated, some standing. In and outside the theatre, Hamra is very quiet. There is a kind of disgust with everything in the air. [The rapper] Ja'far bursts from behind the red curtain and straight off the stage. He seems embarrassed

or uncomfortable. He moves quickly and sporadically, rapping almost to himself [...] A DJ and producer [the well-known rapper Osloob of the group Katibeh 5, discussed below] stands on stage with a mixer and a laptop. He suggests multiple times, in different tones, some commanding, some more jocular, that Ja'far slow down or repeat a verse, so that people can understand the words. Ja'far refuses [...] Indeed, many audience members already know the new tracks by heart. Despite being treated with ostensible derision by the performer, they are eager to sing along with him. Ja'far frequently turns his back on the DJ and the audience [...] He tosses the microphone away dismissively when the sound accidentally cuts out of it and screams his verses into the void of the half-filled house without a mic. The audience shouts their approval [...] When he has finished his set he leaves the stage quickly. He seems tired, irritated, fed up. There is no encore [...]

Outside, after the concert, in front of the theatre, a young woman who attended the performance asks to stand next to me until her ride arrives. It's not safe at night, she explains. 'People here [in Hamra] are rude,' she says, and explains matter-of-factly they'll make fun of her for wearing a veil. I ask her what she thought of the performance and she bubbles over with enthusiasm. She has raps of her own she has shared with Ja'far.[27]

In any language, rappers (like good actors) literally spit to enunciate, but spitting in rap also conducts specific symbolic and affective energy. Rappers spit their verses in the *cipha*, or improvised performance battle and onto recordings. To read 'spitting' affectively recognises that in addition to their lyrics, rappers conduct energy on stage that is related to the content of their work and that specifically responds to various environmental factors such as the venue, the crowd that has gathered, or current events. Ja'far's gestures at Metro that night could be imagined like a *tfeh!* - a disgusted spit - or a series of them - that affected the immediate environment in which the rapper found himself. This happened at the same time that the lyrical spitting addressed the wider political, environmental and social horizon of which both performer and audience were aware.

During the concert in Hamra, Ja'far's pieces, like much of Touffar's work generally, addressed a range of class-based grievances lyrically, incriminating 'polite' Lebanese society. On top of these lyrics, Ja'far performed physical gestures of distaste that performatively generated temporary community during the performance. This enactment of distaste created temporary ties between audiences and performer – not based on education, class or literacy, as Bourdieu's formulation of taste prescribes, but affectively.[28] The performer from Hermel almost seemed to be resisting the audience itself, if not the very fact that he was performing. He turned his back on them, denied requests from them, complained loudly about sound or light onstage, and so on. Moreover, it seemed to be understood that this hostility was not directed at audience members or sound technicians, but was ostensibly part of the politics of the performance itself. We might call this performing a political feeling of objection. When Ja'far performatively relied on enacting a feeling of distaste, he pronounced a specific politics that may be interpreted in his lyrics, but which are not always a part of the aesthetics of the venue, nor the hip part of Hamra where the venue was located. The audience gathered in Metro that night were largely fans of the performer – a considerable number of them his family, extended kin and others from Hermel who had explicitly come to hear him, despite the tense and unpleasant political malaise that had settled on the area of Ras Beirut that night. When Ja'far performed disgust, when he appeared irritated, fed up, disappointed or otherwise unimpressed with his surroundings, he was specifically connecting with this audience, who also may have been sceptical of the hipsteresque dynamics of the (both literally and metaphorically) underground theatre in which he was performing. In the transmission and reception of this feeling of objection, audience and performer embodied a raised middle finger that accompanied the lyrical one, which denounced how cosmopolitan and upper middle-class Beirut actively 'others' the Bekaa. The vociferous approval that received Ja'far's gestures of distaste completed this affective exchange. In this sense, it is important to note that the affective exchange is distinguished from the lyrical one, it does not merely reflect the meaning of the words that Ja'far shouted.

It is also evident in the stance of the young fan outside the theatre. As she lingered next to me, a stranger, until her ride arrived, she objected to the bustling cosmopolitan vibe as being inclusive or festive, trying instead to protect herself against it. Indeed, her interest in carrying on a conversation and her relative comfort with me (an unaccompanied, unveiled, Arabic-speaking woman) performs a similar enactment and exchange of feeling to the one in the theatre, where fans celebrated being in the presence of, or having, one of their own taking the stage within an environment they nevertheless critiqued. That is, her initial mode of reaching out to me was one of expressing distaste or distrust, even as she overcame it to engage with me. Documenting this presence of political feelings provides a way to understand how individuals and communities navigate the seeming contradictions of urban life. While not always manifest in direct action or consistently expressed activity (for example, an organised boycott of a performer or venue), considering this political feeling of objection helps understand the shape of the subcultural experiences of both audience and performer.

Confrontation

It is precisely the contradictions of urban life that appear dynamically when we seriously consider the political feelings that are conducted when individual bodies gather in specific spaces. *The Free Dictionary* defines confrontation as being, among other definitions, 'a meeting of persons face to face'.[29] What interests me in exploring confrontation is the forced recognition of another face: that is, the recognition of difference and tension *within* a performance site. This is something that is often elided in the discourse of resistance, which necessarily assumes a more or less united front against a single, hegemonic foe. In exploring instances of confrontation, I do not mean violence: bar fights or voiced conflicts between performers, audience and venue owners. This is an important distinction. Without it, we are in the realm of subject-based agency that looks to the spectacular event (the strike, the fight) as representing the presence of specific politics. Moreover, noting these forced recognitions of another face need not reinscribe the sometimes restrictive identity positions of participants. Nonetheless, they do reveal the multidimensional space that the discourse of resistance flattens in the construction of a symbolic or 'magical' field of politics.[30]

It is also important to specify that the presence of a political feeling need not necessarily signify a liberating experience. Indeed, the expectation that the things noted in cultural production as being political are necessarily emancipatory is precisely the limiting framework of tracing a narrative of resistance that I have critiqued above. That political feelings be necessarily radical would reiterate the appearance of resistance, previously represented in speech and action. Therefore, it is not that political feelings, their enactment or exchange are necessarily emancipatory; rather, that that they illuminate a multidimensional space within which relationships and behaviours are structured. This is the difference between a political ethnography of subcultural practice, and a narration that locates resistance from a series of recognisable actions within that practice.

The rap collective Katibeh 5 is made up of five emcees who, until 2013, were based in Bourj el Barajneh refugee camp in the southern suburbs of Beirut. The camp is inhabited mostly by Palestinians who fled Zionist forces in 1948 and 1967, their children and grandchildren, and also by poor Lebanese people and refugees from neighbouring countries. The situation for second and third-generation Palestinians in Lebanon, especially those living in refugee camps, is difficult. The majority of Palestinian refugees do not have the papers to work, vote or travel, despite being born in Lebanon. Neither does the Palestinian Authority (nor Israel) recognise them or provide them with travel documents. In 2013, the group was invited to perform at the Liverpool Arab Arts Festival in the UK. Four out of the five members of Katibeh 5 went there to perform, after which they applied for and received asylum. They have been there ever since.

In 2010, the group released their second album, *Al Tareeq Wahad Marsoum* (*One Way Decree*). The release party was held at Masrah Beirut (Beirut Theatre) in the Ain El Mreisseh neighbourhood. The group, which had been together since 2000, has a large following in the refugee camps. For many years, they held their *haflat* (concerts) in the camps themselves, playing directly for the audiences to whom their lyrics spoke. This was not without its difficulties, as overcoming local conservatism against a type of cultural production perceived to be 'Western' was not always obvious. However, the release party for the second album, like an increasing number of their *haflat*, was held in Ras Beirut at the then prominent Masrah Beirut.[31] For these performances, *el shabab* ('the guys'), as they are often referred to (and refer to themselves), coordinated a carpool of sorts in order to facilitate their audience getting to the venue. Without this coordination, the venue would be less accessible – if not inaccessible – for their young fans who reside in the camps.[32]

As crowds gathered outside the theatre, waiting for entry and the concert to begin, tension grew between youths from the camps who had come for the concert and the owner of a nearby store. It was not long before the army, which maintains a presence in the neighbourhood (as it does throughout different parts of Ras Beirut) arrived on the scene. The scuffle, which amounted to some pushing and yelling and did not come to blows or bloodshed, pitted

Palestinian youths against local residents historically affiliated with the political group Amal, who had rallied behind the shopkeeper.[33] As the army descended on the theatre, the artists and crew succeeded in intervening to hurry the majority of the audience inside, dismiss the troublemaking youths and convince local residents and the army that the concert should carry on – it then began and concluded smoothly.

The tension recounted by participants and witnesses points to specific historical and ongoing material conflicts, which generally inform the lyrics of the rap that Katibeh 5 delivers, but which they do not specifically address. Katibeh 5's lyrics are more concerned with the contemporary conditions of life in the camps, the hypocrisy of non-governmental organisation work and corruption, rather than with historical or ongoing disagreements and collaborations between specific political parties or religious sects. The historical confrontation between affiliates of the Shi'a group, Amal and the Palestinian refugees of Lebanon – especially those in the refugee camps, where massacres of Palestinians by Amal and Phalangist forces took place in the mid-1980s – is not something that Katibeh 5's lyrics specifically address. Their lyrical concern is for the general status of the second-generation refugee in Lebanon, and the webs of corruption and repression that make for such dim prospects for so many Palestinian youths in Lebanon. The group's work is received by many young people as empowering, and the artists themselves speak of producing music that speaks to, and resonates with, their audience.

The arrival and performance of Katibeh 5 in the established and distinguished venue of Masrah Beirut can be read as a progress narrative, pointing to the group's success and the growth of the Beiruti art scene more generally. Indeed, welcoming Katibeh 5's perspective from the camps into the more cosmopolitan centre of Beirut was, and remains, a progressive venture. One can read the performance at Masrah Beirut as a validation of Katibeh 5's testimony of the lived experiences in some of Beirut's marginalised ghettos. However, the affective dynamics outside the theatre illustrate that such a presentation of events is, perhaps, too simple. Even if the theatre's curators and programmers sought to celebrate and welcome the work of these artists from the camps, at the same time expanding the resistance perceived in their work and a cultural capital of solidarity, the working-class neighbourhood of Ain El Mreisseh where the theatre was located, and the disenfranchised youths who came to attend it, carried in their bodies the residue of the material realities that they live, and which cannot be reduced to a narrative of resistance.

Aseel Sawalha has discussed how the neoliberal property development of the Hariri-backed property company Solidere has exercised tremendous pressure on the working-class neighbourhood of Ain El Mreisseh. The neighbourhood, traditionally dependent on fishing, is now increasingly closed off from access to the Mediterranean.[34] Residents of Ain El Mreisseh find themselves wedged between the quickly gentrifying neighbourhood of Hamra around the American University of Beirut, and the 'ground zero' of Solidere's transformation of postwar Beirut in the downtown area. As such, they are living their own struggle against the cosmopolitan pressures that estrange them from their own neighbourhood. At the same time, the stakes for Palestinian youth, who rarely have the opportunity to travel to, or move around in, this part of the city, are also high. As a witness to the event described above told me, with only a little embellishment, the kids coming from the camps may just as well have been 'visiting Paris'.[35] In work as nuanced as Katibeh 5's, written from the experiences they have lived, there is no single source of oppression, no single thing to resist. This does not mean that conflict and tension do not exist, neither that individuals are apathetic or disempowered. On the contrary: the event I have described testifies to the presence of multiple agencies facing each other. Can insisting on noticing political feeling lead to a methodology that is able to recognise these different positions as being equally powerful? Can it lead to a theory that thinks about how to face and challenge the material realities that distinguish them?

I do not mean to suggest the concert was a mistake, or that an effort to expand the range of audience for Katibeh 5's work by hosting their concert at Masrah Beirut was a failure. Rather, in conducting a political ethnography of this subcultural event, I mean to highlight the futility of searching for a single narrative of resistance. The experiences of participating in these events points to intertwined, complex and in-flux dynamics.

Another example in a very different context will illustrate further how considering the presence of political feelings, particularly those of confrontation, is a way to analyse how gathering around cultural production points to the texture of power.

Shrine is a world music venue in Harlem, New York. At 113th Street and Amsterdam, it is in the heart of a neighbourhood that, in the past 30 years, has gone from perhaps the most notorious ghetto on the East coast of the US to a haven of increasingly valuable real estate.[36] In November 2011, the British-Palestinian emcee Shadia Mansour performed there with DAM, a group of Palestinian rappers based in Lyd, Israel.[37] Before Mansour took the stage, Harrabic Tubman, leader of the non-profit group Existence is Resistance which hosted the event, began an audience warm-up of her own. She took the microphone between opening acts and

> called out to the audience, in a mix of Arabic and English, 'Who here is *falasteeni* [Palestinian]? Who here is from *falasteen* [Palestine]?' A few enthusiastic shouts of solidarity and hands shot up from the crowd. She repeated the question to a slightly more enthusiastic response and then asked 'Who here is from *masr* [Egypt])?' You could tell she was preparing to run through a short list of countries and the performance space and the bar quieted slightly waiting to hear who would be called on next. In the pause, from the bar, a middle-aged African American man, seated with a friend hollered back in response, 'Harlem! From Harlem!' When she ignored the outburst, his friend continued 'Yea, from Harlem! Speak English!' The interaction effectively ended that tactic of community building which Mansour, when she took the stage, seconds later, quickly countered with an Arabic reference to rap parody videos, encouraging the audience to ignore/forget the outburst.[38]

As with the largely affective confrontation outside Masrah Beirut described above, these moments point to a tension held in the bodies at Shrine that question the narrative of resistance attributed to rap in Arabic. I would like to suggest here that it is irrelevant whether or not the older men seated at the bar identified, understood or sympathised with the political struggle around Palestine and its occupation by Israel, which the artists and the event were endeavouring to make visible. Furthermore, it is similarly perhaps tangential if they identified the rap music being performed as a legacy of African American and other experiences that were expressed by rappers a few miles away and decades before. What is more likely – and more pertinent to a material understanding of what is political about this subcultural event – is that the men from the neighbourhood were responding to an influx of much younger, white and Arab American strangers with different cultural capital in a quickly gentrifying neighbourhood.

It is disingenuous at best to celebrate resistance in solidarity with Palestinians against administrative detention, or the oppression of the Occupation, in a venue such as Shrine while completely ostracising the local clientele. This what I meant when I suggested previously that the discourse of resistance depoliticises cultural production by dismissing consideration of the specific material realities of music practice or performance. While there are certainly lines of solidarity and mutual growth to be drawn between Harlem's increasingly ostracised African American population and the Palestinian struggle against the Israeli Occupation, or between the local residents of Ain El Mreisseh and those of the Bourj el Barajneh camps, this work cannot be done by simply plopping a group of twenty- and thirty-somethings in a bar or concert hall. This kind of presentation of art-as-resistance, whose cultural capital surely increases when it takes place in gritty Harlem, actually perpetuates instead of challenges the neoliberal power that connects these struggles and their lived oppression.

Documenting the presence of political feelings makes these dynamics obvious. In an intellectual and political environment in which solidarity is invoked with alarming alacrity, and in which the studied awareness of oppression stands in for making room for those voices to speak,[39] the simple registration of different feelings may be an initial step towards more dynamic understandings of politics in subcultural production than narratives of resistance can provide.

Repetition

All the examples from the research that I have presented above have dealt with movement in some way: how audiences arrive at, and move within or around performance spaces. Gathering for these events affects the movement within and through a city, sometimes encouraging individuals to traverse boundaries that are rarely crossed, with different results. However, all the events discussed previously were one-off concerts. That is, they were significant because they were one-off occasions: a release party, a stop on a tour, a special gig. The political feelings that were generated in and around them were significant in some ways because of the uniqueness of each event. I would like to turn now to the effects of movement in the city around more mundane gatherings.

In Beirut, starting in late 2011, emcee and producer Edd Abbas of the group Fareeq el Atrash organised a series of open mic events called 'Sha3beh' ('popular' – of the people). At these events, Abbas invited young and developing emcees to perform their rap or spoken word poetry in Arabic or English, in front of a small audience. Usually, one more established DJ or emcee would assist Abbas to host the event. The evenings functioned to build the confidence of a growing group of young poets, who began inviting others to join or share work, eventually hosting alternate gatherings of their own. The events were held at various spaces, such as the News Cafe in the central business district, and at Ta Marbouta in Hamra. Since its opening in autumn 2012 in the developing neighbourhood of Mar Mikhael, Radio Beirut, centrally located on this strip of bars and nightclubs, also has hosted a similar type of series event. Young emcees gather every Tuesday night for 'Hip Hop 101: Open Mic Basics', to share the mic with a seasoned DJ or emcee, and share airtime with produced artists on the international broadcasts that Radio Beirut transmits. Attendance varies at these events. Sometimes folks come to dance, sometimes to listen. Sometimes only a few come. However, there are always young emcees ready to take the mic. They meet each other, creating, on the pavement outside the venue or on the stage itself, an opening into the hip hop *cipha*, the lyrical battleground from which rap's political expression is built. Emcees involved in these serial events speak of the community that it builds through and around them.

> Around midnight at Radio Beirut. Crowd is thin. Groups of friends that came to dance have danced and left or settled into quiet conversation. Edd [Abbas] has come and left. The hosting emcee is still weaving new voices with recordings of more established rappers. A European man wearing a red *keffiyeh* is filming. The bartender, a thin Syrian, has taken to making conversation with me. When he leaves the bar to collect glasses, a young man approaches and introduces himself. He is 19. I can't remember his name but he is keen to assert he is Armenian. I ask him if he raps and he says he is waiting his turn. On the sidewalk outside the bar, the hosting emcee, having wrapped up the evening without getting to my companion, is chummy with listeners and bar-goers. The 19-year-old asks about his turn and the host asks him what he's got. There on the sidewalk, the young man spits a few lines. The host nods and claps him on the back. 'Man,

you don't have any *flow*,' he tells him. He recites a few lines of his own in response. The younger man listens and nods. I can't tell if he feels encouraged or deflated by the response but both seem to enjoy the tiny spotlight, as long as it lasts.[40]

Each event in these series might be productively read as slowly building something affectively. A kind of buzzing, a reverberation. As individuals meet, share with each other, offer critiques, look for and find mentorship and return the following week or the next month, they build familiarity, relationships and rapport with each other and with neighbourhoods in the city. The series hosts a sort of slow-burn, affective energy that gradually accumulates heat. This effect differs considerably from the confrontation at Masrah Beirut, which quickly released energy and from the feeling of objection which communicates subtext and confirms shared, but already more fully developed, understandings. Affective repetition in the open mic events is perhaps closer to the affective construction of familiarity or home, and it essentially functions to make venues and strangers familiar. In a city such as Beirut, with rapidly shrinking public space, affective repetition around a serial event creates a space within which individuals can find common ground through low-stakes collaboration.

Conclusion
Rethinking subcultures through and after the Arab uprisings

At the time of writing, the people of the Gaza Strip are sustaining the 26th day of bombardment from the Israeli Defence Forces in 'Operation Protective Edge'. The Islamic State of Iraq and Syria has taken the town of Sinjar, has destroyed the shrine of Sayyeda Zeinab and is forcing thousands into terrified exile. Every colleague and interlocutor I respect in the Arab world or in diaspora is struggling to make sense of a world that, in three years, can hold all the hope and despair of the Egyptian and Tunisian revolutions, the plundering anew of Iraq, and the dogged determination of Hamas against the overwhelmingly powerful forces of the Israel Defence Forces. In these trying days, theorising the alternative appeal of cultural production and its potential political significance, its ability to express or enact resistance, without facing the limitations, the seeming impossibility and the inherent contradictions of sustaining a radical critique in the face of current events, through art or otherwise, is a hypocritical, detached and especially fruitless exercise.

I have felt, and see in the faces and hear in the voices of others an often exhausting negotiation of hope, cynicism, despair, numbness and anger. It is easier to find resistance in the thick of revolution, easy to romanticise cohesion afterwards, and equally easy to dismiss it as short-sighted euphoria. What I have tried to point to in this chapter is that this way of thinking about politics – as made manifest in spectacular displays of resistance – makes us blind to the radical deliberations and strategies of subversion that do not immediately look like revolution. Attention to how subversion and critique are sustained through subcultural interventions in periods of counter-revolution, during bouts of widespread apathy and in the face of incomprehensible violence, requires making room for the contradictions of contemporary life. It requires patience and respect for the inconsistency and lack of cohesion of radical critique. It pleads for ways – and they must be plural – to ascertain how the assumption of individual agency is encouraged and sustained, and it wants multifaceted strategies to bring people together, overcoming that sense of individual priority.

At the same time, the ubiquitous assertion that everything is resistant fails to recognise how neoliberal power capitalises on this sense of agency. This tendency obscures the ways in which power – vis-à-vis art institutions, cultural venues and academia – incorporate resistance into its own framework. This discourse of resistance attempts to congeal and pacify an audience that is at odds with different parts of itself, and that is capable of (if not already) refusing that same power in effective ways. Paying attention to political feelings in subcultural events can reveal how individuals and groups are at odds with this narrative, and are in the process of conceiving of alternatives.

Notes

1 Hannah Arendt (1958) *The Human Condition*, 2nd edition (Chicago, IL: University of Chicago Press), p. 198.
2 Arendt, *The Human Condition*, p. 7.
3 Speech and action are the two main categories of behaviour that are encompassed by 'political activity'. Arendt explains the mutual dependency in the relationship between the two: 'The actor, the doer of deeds, is possible only if he is at the same time the speaker of words'. Ibid., pp. 178–9.
4 Ibid., p.176, emphasis in original.

5 Ibid., emphasis added.
6 In contradistinction to *zoe*, or 'bare life'. Agamben, Giorgio (1998) *Homo Sacer: Sovereign Power and Bare Life*, trans. Daniel Heller-Roazen (Stanford, CA: Stanford University Press), pp.1–12.
7 Arendt, *The Human Condition*, p. 176.
8 Rancière, Jacques (2004) 'Who Is the Subject of the Rights of Man?', *South Atlantic Quarterly* 103: 297–310, p. 302.
9 Arendt, *The Human Condition*, pp. 180–1.
10 Ibid., p. 182.
11 Frontispiece, in Ken Gelder (2007) *Subcultures: Cultural Histories and Social Practice* (Oxford: Routledge).
12 John Clarke has suggested that while elements of class struggle inform subcultural choices, they actually slip from strategies enacted in subcultural participation. Subcultural agents 'do not mount their solutions on the *real* terrain where the (class) contradictions arise.' John Clarke (1993[1976]) 'Style', in Stuart Hall and Tony Jefferson *(eds) Resistance Through Rituals: Youth Subcultures in Post-War Britain* (London: Routledge), p. 189.
13 See for example, Tony Jefferson (1993[1976]) 'Cultural Responses of the Teds', in Hall and Jefferson *(eds) Resistance Through Rituals*, pp. 81–6.
14 Stanley Cohen (2005) 'Symbols of Trouble', in Ken Gelder and Sarah Thornton *(eds) The Subcultures Reader* (New York: Routledge), p. 163, emphasis in original.
15 Hall and Jefferson, editors' introduction to Paul Corrigan, 'Doing Nothing', in Hall and Jefferson, *Resistance Through Rituals*, p. 103, emphasis added.
16 Lila Abu-Lughod (1990) 'The Romance of Resistance: Tracing Transformations of Power through Bedouin Women,' *American Ethnologist* 17: 41–55, p. 42.
17 Michel Foucault (1990) *History of Sexuality, Volume 1: An Introduction*, trans. Robert Hurley (New York: Vintage Books), p. 104.
18 Sam Gindin and Leo Panitch (2013) *The Making of Global Capitalism: The Political Economy of the American Empire* (New York: Verso).
19 He takes as an initial, spectacular example: the revolt of mill workers in Florence that culminated in 1378 in their taking over state power. They placed one of their own, wool- comber Michele di Lando, as head of the republican government, but the revolt was quickly crushed by the workers' capitalist employers. When the proletarian mill workers returned to riot for bread, it was none other than di Lando who delivered them their defeat. Arrighi quotes the historian Ferdinand Schevill as saying that this struggle of labour in fourteenth-century Florence 'constitutes an early chapter in the very modern conflict between capital and labor'. Arrighi suggests that the workers' revolt and brief seizure of power actually encouraged, instead of weakened, the inclination to make the workers redundant. Giovanni Arrighi (2010) *The Long Twentieth Century: Money, Power and the Origins of Our Times* (New York: Verso), p. 104.

20 Joseph A. Schumpeter (2003) *Capitalism, Socialism and Democracy* (London: Routledge), p. 83. Arrighi, David Harvey, Gindin and Panitch and others take pains to illustrate constancies over the course of capitalism's history while simultaneously singling out the present moment of neoliberalism as unique. Arrighi, *The Long Twentieth Century*; David Harvey (2007) *A Brief History of Neoliberalism* (Oxford: Oxford University Press); Gindin and Panitch, *The Making of Global Capitalism*.
21 Wendy Brown (2006) *Regulating Aversion: Tolerance in the Age of Identity and Empire* (Princeton, NJ: Princeton University Press), p. 83.
22 Ibid., p.8.
23 In Arabic, *hamas*, which means 'enthusiasm', is also an acronym for *Harakat Al-Mouqawameh Al-Islamiyeh* (Hamas, or the Islamic Resistance Movement).
24 Lebanon has also absorbed a large number of Syrian refugees into its own modest population, which has threatened to disrupt an already precarious economy and further challenge a delicate and utterly dysfunctional balance of power in government. In early 2013, the number of Syrian refugees awaiting registration with the United Nations High Commission for Refugees (UNHCR) numbered 849,565 and was expected to exceed 1.5 million by the end of 2014. UNHCR (2014), 'Lebanon'. Available at www.unhcr.org/pages/49e486676.html (accessed 8 August 2014). In April 2014 the 1 millionth Syrian refugee was registered, making Lebanon a country of 4 million, 'the country with the highest per-capita concentration of refugees recorded anywhere in the world in recent history', according to the United Nations. Barbara Surk (2014) 'UN: Syrian Refugees Hit One Million Mark in Lebanon', *Global News*, 3 April. Available at http://globalnews.ca/news/1247786/un-syrian-refugees-hit-million-mark-in-lebanon/ (accessed 8 August 2014).
25 To be sure, Lebanon has long been intimately affected by the shifts in power in neighbouring Syria. It was less than a decade earlier when Syrian troops finally left Lebanese soil in the aftermath of the assassination of then Prime Minister, Rafiq Hariri. The civil uprising against Bashar al-Assad, which has turned into an especially violent sectarian civil war, has overflowed deep into Lebanon. The Lebanese people feel the effects of the developments in Syria, whether or not they are reflected in immediate violent repercussions – be those the hypothetical intervention of the US, which has not yet materialised, or the waves of suicide bombings concentrated in the Dahieh, the southern suburb of Beirut where the political group Hezbollah has strong support. Suicide bombings are frequently claimed by fundamentalist Islamic groups fighting against the Assad regime. Since May 2013, Hezbollah has supported Bashar al-Assad and the Syrian army with fighters and supplies. See Bassem Mroue (2013) 'Hezbollah Chief Says Group Is Fighting in Syria', *Yahoo! News*, 25 May. Available at http://news.yahoo.com/hezbollah-chief-says-group-fighting-syria-162721809.html (accessed 30 July 2014).
26 Interviews with Hamra residents and store and cafe owners. Information International has documented that property investments slumped slightly in 2013 but were again on the rise in 2014. Information International (2014) 'Real Estate

Prices April 2014'. Available at www.information-international.com/info/index.php/the-monthly/articles/1022-real-estate-prices-april-2014 (accessed 10 August 2014).
27. Author's field notes, 27 August 2013.
28. Pierre Bourdieu (1984) *Distinction: A Social Critique of the Judgment of Taste*, trans. Richard Nice (London: Routledge).
29. 'Confrontation', definition in the *The Free Dictionary*. Available at www.thefreedictionary.com/confrontation (accessed 10 August 2014).
30. See Dick Hebdige (1979) *Subculture: The Meaning of Style* (London: Routledge); Phil Cohen (1972) 'Sub-Cultural Conflict and Working Class Community', *Working Papers in Cultural Studies No. 2 (Birmingham: Centre for Contemporary Cultural Studies, University of Birmingham)*, p. 2.
31. The theatre closed in 2012, due to financial difficulties, after much protest and fanfare.
32. Movement for young residents of the camps, Palestinian or otherwise, is difficult due to the almost total dearth of public transport in Beirut. The vast majority of these teenagers do not own their own vehicles.
33. The animosity between these groups dates back to the so-called 'War of the Camps' (1985–7) during the Lebanese Civil War (1975–90). See Julie Peteet (2005) *Landscape of Hope and Despair: Palestinian Refugee Camps* (Philadelphia, PA: University of Pennsylvania Press), pp. 151–5. On the class dynamics of the Ain El Mreisseh neighbourhood and the role of Amal within them, see Aseel Sawalha (2010) 'Ayn el-Mreisseh: The Global Market and the Apartment Unit', in *Reconstructing Beirut* (Austin, TX: University of Texas Press).
34. Sawalha, 'Ayn el-Mreisseh'.
35. Interview with Aseel Sawalha, 23 January 2014.
36. Property values in Harlem were on a steady climb before the 2008 financial crash. Developers and investors are enthused to see the market returning (showing gigantic jumps in asking prices – asking prices for units in a single building on 5th Avenue and 120th Street, for example, leapt from $10,000 to $953,000 in one year, 2012). These changes in property values have significant effects on the demographics of the neighbourhood, making it increasingly inaccessible to the city's poor, who feel less welcome. Joseph Berger (2011) 'As Tastes Change in Harlem, Old-look Liquor Store Stirs a Fight', *New York Times*, 1 December. Available at www.nytimes.com/2011/12/02/nyregion/in-reborn-harlem-liquor-store-draws-complaints.html?_r=3&ref=nyregion; Julie Satow (2012) 'After a Short Nap, Harlem Is Back' *New York Times*, 22 March. Available at www.nytimes.com/2012/03/25/realestate/harlem-back-after-a-short-nap.html?pagewanted=all&_r=0 (accessed 10 August 2014).
37. The concert was part of a promotional tour in several US cities for the documentary film *Hip Hop Is Bigger than the Occupation*, filmed and produced by

the non-profit group Existence is Resistance. See: www.existenceisresistance.org (accessed 10 August 2014).
38 Author's field notes, 19 November 2011.
39 Kayla Kumari Upadhyaya (2014) '"I Have a Cultural Studies Degree" Is the New "I Have Black Friends"', *The Archipelago*, 29 July. Available at https://medium.com/the-archipelago/2be4d371cbcb (accessed 4 August 2014).
40 Author's field notes, 7 January 2014.

Bibliography

Abu-Lughod, Lila (1990) 'The Romance of Resistance: Tracing Transformations of Power Through Bedouin Women', *American Ethnologist* 17: 41–55.
Agamben, Giorgio (1998) *Homo Sacer: Sovereign Power and Bare Life*, trans. Daniel Heller-Roazen (Stanford, CA: Stanford University Press).
Arendt, Hannah (1958) *The Human Condition*, 2nd edition (Chicago, IL: University of Chicago Press).
Arrighi, Giovanni (2010) *The Long Twentieth Century: Money, Power and the Origins of Our Times* (New York: Verso).
Berger, Joseph (2011) 'As Tastes Change in Harlem, Old-look Liquor Store Stirs a Fight', *New York Times*, 1 December. Available at www.nytimes.com/2011/12/02/nyregion/in-reborn-harlem-liquor-store-draws-complaints.html?_r=3&ref=nyregion (accessed 10 August 2014).
Bourdieu, Pierre (1984) *Distinction: A Social Critique of the Judgment of Taste*, trans. Richard Nice (London: Routledge).
Brown, Wendy (2006) *Regulating Aversion: Tolerance in the Age of Identity and Empire* (Princeton, NJ: Princeton University Press).
Clarke, John (1993[1976]) 'Style', in Stuart Hall and Tony Jefferson (eds) *Resistance Through Rituals: Youth Subcultures in Post-War Britain* (London: Routledge).
Cohen, Phil (1972) 'Subcultural Conflict and Working Class Community', in *Working Papers in Cultural Studies* No. 2 (Birmingham: Centre for Contemporary Cultural Studies, University of Birmingham).
Cohen, Stanley (2005) 'Symbols of Trouble', in Ken Gelder and Sarah Thornton (eds) *The Subcultures Reader* (New York: Routledge).
Foucault, Michel (1990) *The History of Sexuality, Volume 1: An Introduction*, trans. Robert Hurley (New York: Vintage Books).
Gelder, Ken (2007) *Subcultures: Cultural Histories and Social Practice* (Oxford: Routledge).
Gindin, Sam and Panitch, Leo (2013) *The Making of Global Capitalism: The Political Economy of the American Empire* (New York: Verso).
Hall, Stuart and Jefferson, Tony (eds) (1993) *Resistance Through Rituals: Youth Subcultures in Post-War Britain* (London: Routledge).

Harvey, David (2007) *A Brief History of Neoliberalism* (Oxford: Oxford University Press).
Hebdige, Dick (1979) *Subculture: The Meaning of Style* (London: Routledge).
Information International (2014) 'Real Estate Prices April 2014'. Available at www.information-international.com/info/index.php/the-monthly/articles/1022-real-estate-prices-april-2014 (accessed 10 August 2014).
Jefferson, Tony (1993[1976]) 'Cultural Responses of the Teds', in Stuart Hall and Tony Jefferson (eds) *Resistance Through Rituals: Youth Subcultures in Post-War Britain* (London: Routledge).
Kumari Upadhyaya, Kayla (2014) '"I Have a Cultural Studies Degree" is the New "I Have Black Friends"', *The Archipelago*, 29 July. Available at https://medium.com/the-archipelago/2be4d371cbcb (accessed 4 August 2014).
Mroue, Bassem (2013) 'Hezbollah Chief Says Group Is Fighting in Syria', *Yahoo! News*, 25 May. Available at http://news.yahoo.com/hezbollah-chief-says-group-fighting-syria-162721809.html (accessed 30 July 2014).
Peteet, Julie (2005) *Landscape of Hope and Despair: Palestinian Refugee Camps* (Philadelphia, PA: University of Pennsylvania Press).
Rancière, Jacques (2004) 'Who Is the Subject of the Rights of Man?', *South Atlantic Quarterly* 103: 297–310.
Satow, Julie (2012) 'After a Short Nap, Harlem Is Back', *New York Times*, 22 March. Available at www.nytimes.com/2012/03/25/realestate/harlem-back-after-a-short-nap.html?pagewanted=all&_r=0 (accessed 10 August 2014).
Sawalha, Aseel (2010) 'Ayn el-Mreisseh: The Global Market and the Apartment Unit', in *Reconstructing Beirut* (Austin, TX: University of Texas Press).
Schumpeter, Joseph A. (2003) *Capitalism, Socialism and Democracy* (London: Routledge).
Surk, Barbara (2014) 'UN: Syrian Refugees Hit One Million Mark in Lebanon', *Global News*, 3. April. Available at http://globalnews.ca/news/1247786/un-syrian-refugees-hit-million-mark-in-lebanon/ (accessed 8 August 2014).
United Nations High Commissioner for Refugees (UNHCR) (2014) 'Lebanon'. Available at www.unhcr.org/pages/49e486676.html (accessed 8 August 2014).

Interlude: Performative Interventions in Public Space

An Interview with Dictaphone Group

Layal Ftouni

Dictaphone Group is a research and performance collective that creates live art performances based on a multidisciplinary study of space. It is a collaborative project initiated by live artist Tania El Khoury and architect and urbanist Abir Saksouk. Together with various collaborators such as performer and producer Petra Serhal, they have been creating site-specific performances informed by research in a variety of places such as a cable car, a fisherman's boat and a decommissioned bus. This conversation was conducted in Beirut in May 2014 between researcher Layal Ftouni and Tania El Khoury, Abir Saksouk and Petra Serhal from Dictaphone Group.

Layal Ftouni (LF): Why and how did you get together as a collective?

Abir Saksouk (AS): What brought us together is a shared interest in space. Space is political and ideological. For us, performances or interventions in space are, themselves, ways of reclaiming the city. Therefore, our practice is very much linked to our relationship to the city and the privatisation of public space, among other issues. On a different level, research on space is very much confined within institutional and academic bodies. So we also aim to make it accessible outside the confines of the institution.

Tania El Khoury (TK): I personally never created work for theatres or 'neutral' spaces. I am interested in devising work that is site-specific, and that uses the city's landscapes as scenography. We started our collaboration in 2009. We wanted to bring together two quite different mediums – urban research and live art – to produce knowledge about our relationship to the city and its public spaces. Simultaneously, we wanted to act and interfere in that space. We find matters concerning accessibility to public space integral to our right to the city. For example, it is unacceptable that our access to the sea in Beirut is restricted and limited. Making site-specific performances based on multidisciplinary research on space is our chosen medium of info-activism. I believe in making art-as-politics, the sort of art that not only discusses politics, but constitutes a political event in itself. For this to take place in contested places such as Lebanon's public spaces, our art had to be informed by research, and it had to engage in writing history of places from below, from the experiences of its users and those rendered invisible by neo-liberal development policies.

AS: I also think that Lefebvre's famous dictum that 'space is political' provides an interesting entry point to our work. How space is made reflects and reproduces social, economic and political formations. The choice to dwell on the politics of space in Dictaphone Group's projects stems from a belief that any intervention in space is the stake and site of political struggle. It is a struggle between those who control space, and those who are subject to this control: between the powerful and the powerless.

LF: Your intervention is therefore mobilised by a certain ethic but also a politics, and is informed by the history of that space? Are you referring here to your performance *This Sea is Mine* (2012)?

TK: Yes, in *This Sea is Mine* we combined multidisciplinary research on space (looking at regulations, illegalities and social practices) with recurrent visits over a period of time to Beirut's coastline from Ain El Mreisseh to Ramlet al-Baida, meeting and interviewing local fishermen. While Abir was the primary researcher, Petra was also meeting with local fishermen. Actually, one of the fishermen she met with became an important collaborator in the project, appearing in the actual performance.

PS: I would regularly meet the fishermen who worked at the harbour. During these visits, I collected oral histories of the fisherman and the harbour that were otherwise forgotten. Abir and I would then synthesise these stories with the research she was conducting on laws and property, and move on from there.

Figure 2 *This Sea is Mine*, performance by Dictaphone Group, Ain El Mreisseh fishing port, Beirut, September 2012
Source: Courtesy of Dictataphone Group

AS: We were attempting to write the history of Beirut coastline. The performance takes place on a fishing boat. The journey allows the audience to experience and relate to the coast differently than they usually do. How to represent space is a question that preoccupies many disciplines, and is approached through multiple methods of enquiry from geography to sociology and anthropology. We approach it through performance. For us, performance is another way of representing space and embodying it, and this is what we do.

LF: There is a whole body of literature that, for the last 20 years, has argued for reclaiming space and spatiality as a dynamic component of social life. Edward Soja and Doreen Massey's work has been so influential in rethinking space as central to the construction and configuration of our socio-economic, political and cultural geographies. *This Sea is Mine* does that through performance. Am I right in thinking that?

TK: That is right. Our project is primarily about reclaiming our city and claiming our right to it. In a sense, taking the audience on a boat ride and attempting to enter part of the coast that we have been banned from is, in itself, an act of reclaiming space. The performance ends at Dalieh, one of the last remaining, publicly used open spaces on the seashore in Beirut. Being there with the audience meant that we collectively refuse to lose that space to a private resort. It was a way of protesting future plans that would make such a performance no longer possible.

LF: As you know, the volume we are editing is the first attempt at conceptualising and studying Arab subcultures. Two key questions always popped up: what are Arab subcultures? and how do they establish a sense of self-identification, against what parent or dominant culture? First, would you identify with the term 'subculture' – that is, ثقافة فرعية (subculture)? Second, what mobilises your critico-political practice? Is there a particular dominant culture that you denounce, reject or protest against? Is it neoliberalism, patriarchy, racism, heterosexism, authoritarianism, the state?

PS: The system.

TK: There is no 'Other' that is already set for us. Obviously, we take issue with the system, as Petra said – how it functions, especially the role of the state in Lebanon. Clearly, we are against all forms of oppression, repression and subordination such as racism, patriarchy, heterosexism and class hierarchy. However, there is no pre-existing Other that we oppose. Also, as a collective, our work is not about simply campaigning or protesting.

When we started working on *This Sea is Mine*, we did not know that former Prime Minister Rafiq al-Hariri had bought up the majority of the plots that make up Dalieh and took control of that part of the coastline. We were mobilised by our concern with the implications of privatisation on people's access to public spaces, and not by a political opposition to Hariri per se. People might think we are anti-Hariri, especially in the context of the Lebanese political scene. I am not saying we are not or should not be, but this is not our approach.

While working on *Nothing to Declare*,[1] we knew that we would confront different forms of state control and censorship. *Nothing to Declare* is a research-based lecture performance that explores the shifting borders of, and within, Lebanon by tracing the non-operational national railway system. We discovered that the Syrian army had occupied a major train station and turned it into a torture site during the Lebanese civil war (1975–90). As a result, many thought of the performance as being anti-Syrian regime, which was not a position we initially intended to communicate in the performance.

PS: During our research for *Nothing to Declare*, we discovered that train stations fall under the category 'state-owned private property' (rather than

Figure 3 Map of Beirut's seafront: ownership and private exploitation

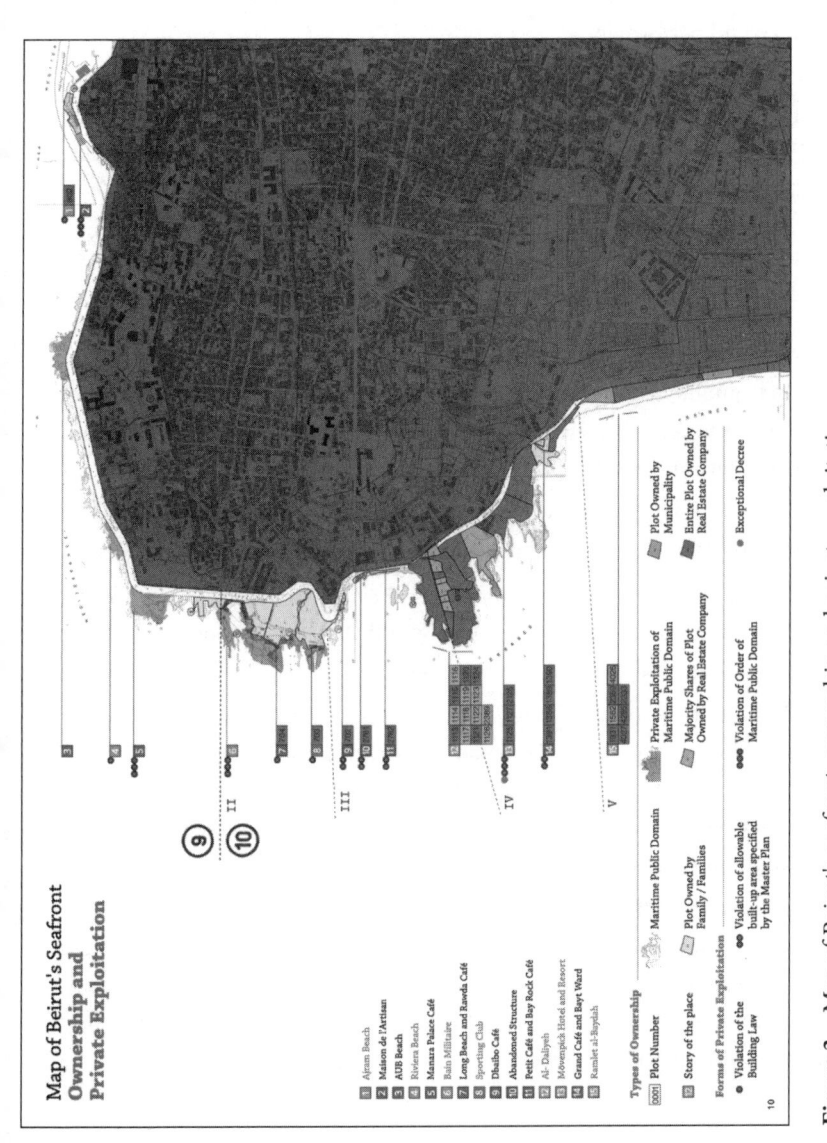

Source: Courtesy of Dictaphone Group, originally published in 2012 in *This Sea is Mine* booklet (in collaboration with Nadine Bekdache)

public domain). But in either case, the station is a public facility. When I went to the Mar Mikhael train station in Beirut to get permission to film for our project, I was asked by the Railway and Public Transportation Authority to pay $600 in order to get access to the site. So here we have a specific case in which public facilities are being rented out for large sums of money in the service of private events (parties, video production, etc.) rather than serving public interests. We cannot ignore this information and its relevance to our research and performance.

TK: When looking into the privatisation of the coastline, those involved in private construction and development were not responsive and refused to disclose any information to Abir – but we did not give up, and resorted to all sorts of methods to get the information needed.

LF: So, certain sociopolitical issues drive your activism and then you proceed to undertaking research accordingly?

AS: In dominant discourses within Lebanon, the issues are seemingly clear: everyone agrees the sea is privatised, that there are no public spaces, and that public transportation is dysfunctional. What concerns us is the approach we take in raising these issues, and evoking new ways of thinking through them and acting upon them.

LF: Do you think that your work has a shared feminist ethos particularly in relation to issues of access and interventions in public space?

TK: While we believe in feminist politics, they are not the sole or primary guiding principles for our work. Having said that, we cannot ignore how public space is gendered and dominated by men.

PS: The fact that we are doing these projects as women implicates us in feminist politics. For example, when we performed *Nothing to Declare* in New York, the first thing the audience picked up on was our experience of crossing checkpoints as women, and how that entailed specific possibilities and limitations.

AS: I think identification is at the heart of this: who we identify with as women and against whom. This is very much linked to the politics of location. For example, as a woman, when I go to Ramlet al-Baida public beach, I identify with the experience of a Syrian worker. We are subjected to the same hostility and verbal abuse.

Figure 4 *Nothing to Declare*, lecture performance by Dictaphone Group, Ashkal Alwan, Beirut, September 2014
Source: Courtesy of Dictataphone Group

LF: Why do you insist on working as a collective and not as individuals who collaborate (artists, researchers, producers) on projects? What implications does this have on the role of the artist as author?

TK: I do work as a solo artist independently from the collective, but it is a totally different experience. The idea of this collective was the result of our interest in multidisciplinary approaches to space, both as artists and researchers. I am interested in working across different media.

AS: I agree with what Tania says, but I have two annotations to it. For me, I have a problem with rigidity and with cliquey cultures: that is, with academics only mixing with other academics, and artists only mixing with other artists. On a personal level, I never wanted to just be an architect or just a researcher. I am an architect, a researcher, a citizen, a member of Dictaphone Group, among other things.

LF: I was talking to Abir earlier about artists being attached to, or 'represented' by, art institutions. The attachment of individual artists to institutions, one can argue, is a result of the logic of neoliberal art – that is, by capitalising on the artist as celebrity. Are you purposefully distancing yourselves from the logic of the market by working as a collective outside institutional affiliations?

TK: Not only are we a collective, we are a non-hierarchical collective. People often ask us who is in charge; people are used to thinking about performance through a hierarchical lens including director, dramaturge, stage manager, actors, etc. I was personally never comfortable with such structure. Our process is built on trust: we have a lot of open discussions about the function and form of our work. Being an all-women collective brings with it its own set of gendered misconceptions – it is interesting (and sometimes infuriating) to notice how we are categorised and perceived by each of the artistic, the academic and the activist scenes. We enjoy borrowing tools and methods from all these scenes while comfortably existing on the margins of institutionalised art and knowledge production. Just like a soldier at an army checkpoint would perceive the three of us as apolitical beings and unthreatening 'good girls', we found that the art or academic world can share similar misconceptions regarding our work.

LF: We briefly talked earlier about the political in your work. I would like us to elaborate a little more on this. Your work is strongly engaged both with Politics and the politics of the every day. It seems to me that your work prioritises the political over common understandings of relational and participatory art as establishing intimate forms of sociability and human interaction. I am thinking here particularly of Bourriaud's work on relational aesthetics, which was criticised for sidelining the political and overplaying the social bond that performance initiates. Where do you stand in relation to that?

TK: We differentiate between politics-as-content and the political-as-form. We may identify in our practice with relational art (Bourriaud) as such, but this is not the end point. We do not just relate to residents/inhabitants of spaces or to the audience. Rather, we collaborate with them.

In performances such as *Bit Teleferique* (2010) and *This Sea is Mine*, we had a small audience so it was quite intimate. Every individual's personality and interests affect how the performance unfolds. We encourage that and do not try to control for it. Control imposes discipline on participation, like telling the audience: 'We are in a conversation, but you cannot talk.' In this sense, we work differently from big production, site-specific performances in which performers control every aspect of their relationship to the audience.

AS: Space in itself is political – it is loaded with politics and ideology, and any intervention in it is political. To acknowledge power relationships in relation to space is in itself a political act. On another level, we produce material that acts as political tools for activists or any person concerned in having a say about the development of the city. For instance, mapping land ownership along the coast, and disclosing the fact that real-estate companies had bought all seaside properties, was a very strong document that took on another life beyond our project, informing activism and political demands.

Figure 5 *Nothing to Declare*, lecture performance by Dictaphone Group, Tranzquartier, Vienna, June 2013
Source: Courtesy of Dictataphone Group

LF: Tell me more about *Nothing to Declare*. How did it start, the ideas behind it and why you chose to present it as a lecture performance?

TK: It all started when we were invited to the regional Arab bloggers' meeting planned for Tunisia in 2012. Abir was able to attend, but I could not, my visa was delayed. Palestinian bloggers were denied entry visas and could not attend the meeting – and this was post-revolution Tunisia. This sparked a conversation about the effects of borders between Arab countries on mobility and solidarity. Later, ArteEast invited us for a residency at Watermill Center (New York). We used that time to develop our ideas. We were also interested in working with the form of a lecture performance in which we all took the stage.

AS: We wanted to start with the thing that we knew best: space. We went on a journey and filmed three different journeys following train tracks that once linked Lebanon with its neighbouring countries. Each one of us went on a journey that took her back to where she was originally from: I went south, Petra went east, and Tania went north. In the lecture performance, the three of us share our personal journeys with the audience: behind us there is a three split-screen video projection.

TK: The videos showed the three journeys in which we filmed the train tracks and the stations that were either destroyed or demolished, or occupied by the army.

AS: The importance of this project is that it brought up issues we did not plan to address, such as the urban–rural divide, the marginalisation of peripheral landscapes and communities that are neglected by the media as well as by existing research.

TK: Art production in Lebanon is very Beirut-centric. Beirut in comparison to other areas in Lebanon is over-researched and over-represented.

AS: What started as a project on borders between nations also exposed borders inside the nation. We also discovered along the work process that there is a much-needed conversation about the railway within Lebanon, and the ways in which it summarises the story of the Lebanese state: the illusion of a weak state that is in fact actively intervening to cater for private interests, rather than the common good.

LF: This is very interesting. Also, by tracing these routes you went on a journey (physically and imaginatively) that is unknown to many of our generation, who did not grow up using trains as a means of transport within Lebanon and across borders. You also collected interviews and spoke to local residents living in nearby villages and former railway employees, right?

PS: Yes – we interviewed former employees at the Railway and Public Transportation Authority, along with ex-commuters and current residents who live by the railway or inside the stations.

LF: Who is 'the public' or 'publics' of your performances?

TK: It varies: they can be the interviewees, the audience and the participants. As I mentioned earlier, some interviewees end up collaborating with us in the performance.

PS: We tried to reach out to a diverse public though our professional and personal networks, the contacts we developed as part of the project (including interviewees) and through social media and internet platforms. We also distributed the research booklets in cafes and along similar lines. We know, for example, that many in the fishing community we had worked with on *This Sea is Mine* found the booklet very informative and enjoyed reading it.

AS: I think that our projects gain an afterlife in the form of articles, booklets, sound pieces, pictures, etc. These afterlives go beyond the project itself, and in this sense reach a very diverse public. This 'public' is different from the audience that actually plays an active role in the performance; in our intervention in space, the audience takes part in the experience itself.

TK: We are also currently working on producing the performance script into an audio piece, which would be available to everyone to download and experience the journey at home or while on a boat trip with one of the fishermen who offer boat trips to the public.

LF: Your performances are site-specific and durational. How does that impact on your practice and the durability of the issues you raise?

TK: The nature of performance is ephemeral, and that is what is interesting about this medium. That said, we feel that our projects never really end: we open conversations, but we do not close them. We are currently writing about *Bit Teleferique*, which was our first project conceived in 2010.

PS: I would add that it is important to recognise that public spaces are in continuous transformation: their ownership and use might change at any point. What is now publicly used can become private, and we would no

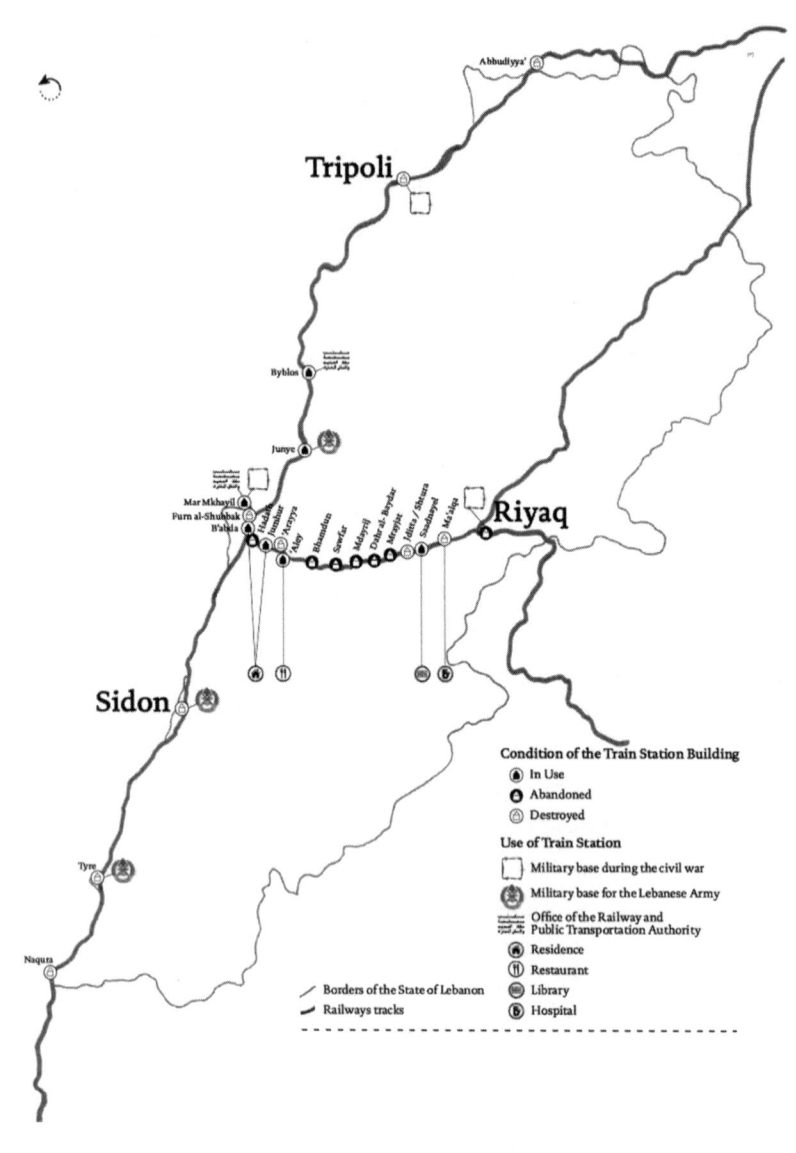

Figure 6 Map of the railway, condition of the train stations, and their current use

Source: Map courtesy of Dictaphone Group, originally published in 2014 in *Nothing to Declare* booklet (in collaboration with Nadine Bekdache)

longer be able to access these spaces. So, all research and art practice is contextual and subject to change.

AS: Our projects invite audiences to build a new collective memory with places, and this is a long-term process. Collective memory is a form of ownership, communal ownership. When dealing with issues such as the loss of shared or public space, using these sites and building a relationship with them is the first step in gaining ownership over them, and consequently reclaiming them.

LF: Thank you.

Note

1 Dictaphone Group, *Nothing to Declare*, Edinburgh Festival Fringe, 16–21 August 2013.

5

Cosmopolitans, Nationalists and Fundamentalists in the Modern Middle East

Sami Zubaida

In the last two or three decades of the twentieth century, with the rise of identity politics in many regions, and specifically of Islamic political advocacy in the Middle East, the public mind has viewed this region as having religion as its essence. This association has been strengthened after 9/11 and other violent attacks. The impression has been created that the societies in this region have always had religion as their essence, and their history is being read backwards. In this chapter I shall offer a different history that comprises lively and varied social and cultural formations in which religion is only one element – and one which, for most of the twentieth century, was not dominant.

Cosmopolitanism

'Cosmopolitanism' is not a precise concept: it slips between different discourses and associations. It is embroiled in ideological contests: construed by some as designating inauthenticity, rootlessness and moral corruption; for others, it connotes desirable diversity, tolerance and sophistication as well as 'fun'. In recent decades, in various corners of the Middle East, it has been the stuff of nostalgia: with the rise of Islamic ideologies and regimes in the region, intellectuals, liberals and revellers have engaged in nostalgic trips to a romanticised past of cosmopolitan and bohemian spaces and sociabilities. Facing an influx of rural and provincial migration and, with these, of narrower cultures and outlooks, well laced with religious disciplines, Istanbul, Alexandria and Beirut hark back to this golden past of cultural vitality, diversity and tolerance. Is it, then, the nationalists and fundamentalists who have stolen this past? Let us delve into aspects of relevant histories to respond to this question.[1]

Empires

The phenomena of cosmopolitanism are the product of empires. They bring diverse peoples together into their urban centres who are engaged in various relationships, economic and political. The association of cosmopolitans with imperialism is one reason nationalists and fundamentalists have found for denouncing it. The two pertinent empires for the modern history of the Middle East (since the mid-nineteenth century) are the Ottoman and the British, which had important inputs both from French language and culture and from German nationalism.

The Ottoman Empire is sometimes described as cosmopolitan in that it brought together diverse peoples, ethnicities and religions which, for the most part, coexisted peacefully. The '*millet* system' is cited as a model of tolerance and harmony; however, the non-Muslim *millets* (and non-Sunni Muslims, not classified as separate *millets*) were always legally inferior, and burdened by restrictions on residence, dress, comportment and worship. They were subject to extortion by rapacious governors and mamlukes (slave dynasties that ruled in Egypt, Syria and Iraq intermittently). The eighteenth-century Egyptian chronicler al-Jabarti tells us that, at one point in the late century, a mamluke prince proclaimed that henceforth, Jews and Christians were to be prohibited from carrying the personal names of prophets. Given that the Qur'an celebrates all Jewish and Christian prophets and biblical kings, this meant that people with the names of Abraham, David or Joseph had to change their names. (Of course, this was only a ruse to extort money, and a suitable sum was agreed after strenuous bargaining.)[2]

In any case, the co-presence of diverse peoples does not necessarily entail social and cultural mixing. For the most part, individuals were confined within their own social boundaries and often the topographical locations of their communities, under the authority of their religious chiefs who, in turn, were supported by the power of the sultan. Even when diverse peoples are free under a liberal regime, the coexistence of different ethnicities and cultures does not constitute what is meant or connoted by 'cosmopolitanism'. For example, on my first visit to Toronto in the mid-1970s, the wide range of ethnicities and nationalities in its population impressed me: Hungarians, Portuguese, Chinese, Indians, with their own colourful districts and markets. Yet this was not 'cosmopolitan': people from all over the world brought their families to this place of prosperity and security, and were enclosed within their homes and communities, having little to do with others except in the marketplace. Of course, this was generally the case with migrants everywhere, including in major metropolitan centres such as Paris or New York. What makes those cities (and perhaps also Toronto in later decades) 'cosmopolitan' is the presence of particular milieux of social and cultural mixing and hybridity across communal boundaries, and indeed the permeability of these boundaries.

Cosmopolitanism as social promiscuity

It was only during the course of the nineteenth century and into the twentieth – with a combination of the processes of modernity and capitalism under the increasing hegemony of European powers, especially Britain and the responses of Ottoman reforms – that communal barriers became more permeable, especially in the main centres of power, commerce and culture. The new print media, the creation of public opinion, the spread of literacy and reading to wider sectors of society and attractive European models of public and cultural life – all of these combined to bring about new strata and associations, many of which cut across communal barriers, at least for some of the elites. The ideas and aspirations of the Enlightenment stimulated intellectuals from the *millet* to reject 'backward' religious and communal authority. This was further stimulated for the Christian *millets* by the attractions of the Anglo-Saxon Protestant missions and their educational and cultural activities.[3] These missions played an important part in the revival of Arabic language and culture in Syria and Lebanon, and are credited with stimulating the beginnings of Arab nationalism among Christian Arabs. The Alliance Israélite Universelle played a similar role for the Jewish communities of the Empire. The products of these educational institutions cultivated notions of citizenship and active participation in public life, which was satisfied partly by the emergence of the modern sectors of state bureaucracy, education and commerce. The railways and telegraphy were crucial not only in facilitating the opening up of isolated regions and integrating them into the capitalist market, but also in providing employment for the literate.[4]

Cosmopolitan milieux

Alexandria, Beirut, Cairo and Istanbul became the locations where economic and cultural modernity flourished from the latter part of the nineteenth century. While some new intellectuals and statespeople were ideologically attached to Islamic and Ottoman roots, most had adopted new lifestyles and associations and explored new horizons, stimulated partly by the painful realisation of European superiority in wealth and arms. One enclave of cultural as well as political endeavour was that of the Young Ottomans, a group of intellectuals versed in European languages and ideas but seeking a renaissance of Islamic and/or Ottoman civilisation.[5] Their prominent member, Namık Kemal (1840–88), a poet, essayist and liberal political philosopher, was deeply influenced by European currents: he translated Charles-Louis de Secondat, Baron de Montesquieu, debated Voltaire and Nicolas, Marquis de Condorcet, followed the nationalist models of Giuseppe Garibaldi and Giuseppe Mazzini (the Young Ottomans had personal and political connections with Italian nationalists and the Carbonari societies). Kemal and many of the others spent periods of exile in Geneva, London and Paris, where they published the journals that were prohibited in Istanbul, intriguing with patrons and factions in and out of government. Intellectually and politically, these were 'cosmopolitans'; yet Kemal was firmly attached to the idea that a revived Islam must form the basis of society and government. He tried to find Islamic idioms for expressing the main ideas and concepts of the Enlightenment – those of Jean-Jacques Rousseau, Montesquieu and the natural law tradition. He was highly critical of the ruling functionaries of the Porte[6] for its blind imitation of Europe. The Tanzimat[7] was denounced not for its reforms, but for failing to institute a liberal constitution empowering the people as citizens – ensuring liberties supposedly granted by God, as against reforms imposed from above by an autocratic government. For these intellectuals and reformers, Islam became an ideology of national authenticity rather than of ritual observance and their disciplines – a kind of cultural nationalism that persists.[8]

Freemasonry

Many of the members of the Ottoman elites, including politicians and high functionaries and some Young Ottomans, became members of Masonic lodges first started by Europeans with their own rival lodges in which political and personal factions and intrigues, as well as the interests of European powers, were pursued. A similar situation prevailed in Egypt in the nineteenth and twentieth centuries. The most renowned Muslim reformer of the time, Jamal ad-Din al-Afghani ('Asadabadi' to the Iranians) (1838–97), was a member (by some reports, a master) of such a lodge in Egypt. In the figure of al-Afghani, we have a remarkable cosmopolitan.

Freemasonry featured prominently in the cultural and political life of the Ottoman world in the nineteenth and early twentieth centuries, and constituted an important aspect of the cosmopolitan milieu.[9] Branches of British, then French and other continental lodges were established in Istanbul from the early nineteenth century, often by diplomats, including ambassadors from these countries. Initially their membership was confined to Europeans, officials and merchants, and then open to non-Muslim Ottomans; however, from the 1860s this was opened fully to Muslim Ottomans, statespeople, intellectuals and other public figures. Alexandria, Cairo, Istanbul, Izmir and Salonica were prominent centres for Masonic lodges, but they also spread to Syrian and even Iraqi cities.

Masons included some of the main reformers and intellectuals, including Mustafa Reşhid Pasha (1800–58) and Midhat Pasha (1822–84) and the aforementioned writer and intellectual, Namık Kemal. Masonic lodges, especially the French ones, came to foster Ottoman reforms, liberalism and constitutionalism.[10] Sultan Murad V, who ruled briefly in 1876 before being deposed and imprisoned by his brother, Sultan Abdul-Hamid II, was a patron of the liberal constitutionalists as well as a Freemason.[11] A failed conspiracy to liberate and restore Murad emerged from Masonic networks, which incurred Abdul-Hamid's wrath.[12] The long reign of Abdul-Hamid (1876–1909) was one of reaction against liberalism, suspension of the nascent constitution and exile of prominent reformers and liberals, notably Midhat Pasha and Kemal. His reign was marked by repressive measures, censorship and strict regulation of associative life. Masonic lodges came under scrutiny and occasional interdiction. (As we will see later in this chapter, the sultan was correct in distrusting the lodges, as the Young Turk conspiracy that deposed him in 1908 was hatched partly in an Italian Masonic lodge in Salonica.)

However, not all Freemasonry harboured liberals. There was a parting of the ways between the British lodges, which were more conservative and cautious, and the French Grand Orient network, animated by the spirit of the French Revolution. A crucial split came in 1877, when the French jettisoned what had been a founding clause in the Masonic constitution specifying a belief in the 'Supreme Being' and the immortality of the soul as conditions of Masonic affiliation. This formulation was aimed at religious universalism, thus opening up membership to people of diverse religions. However, an unspecified religious belief of some kind was a condition of membership until its termination in the French lodges. This became a clear issue of controversy between the British and the French, with implications for Ottoman membership. The main avant-garde lodge that welcomed Ottoman membership was *i Prodos* (Greek for 'Progress'), an offshoot of the Grand Orient founded in 1868. It was there that the liberal intelligentsia, including Namık and Midhat Pasha, were affiliated. It soon introduced rituals and proceedings in Turkish.[13] It is interesting to note that most of the Ottoman intelligentsia who were Freemasons continued to adhere to the French and Italian lodges, despite – or perhaps because of – their more secular stance, deemed 'atheist' by their detractors. Indeed, some Muslim clerics were affiliated to those lodges, including – in the later period of the Young Turk *coup d'état* – no less a figure than Shayk ul-Islam Musa Kazim.[14]

Salonica at the turn of the twentieth century presents interesting examples of the paradoxes of multi-ethnicity and cosmopolitanism. It was home to a bewildering variety of ethnicities and religions: Jews, Donmeh,[15] Greeks, Bulgarians, Albanians and Ottoman Muslims (a diverse category of ethnicities ranging from Circassians to Sudanese, many Turkish speaking).[16] In many respects this diversity constituted a 'mosaic' society of distinct communities, which were closed in on themselves and had little to do with one another. The rise of Balkan nationalism in the nineteenth century contributed to this insulation, and indeed generated fierce hostilities, especially between Greeks and Bulgarians fighting over the national identity of Macedonia. Yet in the associations and events of the Young Turk revolution of 1908, we see an episode of enthusiastic common participation by individuals from the various communities, in a rare political and cultural identification with Ottomanism in what promised to be its liberal constitutional evolution.

The Masonic lodges played a prominent part in both the plotting of the revolution, and the cosmopolitan surge that accompanied it.[17] The Salonica branch of the Committee of Union and Progress was the main mover of the revolution, with its military members manoeuvring the Third Army in a *coup d'état* against Abdul-Hamid's autocratic regime, in favour of restoring the constitution and parliament. Its initial ideology was one of liberal Ottomanism, embracing all the ethnic and confessional elements of the population in an attempt to preserve the shaky Empire. The plotting was carried out largely in the Italian Masonic lodge, Macedonia Risorta, which followed the Italian Grand Orient and shared the liberal and secular ideology of its French counterpart.[18] The lodges afforded the conspirators secrecy as well as the protection of foreign connections, immune under the capitulations[19] from Abdul-Hamid's vigilant intelligence networks, which were active in Salonica but frustrated by the immunities of foreigners sheltering the plotters. Officers and civil servants who subsequently became prominent statespeople included Talaat Bey and Enver Bey (later pashas). They cultivated Greek notables to help in their plans and involved some notable Jews who became public figures, including the journalist Nissim Rousso and the politician Nissim Mazliah, as well as the Donmeh, Mehmed Javid Bey. A prominent figure was the President of Macedonia Risorta, Emmanuel Carasso, an Italian Jew.[20] Even at that stage, the involvement of Jewish individuals in these Masonic contexts elicited accusations of Zionist conspiracies, which have more recently become prevalent (as we shall see presently). In fact, the Jewish people in question were not sympathetic to Zionism, seeing it as incompatible with the Ottomanist patriotism that was their basic ideology, as well as that of the Young Turks.[21]

The ideological cosmopolitanism of the Young Turks – embodied in their Ottomanism, which embraced all elements of the Ottoman population – was soon to be assailed by catastrophic wars and strident nationalism, both in the Balkans and in the Turkish heartlands.[22] Already, in 1909 a 'national' Masonic lodge had been founded: the Ottoman Grand Orient, which embraced the main actors in the Committee of Union and Progress,[23] but maintained affiliation with the Grand Orient of France. The Balkan War of 1912 spelled disaster for the Empire, with the combined forces of Greece, Serbia and Bulgaria displacing the Ottomans from almost all their European territories and, at one stage, threatening Istanbul itself.[24] The dominant ideology and policy of the Young Turks in government turned towards Turkish nationalism, confronting the ethno-national movements combining to assail the Empire. World War I brought defeat and ruin, the flight of the remaining Young Turk leaders and the ultimate dissolution of the Empire; then, after the war of liberation from the occupying Allies, the rise of a highly nationalist Turkish republic. Along with many other forms of associational life, freemasonry was banned by the Atatürk regime; it was licensed again in 1948, but with little political or ideological effect.

In the late nineteenth century and into the twentieth century, Egypt had a strong Masonic presence. The British Grand Orient was the first and main lodge and recruited many of the prominent public figures of the time, including at one point Mohammed Tawfiq Pasha (Khedive (ruler) of Egypt), who served as its honorary president. It also included many intellectuals and statespeople, including Boutros Ghali, scion of a major Coptic family and a prominent jurist; Sa'ad Zaghloul, a prominent nationalist who led the al-Wafd independence movement in 1919; Lutfi al-Sayyid, another prominent nationalist intellectual; and many of the ruling circle and army officers. However, most interesting was the active membership of the most prominent Islamic reformers of the time, al-Afghani and Muhammad Abduh.[25] Ali al-Wardi cites al-Afghani's letter of application to join the Grand Lodge in 1875,[26] in which he addresses the Masons as *Ikhwan al-Safa* ('brothers of purity'), the title of a group of rationalist intellectuals in early Islam. He was admitted and proceeded to the rank of president of one of the lodges in 1878. Many of his disciples were also Freemasons, including Muhammad Abduh. Al-Afghani counted among his disciples the Christian Adib Ishaq (1856–85) and the Egyptian Jew, Yaqub Sanu (James Sanua) (1839–1912),[27] which indicates the wide cosmopolitan milieu of which they formed a part, and the attraction of Freemasonry in offering a tolerant congruence between religions and ethnicities. While charismatic and charming, al-Afghani was also a sharp polemicist who made many enemies. He clashed with the authorities of the Grand Orient over his politicisation of Freemasonry in opposition to Khedive Ismail, then to his successor Tawfiq (a Freemason). It is not clear whether he left that lodge or was expelled, but he soon founded another under the tutelage of the Grand Orient of France.[28] Al-Wardi cites extracts from his letter of reproach to the British Masons, in which he denounced their 'cowardice' and refusal to pursue the

Masonic ideals of liberty, equality and fraternity against oppression and corruption, for the benefit of the whole of humankind. Subsequently, in the aftermath of the failure of the Urabi military revolt of 1882, Abduh and other disciples were exiled from Egypt for complicity in the revolt and eventually found refuge in Beirut, where they were welcomed and assisted by the lodges of that city.[29]

Al-Afghani was a maverick character who dissimulated his ideas and identity to achieve maximum influence in different contexts. Although almost certainly of Iranian Shi'ite birth and formation, he assumed the identity of an Afghani Sunni, dressing in the manner of Sunni *ulama* from that country when he was in Turkey and Egypt, but dressing as a Shi'ite cleric when in Iran, and even assuming Arab dress in Hijaz. His main designation was al-Afghani, but at times he also called himself 'al-Husseini' (the title of descent from the Prophet through Imam Hussein) when in Shi'i Iran, and even 'Istanbuli', depending on his target audience. His Islamic adherence was challenged by many of his adversaries, but also by scholars and historians – notably Elie Kedourie, who argued that he and Abduh were positivist rationalists, if not atheists, and pretended a belief in Islam for political reasons. Al-Afghani's Islamic modernism certainly favoured reconciling religion with science and rationality, but he was not consistent. In India he denounced Syed Ahmad Khan, the religious reformer and modernist – although he espoused similar views to those that al-Afghani himself held – because Ahmad Khan adopted a conciliatory attitude to British colonialism, seeing it as a progressive stage in the advance of Indians and Muslims into modernity. In Istanbul, al-Afghani was denounced by orthodox clerics for lecturing on the congruence of religion with rational philosophy.[30]

Like that of the Young Ottomans, al-Afghani's pan-Islamism was aimed at the restoration of Islam to its pristine origins, which then would make it superior to European creeds in political order and civilisation. However, the intended reforms would result in polity, law and society looking remarkably like idealised European models. Politically, his objective was a pan-Islamic unity that, armed with a reformed religion, society and polity, would stand up to European domination and revive the strength and glory of historical Islam. Like all reformers of his time, he sought to influence the elite – primarily, the princes and kings of Islam. They welcomed him at first, flattered by his attentions, but soon realised the import of his advocacy and sought to get rid of him – at which point he turned to dissident intellectuals and constitutionalists to propagate his ideas, which landed him in exile.

The cosmopolitanism of al-Afghani spanned not only the boundaries between Islam and Europe, but also those between different Muslim cultures. He operated between British India, Iran, Egypt and Turkey, as well as from European capitals. He worked in Persian, Turkish and Arabic and knew English and French. He debated with Indian Muslim reformers and Arab clerics, and his best-known work was a polemic with the French writer Ernest Renan. In this later work, al-Afghani advanced a rationalist explanation of the formation and history of religion and its social functions: arguments that led to accusations of 'atheism' by opponents in the Muslim world (who had access to the French publication), and by European commentators who sought to detract from his reformist project.[31] His cosmopolitanism extended to aspects of culture and lifestyle: apart from his membership of Masonic lodges, he was also known to frequent cafes and clubs, to be fond of cognac, and was rumoured to have illicit sexual encounters. Recent Arab historians who have written on these aspects of his life – especially his Freemasonry – have been attacked by orthodox Muslims who still claim him as an early advocate of their reforms.

We may now ask what the attractions of Freemasonry were for the elites of the Ottoman lands in the nineteenth and early twentieth centuries. First, it offered clear instrumental advantages: contacts, networking and mutual aid in relation to positions, promotion and business dealings. Second, Masonic lodges offered a means of secrecy and dissimulation for political planning and campaigning, as well as plots and conspiracies – as we saw in the case of the Young Turks and al-Afghani's clique (and as noted previously, foreign involvement in Salonica also afforded protection for the Young Turk conspirators). However, apart from these instrumental benefits, there were clearly ideological and aesthetic attractions. Thierry Zarcone argues that the mode of sociability of Masonic lodges – as secret brotherhoods, with their elaborate rituals and hierarchies of initiation and promotion – had close affinities with Sufi orders and lodges as a form of sociability and brotherhood. In particular, the interdiction and then clandestine flourishing of the Bektashi Orders after the destruction of the janissaries in 1824, generated forms of secret organisations that attracted intellectuals who combined modern enlightenment with heterodox mysticism, distinguished by its adherents as 'enlightened Sufism' – a combination we may also observe in the case of Iranian secret societies of the time. Zarcone further argues that there was an overlap of personnel, institutions and ideas between the two forms of association. He shows that many of the people involved in the politics of the Young Turk period and afterwards were adepts of both Sufi orders (mainly Bektashi and Melami) and Masonic lodges.[32]

Zarcone devotes one section of his book to the life and work of Riza Tevfik Bölükbaşı – a prominent intellectual, philosopher, teacher and politician of the Young Turk era who wrote, among other things, a dictionary of philosophy. Tevfik declared himself a follower of both Ibn Arabi, the source of much Sufi philosophy and mysticism, and of Herbert Spencer, the English evolutionist philosopher and social theorist. From our point of view, the link that Tevfik forged between the two philosophies was tenuous and to do with a scepticism that he identified in them both, in relation to the theory of knowledge (the elaborate arguments he put forward need not concern us here). What is interesting is Tevfik's mentality or outlook, which was not uncommon among modernist Turkish and Iranian intellectuals of the nineteenth and early twentieth centuries who subscribed to European Enlightenment currents that were mainly positivist, rationalist, evolutionist and sceptical of religious verities, as well as to mystical philosophies with a Muslim and Greek heritage. They also were liable to form and affiliate to secret societies, including Freemasonry. What these diverse currents seemed to share was a rejection of the verities and disciplines of orthodox Islam, and the authority of its *ulama* (scholars) and institutions. Above all, it was the idea of the *Shari'a* (Islamic law) as the basis of social order – buttressed by the authority of *ulama* and *mujtahids* (scholars in, and authorities on, Islamic law) and enforced by absolute rulers – that was rejected and seen as the cause and hallmark of the stagnation and backwardness of their societies and polities. Further, that orthodoxy had forbidden free philosophical enquiry, in which the modern intellectuals were finding exciting truths and programmes for renewed conceptions of social and political life. Montesquieu, Rousseau, Spencer, Charles Darwin and John Stuart Mill were the prophets of this Enlightenment, and the inspiration for a dreamt modernity of liberty and rationality. Many of the intellectuals of that generation stopped at that; rejecting the religious baggage of their Ottoman heritage, they embraced unencumbered positivism and scientism. However, many others attempted to find a link between the European Enlightenment and elements of their philosophical heritage, linked to mostly heterodox Sufism, which metamorphosed in nineteenth-century intellectual and political contexts into Bektashism. These currents, or torrents, of ideas and programmes were socially embedded in the secret societies and rituals of Freemasonry and Sufi lodges – with a healthy traffic between them, according to Zarcone.

We may speculate that a crucial element of the appeal of Freemasonry to those intellectual and political elites was the *imaginaire* of participation in a milieu of the civilised world (*medeniyat*), a regular theme in the discourse of modernity and reform at the time. The 'brotherhood' with similar elites in the 'civilised' world, participating in their spheres of sociability and in their discourses and intrigues and the universalism of their world – these were powerful draws, taking the form of an active cosmopolitanism.

Freemasonry, along with other cosmopolitan and liberationist currents in the Middle East, was to gradually dwindle in the course of the twentieth century, confronting increasingly strident nationalisms and ethno-religious movements and the authoritarian regimes that fostered them. In these contexts, secret societies were always suspect – perhaps rightly – as the locations of conspiracies. Added to that were the cosmopolitan dimensions of Freemasonry, emphasising human communalities and the basic unity of all religion – a basic universalism – as the exclusive claims for the allegiance of both orthodox religion and nationalist regimes. After all, that was why Pope Clement XII had declared his ban on Freemasonry in 1738, soon after its foundation: its secrecy and universalism were a threat to the exclusive allegiance of the faithful to their Mother Church.[33] As we have seen, Atatürk banned and dissolved Masonic lodges, which were revived after his death; however, we should note that after that charismatic period of intellectual and political effervescence in the late nineteenth and early twentieth centuries, Freemasonry, where it survived, appears to have been 'routinised' into its predominant form in the modern world – as merely an instrumental medium for promoting its members' interests in business and public life, with its intellectual and spiritual dimensions reduced to formulaic affirmations. Even so, its secrecy and refusal to be supervised by the monitors of the authoritarian regimes resulted in its being interdicted in most Middle Eastern countries. Nasser's Egypt banned and dissolved Masonic lodges in 1964, ostensibly because the lodges refused supervision and regulation by the Ministry of Social Affairs.[34] Freemasonry was banned in Syria the following year, but survived in the more liberal and bourgeois Lebanon.

Everywhere, 'Masonry' and 'Zionism' became twin evils, weaving imperialist conspiracies against the Arab and Muslim nations. In Iraq, after the 1958 revolution that toppled the monarchy, the show trials of the luminaries of that regime included indictments for Masonry, famously against Fadhil al-Jamali, a statesman of the *ancien régime* and actually a Mason. In his interrogation by the revolutionary judge, al-Jamali defended Masonry as a universalist humanism, respectful of national interests and innocent of complicity with Zionism.[35] Under Saddam Hussein, being a Mason became one of many capital offences, and accusations of Masonry were flung at members of the old bourgeoisie who were disliked by the regime.

Drinking cultures

Masonic lodges, cafes and salons were among the milieux of cosmopolitanism, but in nineteenth-century Istanbul, these also included taverns and a drinking culture. The prohibition of alcohol is iconic for orthodox and political Islam as a marker of authenticity and distinction from the dissolute other – i.e. 'the West'. It also has contributed to the intrigue and romance of drink throughout the history of Middle Eastern societies: in poetry, Sufism (mysticism) and *belles lettres*. Drinking cultures were high and low: the sumptuous wine tables of the rich and the taverns of the soldiery and *awbash* (rabble).

The janissary corps, the military mainstay of the Ottomans who, as we have seen, were intertwined with the Bektashi Order, were well-known drinkers: many of their entertainments, as well as intrigues and conspiracies, were conducted in taverns. Dancing boys dressed as girls and offering sexual favours, were a regular item of entertainment.[36] The disorders and violence perpetrated by the janissaries in their years of decadence in the late eighteenth century, and until their destruction in 1826, were fuelled by drink. However, soldiers and the lower orders were not the only patrons of taverns. One Nihali, a sixteenth-century *qadi* (judge) of Galata and a celebrated poet with the nom de plume 'Jaafar', boasted of frequenting the taverns of that part of Istanbul, which was 'cosmopolitan' even then.[37] For the most part, the respectable classes drank in private, with their own circles of companions. In some Middle Eastern cities in the nineteenth and twentieth centuries, public male drinking cultures became respectable and open – a sign of modernity and *medeniyet* (culture, civilisation). Thus alcohol became an issue in contests of identity and authenticity. François Georgeon has written a fascinating account of the symbolic significance of alcohol for notions of modernity and civilisation in Turkey from the nineteenth century.[38] Sultan Mahmud II (1808–39) was the first reforming ruler who made a serious impact. He modelled himself on other European rulers, and included alcohol as a feature of public occasions such as official dinners and receptions. Champagne, which was not new to the Ottoman court, then came out in public. Over the course of the century and among the modern elites and the official classes, drink came to be associated with being modern and civilisation. Hüsrev Pasha, *serasker* (army chief), would drink 'champagne with an influential European', even though he did not like it and preferred water, 'to show how he had shed completely the prejudices of the old Turkey: he knows full well that the fact will be noted in a newspaper article'.[39] Georgeon adds that the disappearance of the janissaries and their association with alcohol from the public scene after 1826 'permitted a shift to civilian and by extension "civilised" consumption of alcohol'. Later in the century, the state class of the expanded reform bureaucracy became the vanguard of the drinking classes. To cater for them, a new type of refined and opulent tavern (*meyhane*) came into existence, with a professional guild of tavernkeepers and their assistants trained in the arts of serving alcohol and its accompaniment of mezze, and in the skills of nursing a *narguila* (*shisha*, or water pipe). Among the consumers, a new *adab* (etiquette) and lore of drink determined a kind of *savoir boire*.

Much of this new culture of drinking revolved around the newly fashionable *rah/arak*, displacing wine as the favoured drink. It became an identity marker as a specifically native drink, in contrast to the more cosmopolitan and European wine.[40] It acquired the honorific description of *arslan sutu*, and in Arabic (at least in Iraq) of *halib sba'* (both translate as 'lion's milk'). It became the drink of choice in the cafes, clubs and salons of intellectuals and reformers, which included the poet Kemal and the statesman Midhat Pasha. Later in the century, under the more religious and authoritarian reign of Abdul-Hamid II, there was a backlash against this drinking culture, both religious and medical, but with little effect. *Rah* was to feature again as part of the culture of the Turkish republic under Atatürk, himself a noted devotee of the beverage. It is said that old Kemalist stalwarts were still to be seen until recent times at the bar in Sirkeci railway station at sunset, raising a glass to the memory of their hero, accompanied by the classic and austere mezze preferred by the pasha: the *beyaz maza* (white table) of white cheese, melon and yoghurt and cucumber.

Alcohol and drinking culture became an issue concerning authenticity and identity. In the aftermath of municipal elections that brought the Islamic Refah Partisi (Welfare Party) to power in Istanbul in 1994, one of the first issues that arose between the Islamic mayors and the Kemalist bourgeoisie was that of drink. The bars and restaurants of Beyoglu, the cosmopolitan centre of the city, were targeted by the mayor, who did not dare to ban alcohol but made rules restricting its visibility: establishments were requested not to allow drinking on terraces and at street tables, and to hide their drinkers behind curtains. An outcry from the modern bourgeoisie, with demonstrations of street drinking, soon forced the withdrawal of the order. On a more recent visit to Istanbul I came across two new bars in Beyoglu: one named Victor Cohen Sheraphanesi (wine bar), the other going by the equally typical Greek name of Stavros Sheraphanesi. On enquiry, it seemed that both were run by Turkish Muslim entrepreneurs who had acquired the old names to recreate the atmosphere and associations of the old 'cosmopolitan' Beyoglu. Another disco bar in that quarter had the potentially blasphemous name of 'Abdul-JabBAR' (Abdul-Jabbar being a reference to one of the attributes of God). However, more recent reports indicate that in the more conservative parts of Istanbul and other cities, especially in Anatolia, authorities from the ruling pro-Muslim Adalet ve Kalkınma Partisi (Justice and Development Party, successor to the Refah Partisi of the 1990s) are banning or pressuring establishments serving alcohol in areas under their control. Alcohol consumption in today's Turkey has become a potent identity marker in political and cultural struggles between secularism and religiosity. The modern bourgeoisie of Istanbul stands in contrast to the vast Anatolian territory of conservative mores and religious sensibility, now fully present in the city and seen by the bourgeoisie as representing the threatening barbarians at the gates. The contrast is illustrated in the following anecdote:

> [T]wo Turkish women, one veiled, the other not, encountered one another in front of the Ayasofya museum in the old quarter of Istanbul. The short-haired woman, dressed in a skirt to her knees, a trimly fit blouse, and a short coat, asked the other woman who was wearing a black veil, whether this was the line for tickets to the museum. The veiled woman was surprised. 'You speak Turkish?' she asked in amazement. 'Yes, I am Turkish!' asserted the short-haired woman, put off by the question. 'Oh! You don't look Turkish. You look like a Westerner,'

said the veiled woman. 'You don't look Turkish either,' said the other. 'I thought you were an Arab.' 'Oh!' said the veiled woman, 'thanks to God, we are Turkish and Muslim.' 'Well, we are too,' said the short-haired woman.[41]

Egyptian cosmopolitanism

Much of the nostalgia for cosmopolitan milieux in the Middle East relates to Egypt, and in particular to Alexandria. The transformations of the Egyptian economy and society of the nineteenth century, culminating in the British occupation from 1882, brought many migrants and entrepreneurs from Europe and the Levant, who formed a diverse and colourful society: not only opportunists and adventurers, but also Greek shopkeepers and Italian stevedores – a glimpse of which can be seen in the highly romanticised fiction of Lawrence Durrell's *Alexandria Quartet*. There are many things to be said about this society, but let me pick out a contrast between two facets of cosmopolitanism at that point.[42]

The subsequent nostalgia for this golden age conveniently forgets its imperial context. Cosmopolitan Alexandria, for example, included a rigorous system of exclusions for native Egyptians, including segregation or exclusion on buses and trams, and certainly from clubs, some bars and cafes and many social milieux. Native Egyptian society provided servants, functionaries and prostitutes for the cosmopolitan milieu. They were inferiorised and despised. It was no coincidence, then, that the Muslim Brotherhood was founded in 1928 in Ismailiya, in the Canal Zone, and had as its founding programme the rescue of Muslim youth from the corruption of European dominance – drink and prostitution – it is no wonder that it found an echo in Egyptian society.

Conversely, Egypt in the first half of the twentieth century witnessed a flourishing of intellectual and artistic movements and milieux (as well as religious and nativist reactions against them). The new Egyptian university, a lively press, the film industry, an artistic and musical renaissance and intellectual opening – all looked to the wider world for inspiration and innovation. Taha Hussein, a prominent figure in Egyptian letters, declared the Pharaonic and Hellenistic roots of Egyptian culture: it was to the Mediterranean world that it must look for its future.[43] The 1932 Congress of Arab Music in Cairo, attended by musicians and theorists from the Arab world, as well as by major European figures such as the composers Béla Bartók and Paul

Hindemith, debated the links between tradition and modernity, particularism and universality.⁴⁴ Paradoxically, it was Bartók who defended traditional music against the Arab modernists who proclaimed the decadence of the old and the necessity of innovating and evolving in line with the general progress of society and the opening to universal trends and values. The British anthropologist Edward E. Evans-Pritchard was giving his seminal lectures on primitive religion at Egyptian University.⁴⁵ Films portrayed a universe of romance and music in social settings contrasting the old and the new, the popular quarters and Europeanised suburbs. This cultural mix and excitement was cosmopolitan in a much more profound sense than the celebrated European-Levantine milieu of Alexandria.

These milieux and ideas ended with the Nasserist transformation of the country, with the expulsion of most foreigners and Jews following the 1956 tripartite invasion of Egypt. Subsequently, Egypt became a bastion of Arab nationalism, modelled on a Soviet-style command economy, and its internationalism became that of intergovernmental cooperation. Let us now turn to aspects of nationalism and Islamism.

Paradoxes of nationalism and Islamism

The Istanbul bourgeoisie, nostalgic for past cosmopolitanism, are ideologically and socially products of the sternest Turkish nationalism: that of Kemalism. The paradox of Kemalism is that it sought to assert a particularism of Turks – as distinct from Arabs, Persians, Ottomans and traditional Islam – by orienting itself to Europe and modernity. Its official ethos might appear 'cosmopolitan' in relation to the styles that it adopted: the dress code, from turbans and fez to hats and formal European dress, as well as prohibition of the *hijab* and religious garb; the change of script from Arabic to Roman; lifestyles, including Atatürk's insistence on European-style festivities, including balls and ballroom dancing for official occasions; the culture of drink, especially the national *rah*, and so on. However, the actual policies and processes in the establishment of the Turkish republic brought about the homogenisation of its population and culture: the ethnic cleansing of Greek and Armenian populations, then the enforced Turkicisation of Muslim minorities, Kurds and Circassians.⁴⁶ The ideal citizen of the new secular republic was a Sunni Muslim of the Hanafi *madhhab* (school of thought; as opposed to the Shafi'i Kurds and the 'heretical' Alevis). That is why, in spite of the bitter antagonisms between Islamic and secular Turkey, there remains a basic affinity between different groups. At the same time, Kemalist identification with European modernity was explicitly opposed to the culture of cosmopolitanism. Like all nationalist ideologies, Kemalism rejected cosmopolitans as inauthentic and lacking in moral rectitude: its aim was a unitary and homogeneous nation.

German Romantic nationalism (which was the ideological underpinning of many Arab and Middle Eastern nationalisms) was explicitly anti-cosmopolitan. In the opposition between culture and civilisation, it was culture – rooted in the *volk*, in the blood and soil – that was the positive, desirable element. Civilisation was a superficial veneer – artificial, seductive to the weak and fashionable – that undermined the natural rootedness of *volk* culture. For Johann Gottfried Herder, it was French civilisation against German culture. Yet for Herder and his followers, this nationalism was part of a universalist commitment: he was not against other nationalities and cultures, but against mixing, hybridity and dilution; the ideal was for every people to conform to its own culture and roots and be true to its nature, which would fulfil a universal harmony. Cosmopolitanism was hybrid, superficial and immoral – psychologically and even biologically debilitating.[47] Kemalists and Arab nationalists incorporated these notions, often explicitly, into their ideologies and programmes.

Islamism, the cosmopolitan and the transnational

We have seen how the leading Muslim modernist reformers were, in many senses, cosmopolitan. They formed part of the elite circles of intellectuals, aristocrats and politicians, and focused their efforts mostly within these elites. A subsequent generation of Muslim leaders turned to populism and mass mobilisation, deploying a much more puritanical and nativist Islam: notably the Muslim Brotherhood in Egypt under Hassan al-Banna, which emerged in 1928; these were the 'fundamentalists'. Their ideology was one of a return to the purity of early Islam and the first generations (hence 'Salafi' – *salaf* means 'ancestors'), but their politics were essentially those of modern, populist mass mobilisation.[48] Their appeal was largely that of national liberation from foreign rule, but also, essentially, from foreign customs and lifestyles: they rejected not only the Europeans, but also those of their compatriots and co-religionists who adopted European ways, and precisely those forms and styles considered cosmopolitan. In this respect they shared the nationalist quest for authenticity. Indeed, at the present time we see an explicit convergence between forms of Islamism and Arab nationalism (though there is diversity within both) in rejecting the West, seen as the aggressor against all Muslims and Arabs.[49] An essential part of this perceived Western invasion is the cultural component – *al-ghazw al-fikri* – of alien ideas and corrupt lifestyles.

This convergence between nationalists and Islamists on the cultural front is illustrated by the example of the trials of homosexuals in Egypt, the *Queen Boat* episode.[50] This boat was one of the many entertainment venues on the Nile in Cairo suspected of being a gay venue. It was raided by the police and all those present were arrested, some subsequently tried – reportedly after the usual police performance of beatings and maltreatment. This highly publicised episode occasioned public outrage against the victims. The thrust of the press campaign was that homosexuality was a Western corruption, alien to Egypt and Islam. One lawyer beseeched the judge to acquit his client to prove to the world that there was no homosexuality in Egypt. While homoeroticism of various forms has been common and unremarked on throughout the region (see Introduction), these particular groups become a target because of their style and culture: they are engaged in a lifestyle and forms of sociability associated with modern social libertarians – with gay culture – and thus are seen as alien and threatening. They are, in our parlance, 'cosmopolitan'.

What of Islamic cosmopolitanism? After all, Islamic ideologies are directed at a world community of Muslims and at proselytising universally. Indeed, many Islamists have denounced nationalism as being divisive of the universal Muslim *umma* (community). The prominence of Arab Christians in the leadership and ideology of Arab nationalism from Ottoman times has prompted many Islamists to denounce Arab nationalism as a Christian conspiracy with the West, aimed at the destruction of the Ottoman caliphate and Muslim unity. However, in practice, Islamic politics had been oriented towards particular countries and regions, not the world community. Even the Sufi orders, which had generated widespread networks in the past, had become nationalised within state boundaries. This has changed in recent decades, first with the internationalisation of Islamism through the Afghan wars (courtesy of the Americans and the Saudis), then through the spread in migrant and transnational communities and networks. This is a complex phenomenon demanding extensive treatment to do it justice. For the present, let me say that transnationalism is distinct from the thrust and connotation of cosmopolitanism. Transnational networks and ideologies are often directed at social particularism and exclusiveness. While nation states in the Middle East and many other parts have engaged throughout the twentieth century in attempts to homogenise their populations through ethnic cleansing and the suppression of minority cultures, the cities of the West have undergone the opposite process – one of increasing diversification, fusion and hybridity. Within these spaces develop transnational networks with diverse ideologies and cultures. Nonetheless, one prominent element in this mix is what has been called 'long distance nationalism', including exclusivist religious networks. Muslim groups, communities and associations in the West are diverse, and most are secular. There are also Euro-Muslims: those who want their religion to be recognised alongside the other major religions in European society. However, the most vocal and publicised are the Salafi: fundamentalist groups who, while content with a transnational presence, insist on exclusiveness and distance from others.

Cosmopolitanism in the new age

Our own time is marked by the most profound technical revolution in global communications, transcending national and cultural boundaries. At the level of the common people, television soaps from Hollywood, Mumbai and South America are beamed into every home and followed with passion. This is accompanied by international patterns of mass consumption, with global brand names that have become iconic. At the technical and institutional levels, the internet is conquering ever more frontiers: even the most repressive and isolationist Middle Eastern states are connected, but always looking for means of control and censorship. Add to that the enormous explosion in tourism, travel, commerce, international media and the translation and publishing industries, and impressive cross-cultural transactions and mixes are achieved. Alongside this cultural globalisation, we have the most xenophobic and intolerant manifestations of narrow nationalisms and religious revivals, of which political Islam is the most prominent in the Middle East.

Does cultural globalisation represent heightened cosmopolitanism? Is the xenophobia of political Islam a reaction? I would argue that manifestations of cultural globalism have transcended the problematic of cosmopolitanism. The context of the cosmopolitanisms of the first half of the twentieth century were networks and milieux of intellectuals, artists, dilettantes and *flâneurs* in urban centres – deracinated, transcending recently impermeable communal and religious boundaries, daring and experimenting. Or at least that was the projected image – one that defined identities and outlooks. These kinds of networks and milieux persist, and are probably more extensive than ever before, but in the age of cultural globalism they have been routinised and have lost their special identities and charismatic images. At the same time, global means of communication in the form of television, the internet and other media do not necessarily breach communal and particularistic boundaries and spaces. People receive foreign soap operas in their own homes or neighbourhood cafes, dubbed into their own language. They consume them in terms of their own constructions of meanings and lifeworlds.

In another global context, international business creates its own uniform milieux, with its executives and personnel travelling the world and residing in diverse centres, but always in the 'same' hotel rooms or apartments, served by Filipino maids and the same networks of sociability of colleagues and associates.[51] Tourism similarly creates its own milieux: at the cheaper levels, resorts, hotels, entertainments and food that strive for standardisation, from Benidorm to Bodrum. Upmarket tourists pay for a touch of exoticism and local colour, often constructed within the safe and hygienic confines of their hotels: witness the constructions of popular cafes and souks in the Cairo Nile Hilton, complete with Ramadan nights if you happen to stay during the blessed month. What is intriguing is that these constructions are not just for tourists, but attract the native prosperous classes, who also like to engage in ersatz exoticism without rubbing shoulders with their poor compatriots.

Conclusion

In conclusion, we can say that cosmopolitanism in the Middle East – in the old-fashioned sense of communally deracinated and culturally promiscuous groups and milieux – continues to exist in particular corners of urban space. However, these are submerged by the two major forces of the metropolis: the urbanised masses and their transformation of the city and its politics; and the forces of international capital of business and tourism and their towering hotels and offices, their media and the consumption of goods and images that cater to them.

Mass higher education produces a proletarianised, poorly educated intelligentsia, lacking in wealth and resentful, directing its *ressentiment* against the Westernised elites, seen as the agents of cultural invasion. These are the main cadres of nationalist and religious xenophobia currently so powerful in the region.

While some degree of liberalisation has benefited cultural production in Egypt and elsewhere in recent decades, these limited gains have been very insecure, especially now that they are threatened by religious censorship and intimidation, which also extend to the urban spaces, such as cafes and bars, that form the social milieux of intellectuals and artists. Therefore, it is not surprising that the main cultural flourishing of Middle Eastern cosmopolitanism now occurs in London and Paris.

Notes

1 Two collections of essays on cosmopolitanism are Roel Meijer (ed.) (1999) *Cosmopolitanism, Idenity and Authenticity in the Middle East* (London: Curzon Press), and, Steven Vertovec and Robin Cohen (eds) (2002) *Concerning Cosmopolitanism: Theory, Context and Practice* (Oxford: Oxford University Press). Each include an essay by the present author.
2 Al-Jabarti, Abdul Rahman (n.d.) *Tarikh 'Aja'ib al-Athar fi'l Tarajim w'al-Akhbar* [*The History of Wondrous Traces in Translations and News*], 3 vols (Beirut: Dar al-Jil), vol. 1, pp. 633–4.
3 See Albert Hourani (1983) *Arabic Thought in the Liberal Age, 1798–1939* (Cambridge: Cambridge University Press), pp. 245–59.
4 Donald Quataert (2000) *The Ottoman Empire, 1700–1992* (Cambridge: Cambridge University Press), pp. 110–39.
5 See Serif Mardin (1962) *The Genesis of Young Ottoman Thought: A Study in the Modernization of Turkish Political Ideas* (Princeton, NJ: Princeton University Press).
6 The central government of the Ottoman Empire.
7 The reformation of the Ottoman Empire, from 1839–76.
8 For an exposition of Namık Kemal's ideological formulations, see Niyazi Berkes (1998[1964]) *The Development of Secularism in Turkey* (London: Hurst), pp. 208–22.
9 The most comprehensive source on freemasonry is Thierry Zarcone (1993) *Mystiques, philosophes, et franc-maçon en Islam: Riza Teufik, penseur ottoman 1868–1949* (Paris: Maison Neuve), especially pp. 177–300. An unusually objective, but not always accurate, modern Arabic account is Ali Al-Wardi (1992) *Lamahat ijtima'iya min tarikh al-Iraq al-hadith* [*Social Aspects of Iraqi Modern History*], Vol. III (London: Kufan Publishing), pp. 329–83 (see also pp. 266–328).
10 Zarcone, *Mystiques*, pp. 98–9.
11 Ibid., pp. 208–10.

12 Ibid., p. 209.
13 Ibid., p. 99.
14 Ibid., pp. 149–54.
15 The Donmeh are Jews who converted to Islam in the seventeenth century after the failure and conversion of Sabbatai Zevi, the so-called 'False Messiah'. Although formally Sunni Muslim, they divided into distinct sects and communities and were prominently present in Ottoman Salonica. Many of their intelligentsia became enthusiastic supporters of liberal constitutionalism, and then of the Kemalist republic.
16 See Mark Mazower (2004) *Salonica: City of Ghosts, Christians, Muslims and Jews 1430–1950* (London: HarperCollins), pp. 252–7.
17 Ibid., pp. 272–85; Zarcone, *Mystiques*, pp. 241–70.
18 Zarcone, *Mystiques*, p. 241.
19 Privileges and immunities granted to nationals of favoured countries.
20 Zarcone, *Mystiques*, p. 243; Mazower, *Salonica*, pp. 272–3.
21 Mazower, *Salonica*, pp. 282–5.
22 M. Şükrü Hanioğlu (2008) *A Brief History of the Late Ottoman Empire* (Princeton, NJ: Princeton University Press), pp. 150–202.
23 Zarcone, *Mystiques*, pp. 250–4.
24 Hanioğlu, *A Brief History*, pp. 167–77.
25 Zarcone, *Mystiques*, pp. 288–90; al-Wardi, *Lamahat ijtima'iya min tarikh*, pp. 276–80.
26 Which was among al-Afghani's papers that were apparently kept in the archives of the Iranian parliament and published in a book in 1963, cited by al-Wardi, *Lamahat ijtima'iya min tarikh*, p. 276, fn. 22.
27 Zarcone, *Mystiques*, p. 289.
28 Ibid., p. 288; al-Wardi, *Lamahat ijtima'iya min tarikh*, p. 278.
29 Al-Wardi, *Lamahat ijtima'iya min tarikh*, pp. 322–33.
30 Ibid., pp. 283–6, 313–18.
31 In particular, Elie Kedourie (1997[1966]) *Afghani and Abduh: An Essay on Religious Unbelief and Political Activism in Modern Islam* (London: Gass).
32 Zarcone, *Mystiques*, pp. 301–26.
33 Al-Wardi, *Lamahat ijtima'iya min tarikh*, p. 334.
34 Ibid., pp. 379–83.
35 Ibid., pp. 377–8.
36 Godfrey Goodwin (2006) *The Janissaries* (London: Saqi Books), pp. 87–9.
37 Cemal Kafadar (1995) *Between Two Worlds: The Construction of Ottoman State* (Berkeley, CA: University of California Press), p. 150.
38 Georgeon, Francois (2002) 'Ottomans and Drinkers: The Consumption of Alcohol in Istanbul in the Nineteenth Century', in Eugene Rogan (ed.) *Outside In: On the Margins of the Modern Middle East* (London: I.B.Tauris), pp. 7–30.
39 Ibid., p. 17.
40 Ibid., pp. 19–23.

41 Related in Yael Navaro-Yashin (2002) *Faces of the State: Secularism and Public Life in Turkey* (Princeton, NJ: Princeton University Press), p. 19.
42 See Khaled Fahmy (2004) 'Towards a History of Alexandria', in Anthony Hirst and Michael Silk, eds, *Alexandria, Real and Imagined* (Aldershot: Ashgate); (2004) 'For Cavafy, with Love and Squalor: Some critical notes on the History and Historiography of Modern Alexandria', in Hirst and Silk, *Alexandria*; and Robert Mabro (2004) 'Egyptian Literary Images of Alexandria', in Hirst and Silk, *Alexandria*.
43 Taha Hussein (1937) *Mustaqbal al-thaqafa fi Misr* [*The Future of Culture in Egypt*] (Cairo: Matba'at al-Ma'arif).
44 A brief account appears in a booklet accompanying the recording *Congres du Caire 1932* Muhammad al Qubbanji, Dawud Hosni, Muhammad Ghanim et al. (1988), 2 vols, compact disc (France: Édition Bibliothèque Nationale, APN), pp. pp. 33–7, 88–9. See also Ali J. Racy (2003) *Making Music in the Arab World: The Culture and Artistry of Tarab* (Cambridge: Cambridge University Press).
45 Evans-Pritchard delivered these lectures at the Faculty of Arts at Egyptian (later Cairo) University after his appointment there in 1932. A later version was published: Edward E. Evans-Pritchard (1965) *Theories of Primitive Religion* (Oxford: Oxford University Press).
46 See, Erik J. Zürcher (1993) *Turkey: A Modern History* (London: I.B.Tauris), pp. 231–322.
47 These themes in German Romantic nationalism and its emphasis on language are recounted in Kedourie, *Afghani and Abduh*, especially pp. 44–86.
48 There is extensive literature on the Muslim Brotherhood. See the now-classic Richard P. Mitchell (1969) *The Society of Muslim Brothers* (Oxford: Oxford University Press), and Gilles Kepel (1985) *The Prophet and Pharaoh: Muslim Extremism in Egypt* (London: Saqi Books).
49 See Chapter 6.
50 See Human Rights Watch (2004) 'In a Time of Torture: The Assault on Justice in Egypt's Crackdown on Homosexual Conduct', 29 February. Available at http://www.hrw.org/en/reports/2004/02/29/time-torture (accessed 27 April 2016).
51 For interesting insights in some of these areas, see Richard Sennett (2002) 'Cosmopolitanism and the Social Experience of Cities', in Steven Vertovec and Robin Cohen (eds) *Conceiving Cosmopolitanism: Theory, Context and Practice* (Oxford: Oxford University Press), pp. 42–7.

Bibliography

Al-Jabarti, Abdul Rahman (n.d.) *Tarikh 'Aja'ib al-Athar fi'l Tarajim w'al-Akhbar* [*The History of Wondrous Traces in Translations and News*], 3 vols (Beirut: Dar al-Jil).
Al-Wardi, Ali (1992) *Lamahat ijtima'iya min tarikh al-Iraq al-hadith* [*Social Aspects of Iraqi Modern History*], Vol. III (London: Kufan Publishing).

Berkes, Niyazi (1998[1964]) *The Development of Secularism in Turkey* (London: Hurst).
Evans-Pritchard, Edward E. (1965) *Theories of Primitive Religion* (Oxford: Oxford University Press).
Fahmy, Khaled (2004) 'Towards a History of Alexandria', in Anthony Hirst and Michael Silk (eds) *Alexandria, Real and Imagined* (Aldershot: Ashgate).
_____ (2004) 'For Cavafy, with Love and Squalor: Some critical notes on the History and Historiography of Modern Alexandria', in Anthony Hirst and Michael Silk (eds) *Alexandria, Real and Imagined* (Aldershot: Ashgate).
Georgeon, Francois (2002) 'Ottomans and Drinkers: The Consumption of Alcohol in Istanbul in the Nineteenth Century', in Eugene Rogan (ed.) *Outside In: On the Margins of the Modern Middle East* (London: I.B.Tauris).
Goodwin, Godfrey (2006) *The Janissaries* (London: Saqi Books).
Hirst, Anthony and Silk, Michael (eds) (2004) *Alexandria, Real and Imagined* (Aldershot: Ashgate).
Hourani, Albert (1983) *Arabic Thought in the Liberal Age, 1798–1939* (Cambridge: Cambridge University Press).
Human Rights Watch (2004) 'In a Time of Torture: The Assault on Justice in Egypt's Crackdown on Homosexual Conduct', 29 February. Available at http://www.hrw.org/en/reports/2004/02/29/time-torture (accessed 27 April 2016).
Hussein, Taha (1937) *Mustaqbal al-thaqafa fi Misr* [*The Future of Culture in Egypt*] (Cairo: Matba'at al-Ma'arif).
Kafadar, Cemal (1995) *Between Two Worlds: The Construction of Ottoman State* (Berkeley, CA: University of California Press).
Kedourie, Elie (1997[1966]) *Afghani and Abduh: An Essay on Religious Unbelief and Political Activism in Modern Islam* (London: Gass).
Kepel, Gilles (1985) *The Prophet and Pharaoh: Muslim Extremism in Egypt* (London: Saqi Books).
Mabro, Robert (2004) 'Egyptian Literary Images of Alexandria', in Anthony Hirst and Michael Silk (eds) *Alexandria, Real and Imagined* (Aldershot: Ashgate).
Mardin, Serif (1962) *The Genesis of Young Ottoman Thought: A Study in the Modernization of Turkish Political Ideas* (Princeton, NJ: Princeton University Press).
Mazower, Mark (2004) *Salonica: City of Ghosts, Christians, Muslims and Jews 1430–1950* (London: HarperCollins).
Meijer, Roel (ed.) (1999) *Cosmopolitanism, Idenity and Authenticity in the Middle East* (London: Curzon Press).
Mitchell, Richard P. (1969) *The Society of Muslim Brothers* (Oxford: Oxford University Press).
Navaro-Yashin, Yael (2002) *Faces of the State: Secularism and Public Life in Turkey* (Princeton, NJ: Princeton University Press).
Quataert, Donald (2000) *The Ottoman Empire, 1700–1992* (Cambridge: Cambridge University Press).

Racy, Ali J. (2003) *Making Music in the Arab World: The Culture and Artistry of Tarab* (Cambridge: Cambridge University Press).

Sennett, Richard (2002) 'Cosmopolitanism and the Social Experience of Cities', in Steven Vertovec and Robin Cohen (eds) *Conceiving Cosmopolitanism: Theory, Context and Practice* (Oxford: Oxford University Press).

Şükrü Hanioğlu, M. (2008) *A Brief History of the Late Ottoman Empire* (Princeton, NJ: Princeton University Press).

Vertovec, Steven and Cohen, Robin (eds) (2002) *Concerning Cosmopolitanism: Theory, Context and Practice* (Oxford: Oxford University Press).

Zarcone, Thierry (1993) *Mystiques, philosophes, et franc-maçon en Islam: Riza Teufik, penseur ottoman 1868–1949* (Paris: Maison Neuve).

Zürcher, Erik J. (1993) *Turkey: A Modern History* (London: I.B.Tauris).

6

Mediated Imagination, Class and Cairo's Young Cosmopolitans

Heba El Sayed

I clearly remember a summer's day about three years ago, when I was sitting with a group of friends, eating club sandwiches and sipping cappuccinos in what was at that time Cairo's trendiest cafe. While talking animatedly among ourselves, Mariam, a 20-year-old medical student, suddenly turned with a hushed whisper and told us to 'look quickly', as she gestured with her eyes towards a young veiled woman who had just entered the cafe. Our five pairs of eyes keenly followed the humbly dressed woman, clothed in a long dress and *hijab*, as she proceeded quickly towards the staff changing room. Around six minutes later, the woman reappeared and, to my bewilderment, her veiled and conservative demeanour was transformed. She had become a waitress with long, blonde hair (obviously dyed: the signature Western look in Egypt), clad in a fashionable knee-length skirt and the cafe staff's customary orange T-shirt. The waitress happily and obliviously went about taking orders from customers, abundantly using (wrongly pronounced) English phrases with which she had been trained to address customers, such as 'Good evening' and 'We have an offer'. As I stared in disbelief, Mariam informed me that the cafe's management demands that the waitress remove her veil before beginning every shift 'in order to preserve the modern image' that these urban establishments fervently try to maintain. Confronted with such a situation for the first time, I was confused as to why this waitress would willingly choose to work in a place that forces her to abandon her religious principles and (one assumes) preferred form of dress.

Mariam, who knows the waitress personally, informed me that this sartorial transformation is partly a matter of choice, as the waitress wears the veil 'due to family and community pressures'. Hence, this job is one of the few opportunities in which she can move out of her poverty-stricken and restrictive home environment and defy socially acceptable dress codes, as long as she returns to her 'proper' veiled appearance before she returns to her local community. At this point, I could not help but laugh inwardly, as Mariam seemed to miss the irony of her own words, uttered as she was smoking and flirting intimately with her boyfriend: two aspects of her life that she made sure to conceal unless we were in familiar and 'safe spaces'[1] such as this cafe.

Such examples point to the fact that, regardless of class status, Egyptian women are the potential victims of the same deeply entrenched gender ideologies which drive them to police their public behaviour and appearance in comparable ways. The scrutiny, critique and shame that women may be exposed to if they overstep the moral boundaries set up by Egyptian society, in relation to either prevalent protocols of conservative dress or intergender contact, do not discriminate between the privileged and the poor. Thus Mariam and the waitress are united, both in the restrictions they face through their gender identity, and in their intelligent appropriation of urban space as a way of subverting the dominant conservative codes that regulate their public behaviour as Egyptian women. Importantly, although class differences can be temporarily suspended in situations where women of different backgrounds fall prey to the same prevalent gender inequalities, in most other aspects of young Egyptians' lives, class still matters. In relation to lifestyle, access to privileges and the entrée into urban space, class status functions as a palpable social barrier between Cairenes, creating a vast gulf that keeps the very different worlds of the city's inhabitants firmly divided.

In this context, youth-orientated urban enclaves across Cairo, including the cafe in the example above, are not only physical places but highly symbolic and imaginative 'glocal' spaces, located at the juncture between complex and intersecting systems of local moralities and globalised consumer networks that are highly structured around the class, age and gender identities of those who occupy them. These socio-economic factors not only partly determine the unspoken rules of inclusion in, and exclusion from, such spaces, but they work at a more powerful yet subtle level, drawing symbolic boundaries between urban denizens and governing the contours of Cairo's various youth subcultures, thus giving rise to the many different experiences of being a young Cairene.

Drawing on nine months of ethnographic fieldwork conducted in Cairo between 2008 and 2010, this chapter undertakes a comparative analysis between the subcultural experiences of young, upper-middle-class and working-class Egyptians. In doing so, it offers an attempt at the cultural translation of 1970s British youth cultural theories'[2] class-based analyses of subcultural resistance, in relation to the Egyptian context. In contemporary youth-based studies, these classic class-based approaches have fallen largely out of favour. This is partly a result of the changing socio-economic status of youth in the West, yet mainly a response to the class-deterministic approach of these theories, which have tended to underestimate drastically the importance of 'race', culture and gender to the study of subcultures. As a consequence, a new canon of work, often referred to as 'post-subcultural' studies,[3] has marginalised class altogether, while over-romanticising the cultural possibilities, choices and opportunities for agency that face young people in contemporary times. Nevertheless, I take a more critical and holistic approach to the understanding of youth cultures, focusing on the ways in which young Egyptians' 'leisure and cultural lives intersect with wider aspects of their biographies'.[4] In this way, I awaken one of the central arguments that characterised the youth subcultural theories of the mid-1970s, by arguing that structural inequalities related to class position – as they intersect with urban experiences, gender identity and religion – continue to play a central role in organising youth cultural experiences in Egypt. Furthermore, I discuss how subcultures are not centred solely around social exclusion and subordination, and thus are not limited to the underprivileged. Alongside working-class Egyptian youth, I provide evidence of how the young middle class is involved in their own class-based struggles that – although no less meaningful or relevant than those of the working class – lead to the formulation of a very specific type of subcultural experience. This is based on maintaining social class distinction, and conceiving elite spaces of self-expression that disconnect them from the harsh daily reality of a highly conservative, densely overpopulated, poverty-stricken megacity that is largely unkind to its young inhabitants. Such a comparative cross-class analysis will function as a springboard for the broader question of what distinguishes middle-class and working-class subcultures in Egypt, and the extent to which we can place these two varying articulations of cultural resistance within the same theoretical framework.

While making the case for the continuing importance of class, I also introduce the media as primary cultural windows, particularly for the young working class, which play a central role in informing their subcultural experiences. As the majority of these young people have never travelled outside Egypt, the media come to represent their only passport to the outside world, expanding their imaginative horizons and exposing them to alternative realities, lifestyles and modes of expression. Thus, I provide evidence of how a cosmopolitan imagination that is enabled by the media encourages young Egyptians to transform, every day, transnationally inspired youth performances into acts of subversion that disturb normalised practices and prevalent meanings at the local level. On that score, the ensuing discussion on subcultures will be an important path along which to explore the many and complex ways that youth identities, in a Global South context, are being articulated within a world of increased cultural interdependence, intense mediated connectivity and trans-temporality.

In addition, I show how subcultures, although rooted firmly in place, become dynamic multi-node spaces where new relations between the local and the global, self and others, distance and proximity, the virtual and immediate, coalesce – creating alternative avenues where national and religious particularities may be (re)imagined and read in new ways, yet are never completely abandoned. As Nilan and Feixa[5] argue, whereas from an adult or outsider perspective it may appear that young people are caught between multiple contradictory cultural repertoires, for a generation of technologically competent and media-savvy youth, this is integral to their local creative practices and a part of young people's daily struggle to grasp and make sense of a highly complex, interconnected and rapidly changing world. This chapter illustrates how a classed subcultural subjectivity is one way through which young people in Egypt, who stand far from 'the apex of power',[6] attempt to win back space, identity and recognition. I explore the very unique, class-specific ways in which music consumption, fashion choices and the use of technology are appropriated by young Egyptians as signifiers of discontent, allowing them to challenge or question religious moralities and overbearing ideologies that are integral both to their parent class cultures and to wider dominant institutions, such as family, education, the mosque and the state.

Youth marginalisation, media and an imagination away from home

Although the two classed groups that I observed live cheek-by-jowl in the same urban space, they inhabit multiple and usually disconnected, sociocultural youth spheres, and thus diverge strongly in their understanding of what it means to be young, Egyptian, Muslim, yet also cosmopolitan. Nevertheless, despite living divided lives, particularly through having a strong variation in their access to cultural and economic capital, both groups occupy the same national terrain, and are forced to bear the daily consequences of the same widespread, deep-rooted social prejudices. Indeed, although Egypt's demography is now shaped by one of the biggest ever bulges in its youth population,[7] research has illustrated that this cohort remains the most disadvantaged by the severe social and economic restrictions that they face. One year before the 2011 revolution, the Egypt Human Development Report[8] documented how the life chances of young Egyptians were severely restricted by a lack of democracy and respect for human rights, political corruption, lack of civic engagement, decreasing income levels, unequal job opportunities and poor education. Even after the 'Arab Spring', public opinion polls have shown that the revolution failed to realise young Egyptians' aspirations for a more dignified life, since they continue to feel politically, socially and economically marginalised.[9] These trends are compelling indicators of how it may take years – decades, even – for the Arab revolutions to adequately address and challenge the severe inequalities that have long plagued the lives of the younger generation. Yet it is important to comprehend that these young people enjoy the benefits and potential that are made possible by unprecedented access to media and communication technologies, in ways that were not available to previous generations. Indeed, Al-Tawila et al.[10] argue that completing higher levels of education, and having easy access to a diversity of modern media platforms, mean that young Egyptians are now formulating their own unique dreams and imaginings and are occupying and experiencing a youth that is quite different from that of their parents, specifically in relation to their expectations about marriage and gender equality.

The 2011 revolution was a very visible manifestation of the central role that modern forms of media technology can play in helping to shape the demands and social aspirations of the younger generation. In an interesting personal editorial on the events of the revolution, Selim Shahine argues that, online, the young generation have taken part in a world that is very different from that of his older generation, and thus by connecting with other global activists through Facebook and Twitter, 'Egyptian youth came to understand what it might mean to be a citizen in a proper sense'.[11]

My own research, which informs this chapter, was conducted in the three years immediately prior to the revolution, and argues that the role of the media in laying down the foundations for social dissent did not start in 2011, and was not limited to middle-class users of Facebook or Twitter. Instead, through long-term and day-to-day consumption of transnational media, particularly television, young Egyptians have been exposed to the weaknesses of their nation state, to a lack of liberal and democratic values in their everyday lives, to gender inequalities and a lack of women's rights. Over time, this may have slowly contributed to demands for social and political change, finally unleashing the mass rage that propelled the 2011 uprising. As will be shown, in their daily association with, and banal exposure to, a mediated globalisation – and well before the 2011 revolution – made democratic political protest an option. Thus silent subcultures provided spaces for young Egyptians to playfully challenge and symbolically protest against both the limits of social order, and the hegemonic values that are associated with the State, family and religion.

Silent subcultures in Cairo: private spaces for classed resistance

Within Western culture and in academia, the term 'subculture' has long conjured up images of marginalised or minority groups that are distinguished by their 'subaltern, underground'[12] behaviour. Nevertheless, as Sabry argues, the formation of subcultures is a highly contextualised process and must be seen as a 'reaction to specific moments (historical, economic, cultural and political) and anxieties'.[13] I provide evidence of how a time-specific, youth subcultural experience in Egypt exemplifies the way that globalisation is experienced at the juxtaposition of local conditions, giving rise to 'youth cultural strategies',[14] which become coping mechanisms for dealing with the frustrations of daily life in Cairo. I show how young Egyptians come to appropriate particular lifestyle trends such as music, consumption practices and body modifications, as rituals and signifiers of discontent through which to subvert the hegemonic ideologies that dominate their society. I use the term 'cosmopolitan imagination' with reference to how cosmopolitanism, for young Egyptians, takes the form of a dynamic subjective space that is driven by a sense of connection and belonging to the outside world. Such an imagination expands the cultural horizons of young Egyptians, allowing them to engage in a reimagination of local particularities and adopt a more reflexive understanding of the moral limits placed on the self. In this context, I argue how a cosmopolitan imagination, often informed by the media, becomes an important driving force that fuels young Egyptians' subcultural tendencies. In acquainting them with the possibility of alternative realities and ways of being, young Egyptians often develop a reflexive awareness of different sets of moralities that inform social roles. Thus, in their encounter with the outside world, their sense of morality and the self-righteousness of dominant codes of practice in the nation are discussed, addressed and, as we will see, physically challenged through the use of different aesthetic and stylising processes.

Although the media imbue young Egyptians with the democratic opportunities to access and participate in transnational cultural networks, a focus on class allows me to ground my analysis in the specificity of localised experience, and thus to avoid falling into the trap of providing colourful and overly-optimistic portraits of youth agency. Importantly, by engaging with young Egyptian men and women in all the economic, cultural and urban nuances of their contemporary reality, I illustrate how a common subcultural experience centred on the splintering of class into multiple, subcultural micro-practices is defined on the basis of gender and religious identity. Furthermore, I highlight a fundamental difference between the subcultural experiences that have been documented in Western literature and those of the youth subcultures that I witnessed in Egypt, pertaining to the culturally specific nature of subcultures. For example, Hebdige has offered an enlightening analysis of how British punk subcultures sought to exhibit their withdrawal publically from mainstream society, and their disconnection from the capitalist system.[15] This was achieved through an engagement with alternative rock music and by integrating a highly theatrical and colourful use of clothing, hairstyle and jewellery into the routine aspects of their daily lives. Therefore, in essence, their subcultural identity *was* their identity. However, for young Egyptians, subcultural practices take on a much more restricted form, as they are functional primarily in private or isolated spaces, beyond the scrutinising eyes of family and wider society. Indeed, young people in Egypt remain reliant on their parents emotionally and financially until marriage, and thus adolescent experiences are more likely to be characterised by dependency and restraint, and less by rebellion or 'social distancing'[16] from older generations, as may be the case in Western societies. Although I offer evidence on how experimental and defiant youth identities are taking shape in Cairo, I also argue that these identities remain compelled by the very dominant codes and moral frameworks that they seek to challenge. In this context, in lacking the 'confrontational and transgressive styles'[17] that have characterised Western subcultures, youth subcultures in Egypt represent a form of silent protest that is determined by the boundaries of 'territorial space',[18] rather than an open and explicit challenge to dominant and conventional meanings in society.

The remainder of this chapter will provide ethnographic evidence of the ways in which the two versions of a cosmopolitan imagination that I witnessed among young Egyptians give rise to very different classed subcultural experiences. I focus particularly on educational campuses as private and controlled spaces where subcultural practices are exercised.

Generation, class and the implicit imagination

In my discussions with working-class youth, their discourse was always heavily reflective of a strong religious identification that placed great emphasis on the centrality of Islam to their daily lives. My ethnographic encounter with them has revealed a need to abide by familial expectations and hegemonic social structures, which impose Islamic discourse as a strict set of divine values that define the limits of acceptable conduct and physical appearance. In this context, submission to Islamic principles becomes an overbearing moral framework for maintaining social conformity, and as a way for women in particular to uphold what their immediate neighbourhood environment dictates is a 'respectable' and 'honourable' reputation. In the light of such demanding and often constricting expectations, which command that dress, talk and everyday performance must correspond to the norms of Islamic acceptability, I argue that a cosmopolitan orientation can go far beyond a desire for leisurely cultural choices. My analysis of working-class youth reveals that a cosmopolitan imagination often provides a necessary breathing space, an essential (although temporary) moment of survival, for those confined within repressive social and economic circumstances.

Hence, I explore how working class youth often experience an implicit cosmopolitan imagination, which provides a dynamic space not accorded to them in their daily, grounded experiences – where they can draw on a wide repertoire of mediated representations of global youth cultural practices, thus exercising a degree of freedom in how they dress and behave. Therefore, an implicit cosmopolitan imagination becomes a window of escape from these young people's daily reality. In their casual consumption of the media, they come to acquire new modes of self-expression as signifiers of discontent against religious and conservative codes of morality that are imposed by family and community networks. I observed this in a further education institute which, alongside offering intermediate diplomas in computing, primarily to working-class students, is a private and secure space that houses these young people's subcultural practices.

The first time I walked into the institute, I was quite surprised at the sight of men and women defying the gender norms that are associated with their class identity by comfortably standing around in mixed gender groups, laughing and gossiping in ways that often involved physical contact. I was told frequently in my discussions with them how their campus is one of the few places that men and women can have any form of close interaction. When in public, a male participant told me, they must conform to dominant rules of gender segregation, or else 'people talk', and that women in particular may risk 'tainting their reputation'. As 20-year-old Magda told me:

> I watch my behaviour when I'm out in public, especially my neighbourhood, so I don't put myself or family to shame. However, in our campus we are all young people who are fully aware that the world has changed, and so we don't use our parents' old-fashioned standards to judge people's conduct.

As this quotation illustrates, working-class youth face a daily generational battle as they consider their parents to be unversed in modern ways of life, and so their parents continue to impose strict and outdated rules on them. As one woman told me, young people in Egypt only have to read the newspaper or switch on their television to be exposed to stories of women across the world taking up important social and political roles as prime ministers, judges and scientists. She continued: 'Meanwhile our parents ban us from even talking to men!' This demonstrates that, for working-class women, a feeling that their conduct is highly controlled by rigid social expectations may be strengthened through their exposure to the media and an ability to witness alternative representations of gender roles. This was captured in an hour-long discussion on the general treatment of women in Egypt that I had with a group of working class young people, which was influenced primarily by the American sitcom *Friends* (NBC, 1994–2004). For these women, such mediated drama exposes the ways in which women in the Western world are treated respectfully and on an equal footing to men, and are given the space to make their own individual life decisions. In contrast, they discussed how Egyptian women are constantly pressurised into conforming to pre-set societal rules, irrespective of their own desires. Although, in reality, *Friends* only provided them with a fictional snapshot of Western culture, for these women, it represented an accurate and indisputable point of comparison between women's social position and agency in Egypt and in the Western cultures that they talk confidently about, yet have only experienced through their television screens. In this context, a rich repertoire of media spaces to which these women have access makes more opportunities for reflection and interpretation possible, where the self is seen in the light of socially and geographically distant others, in ways that very often defy the moral frameworks of gendered morality that are set by an older generation.

I witnessed this firsthand in what I was introduced to as 'Love Park': a small grass plot annexed to the institute where students go for extra privacy and intimacy. My friend at the institute, 21-year-old Anan, took me there one day, and as I walked in I was met with hordes of couples either picnicking together, taking short strolls while holding hands, or simply cuddling. As Anan told me, security guards and lecturers at the institute have condemned this type of behaviour on campus, and have even threatened to tell parents; so the park was chosen as an extra secure space-within-a-space only for *shabab* (young people), where an older generation and mentality are excluded. Although Anan was very critical of the 'Love Park' and the behaviour that takes place inside it, she introduced me to her friend, 23-year-old Fatima, a frequent visitor to the park with her male colleague and love interest, Mazen, who was present at the discussion. According to Fatima, the older generation regards dating as an immoral Western concept, and so the only legitimate and permitted form of contact between a man and a woman is marriage. Nevertheless, Fatima points out that unlike her parents, who lived a very sheltered and inward-looking existence, she belongs to a 'new generation exposed to the outside world and to contemporary ways of life through computers and television'. These young people have formulated very different needs from their parents, particularly by demanding love and romance as preconditions to marriage. Therefore, partly as an outcome of their daily encounter with the media as the bearers of all things youthful and modern, the working-class young people transform their educational campus into a highly mediated space of imagination that defies the normalised practices that shape their micro-locale – particularly in relation to the dominant codes that regulate gender interaction.

Interrupting the conversation, Mazen asserted that students rarely come to the institute to actually learn. According to him, the institute is supposed to offer them diplomas in computing, yet there are about three computers in each overcrowded class, which are very rarely functional. Furthermore, Mazen added sadly that the diploma they eventually will achieve is 'worthless', compared to the qualifications of the millions of unemployed youth in Egypt who have university degrees. Facing a bleak future with lack of prospects in education, career, healthcare or housing, Mazen tells me how he, and many others like him, come to the institute to detach themselves 'from a harsh reality outside' that constantly dictates how they should live their lives. Mazen adds: 'Even love is prohibited! No one feels what we are going through. We are very exhausted, mentally and physically.' Mazen's words are an audible manifestation of Clarke et al.'s[19] argument that the working classes are involved in a 'double articulation' of youth subcultures that seek to defy their working-class parent culture and, more broadly, a wider dominant culture to which they are subordinate. Indeed, on the one hand, their subversive practices become a way to assert a modern and youthful identity against an older, working-class parental generation that does not accept their contemporary lifestyle choices and, instead, imposes strict religious values and conservative traditions. On the other hand, these acts become temporary spaces for survival and escape against a repressive society that has done little to address the deep-rooted inequalities facing the young working class.

In spite of the poverty that most of them endured, I was surprised that almost every student I saw possessed a mobile phone. According to many of the female students, these phones were bought by their parents to support their censorship and control over these women. Lena, for example, told me how her dad gave her a phone so he could check up on her throughout the day, while Amany said her mother demands that she must call home once she finishes classes to arrange with her brother to pick her up. Nevertheless, safely enclosed within more liberal educational spaces, mobile phones represented multi-tool media both for communicating and entertainment. Phones are referred to as 'el-iPod' when they wish to use them as miniature stereos to listen to Western and Arabic music, or 'el-camera' when they want to take group pictures with friends, or to turn their phone into a keeper of much desired, yet prohibited, romances. Nadia, 21, told me how the secret world of her mobile phone was the only place she could store digital photos of the man with whom she was in love, as she would be too scared to keep hold of any hardcopies that might be discovered by her parents. In addition, common among this group was the fact that often, music was not permitted by their families, on the basis that it was *haram* (forbidden) in Islamic teachings. This was particularly true of Western music, which Ahmed's family, for example, believed represented the 'devil's presence' in their home. By locking their phones with secret pin codes, or by converting their phone's software into English from Arabic, these young people were able to ensure that their parents, who generally had poor knowledge of technology and English, would not have access to their contents. Again, generational differences mean that these young people use their contemporary, highly mediated, technology-savvy ways of life as a means to trouble hegemonic discourses that are upheld by an older, largely technologically illiterate, parent generation. As the above illustrates, whereas mediated representations of the world accessed through television often represent points of reference against hegemonic codes of morality at the local level, new media technologies also are converted into private and mobile spaces of youth agency and subversion.

Despite the subversive acts mentioned above, religion still continued to occupy an important space within these young people's daily performances. For example, this was demonstrated in the way that mobile phones were not only tools facilitating prohibited romances or for listening to music, but were frequently programmed at set intervals, five times a day, to act as an audible reminder of the Islamic call to prayer. Indeed, although many of them fervently rejected the way that their families imposed religion on them in a very didactic way, their faith remained an important part of their self-identity, and of the ways in which they made sense of the world; it particularly allowed them to rationalise their disadvantaged social position. They often acknowledged that they felt bitter at their marginalisation in Egyptian society, yet they also believed that this must be accepted as 'Allah's will', thus transforming their faith into an important coping mechanism, helping them to endure such a ruthless reality with patience.

A reflexive and complex relationship with religion was captured particularly in the style choices and body modifications in which young working-class women engaged. During my time at the institute and after observing hundreds of students, I only came across three unveiled women, one of whom was Christian. I remember one morning visiting the only campus toilet, to be instantly taken aback by the strong whiff of perfume and the sight of a number of women standing opposite the murky mirror, adjusting and/or changing their clothing and applying make-up to bare faces: some women continued to wear the veil, yet took off long jackets to reveal figure-hugging outfits underneath such as leggings or knee-high boots, while others removed the veil altogether before beginning classes. However, significantly, before these women left campus to head home, I always saw them return to a state of appearance and conduct that was socially acceptable in the non-educational environment. Heavy make-up was toned down, while loose jackets were put on again to cover their bodies, as they were about to face the world outside their institute.

In my discussions with these women, I was surprised to hear that many of them had no specific personal reason for wearing the veil, and usually did so to conform to family and community expectations. Indeed, religion plays a crucial role as a moral framework that organises these working-class locales, and the veil takes centre stage as a highly visible and public expression of these women's 'embodied piety'[20] and well 'preserved' honour. Nevertheless, their campus becomes a secure space where such religious norms guarding the female body are relaxed, allowing women to partake in highly globalised and sexualised fashion performances. These performances often exclude the veil, but usually adjust it by revealing part of the hair, chest or silhouette, as a demonstration that these women are in possession of bodily charms. In an interesting discussion, 20-year-old Seham informed me that with no real career prospects, the only foreseeable future for women of her class status is to get married once they leave the institute, and so they need to constantly demonstrate, while in their community spaces, how they are 'untainted' marriage material. Seham adds that what they get up to in their campus 'has to stay in the campus, or else we could risk living our lives as spinsters!'. This is a stark reminder of how the implicit cosmopolitan imagination of these young people truly is implicit: unable to subvert the dominant forms of power, but forced to operate from within them, leading to the articulation of very restricted subcultural acts that are encapsulated within temporally and spatially bounded contexts. As one participant told me: 'It's only in this campus that I can be myself. The world outside has no mercy on us; the government oppresses us, our family control us and the rich look down upon us.' This quotation succinctly and powerfully encapsulates how the subcultural practices of these young, working-class people involve a two-pronged form of resistance that, on the one hand, targets an older generation and mentality that is part of their parent's class culture; and on the other, seeks to escape a broader dominant culture that gives little power or voice to those on the margins of society.

A closed imagination among Cairo's privileged youth

For most of the upper-middle class with whom I engaged, a cosmopolitan openness towards the world is located almost exclusively within a constricted framework of 'First World' belonging. Despite living in Egypt, the upper-middle-class did not consider *themselves* to be located outside of, or on the fringes of, the 'First World'. As Schielke has argued, for the Egyptian middle class, the 'First World' is not a geographical positioning, but an idea and discourse of elite belonging in which they locate themselves. Unlike other Egyptians from a lower social class background, the middle class's wealth, exclusive upbringing and privileged class status places them right at the centre of the 'First World'.[21] Their access to the necessary social connections and cultural capital that are associated with a transnational, elite middle-class identity automatically positions them on a par with other young people of a similar age and elite social status located in the advanced nations of the West. Furthermore, terms of self-description such as 'modern' and 'civilised' were important vocal indicators of the ways in which members of this class often sought to symbolically separate themselves from a wider, uncouth Egyptian populace, while considering themselves to be harbingers of national progress and development. In this light, I use the term 'closed cosmopolitanism' to describe the imagination of the upper-middle-class. Their sense of being part of the world and engaging in transnational cultural practices is associated to a great extent with securing an elite class status in Egypt from which they seek to exclude the lower social class groups, for whom the pristine standards of 'First World' development are not always within their capabilities.

Interestingly, the upper-middle class's parochial understanding of the world around them even extends to their interpretation of the widespread proliferation of religion in Egypt. While most of the upper-middle class admitted to being 'non-practising' Muslims, with only a few considering themselves to be religious, and a small minority labelling themselves as atheists, it was obvious that Islam still represented an important source of spiritual inspiration for most. Many interlocutors within this class were keen to distinguish between 'true religiosity' – which for them, is about pushing oneself to be a better and kinder being on the inside, irrespective of a person's choice to drink alcohol occasionally, or a woman's decision not to cover her hair – and 'religion as a habit'. This latter expression of religiosity, I was told, most widespread in Egypt, involves an uneducated mass mixing outdated cultural traditions with a false interpretation of religious doctrine. They told me that this has reduced Islam to a rigid framework which the majority blindly conform to superficially, yet without a reflexive appreciation of religion's ultimate essence. Therefore, importantly, I do not use the term 'closed cosmopolitanism' to claim that these young elites are hostile to local and religious particularity. Instead, I describe how their interpretation of the world is a closed one, where they place themselves and their elite standards firmly at the epicentre, while using these standards as a primary mechanism by which to judge other groups who may not share identical frameworks of understanding. Through my discussions with them, most of the upper-middle class youth declared that they are proud of their national and religious heritage, yet their elite and highly globalised lifestyle often makes them feel alien in an Egypt that they consider presently to be hijacked by 'widespread religious hypocrisy and imposed customs', from which they seek to distance themselves. Such fluid and complex identities are captured in my observations of one of Cairo's most expensive private universities, where young elite students engage in a nuanced subcultural subjectivity. Their campus becomes a space where they develop distinct class-based styles and performances that allow them to move effortlessly between moments of commitment to, and challenge of, local (tradition) particularity, religious doctrine and a global articulation of culture.

An elite subcultural subjectivity in Cairo's top university

As far back as I can remember, it has always been well-known that stepping into this university is like crossing the Egyptian borders and entering into a completely different country. Approaching the campus for the first time, I was greeted with high walls, security controlled gates and a couple of checkpoints, which made the experience more akin to a busy international airport than a university. Being a world within a world was certainly the initial thought that came into my head, as I looked around the campus and tried to take in the very different reality I had entered. If I had stepped back only 20 metres outside the university walls, I would see nothing but desert, taxi drivers and a few lone pavement sellers struggling to make a couple of dollars in Cairo's soaring heat. However, as I made my way into the campus and walked past Ben's Cookies, McDonalds and a sushi bar, I could not help remembering my encounter with a poor garbage man standing outside the campus, who warned me that the interior was filled with 'people who look so completely different, doing things that are so completely different'.

One of my friends, a student at the university during my research, gave me a tour of the campus and keenly pointed out how it is split into various mini-societies, each representing a distinct mode of expression. At one end of the campus, I was fascinated to see for the first time in Egypt, a small group of students whose appearance was an interplay between goth and hippie style. They were united through a common dress code: baggy jeans (men's underwear on display), black tops, usually sporting multiple piercings and chains dangling out of their pockets, while they sometimes flaunted unusual hair colours. One member of the group always had a guitar and they would usually sit in the centre of the gathering, strumming to American country music, while the rest of their friends enthusiastically sang along. I asked one member of the hippie group, 23-year-old Omar, if dressing so differently made him less able to integrate into Egyptian society. Tying back his long red hair to reveal three small metal spikes piercing the top of his right ear, he replied:

> That's the whole point. I don't really care to integrate with people who live their lives through a very narrow set of outdated principles anyway. I'm not any less Egyptian than anyone who looks 'normal' – I just refuse *their* restricted interpretation of what it means to be Egyptian, or to be a person in general. So I guess my different outside appearance is a reflection of how I feel on the inside. My university is one of the few places I can feel comfortable having long dyed hair, or will not be surprised to see a woman with tattoos.

An initial reading of Omar's unusual style choice may connote a playful challenge to traditional modes of appearance that are prevalent in Egypt. However, his words are also indicative of a more serious intention that runs deeper than fashion. Omar's external appearance is appropriated as a visible expression of resistance, flagging his difference to a mainstream culture dominated by rigid traditions. This is reflected in the words of a female member of the small hippie/goth community, who explained that for young people to be accepted in Egyptian society, they must fit a very rigid mould which 'has not changed much in the last 100 years'. However, every person has the opportunity to break out of this mould, she believes, by using their body and their daily practices as 'weapons' to challenge this societal control.

As illustrated previously in the discussion on the working class, the media are significant tools on which they heavily depend in a daily context for information and entertainment and, significantly, their only window onto the outside world. For the upper-middle class, their frequent international travel and elite education means that they are exposed firsthand to transnational lifestyles, and thus there is less dependence on the media as sources of education and global information. Yet the media remain strongly linked to their personal development and sense of class consciousness by providing a regular and instant point of access to distinct fashion styles (e.g. fashion blogs and purchasing items that are not available in Egypt directly from international online retailers) and niche music genres (e.g. iTunes' subscription and internet downloads). Indeed, on-campus, music was particularly common during my observation experiences at the university which, at the time, frequently hosted student fairs and events. I was especially used to American rap music (never Arabic) infiltrated with lewd language, which usually had something to say about drugs, sex or open relationships. According to 21-year-old Zein, the themes that dominate this genre of music are generally taboo for most Egyptians, but for students at the university they are normal aspects of their lives and youth experiences. Zein adds that even for those who choose to live conservative lifestyles, the nature of their upbringing and their exposure to 'foreign ways of life' means that they have usually come across these practices on campus, or have experienced them through their friendship networks. Thus, for Zein and other students like him, their ability to enjoy this type of music and to identify with aspects of the lyrics, while being tolerant of the obscenities, represents another cultural chasm which distances them further from more traditional

Egyptians, who are likely to dismiss such music as being 'morally unacceptable'. Twenty-four-year-old Habiba takes a different stance, and tells me that such lyrics do not really reflect her personal life, as she chooses not to partake in drugs or drink alcohol. However, according to Habiba:

> In a didactic culture such as ours, when you obsessively tell young people that something is wrong, you achieve the exact opposite. We develop a desire to explore such 'deviant' acts, even if it is just by listening to music, to demonstrate that we oppose these attempts to control our minds.

On the one hand, music becomes a vocal expression of some of these young people's desires to participate in behaviours that are not usually accepted by mainstream Egyptian society. On the other, for those who did not take part in the practices that dominate the songs' lyrics, their campus provides a space where the simple act of being able to openly enjoy such music is an expression of 'harmless rebellion', or of the performance of non-conformity against a society which encourages them to conform in most aspects of their lives.

During one memorable session at the university, my friend took me to what I amusingly learned was 'Gucci Corner', where the seriously (and willing to spend) fashion-conscious students were awarded the privilege of being part of this exclusive group. They visibly and consciously displayed their bodies adorned only with Gucci styles and other top designer brands from head to toe. Gucci Corner made me instantly conscious of the fact that distinguishing between subversion and elitism, within the context of this particular university setting, may be delicate ground on which to tread. Indeed, for members of the Gucci clan, expensive and globalised consumer brands were less about articulating a distinct subversive subjectivity, and more about maintaining an exclusive route to social status distinction from those Egyptians who lack the awareness or ability to obtain such products. Nevertheless, it was particularly interesting to see how veiled women remained a minority on campus, yet were visible at Gucci Corner. Although many students at the university engaged in a vocal and embodied struggle to distance themselves from a wider Egyptian culture that they deemed to have been usurped by cultural stagnation, underdevelopment and an obsession with tradition, religion still informed some of the daily practices of this young elite. Importantly, for the upper-middle-class youth, an engagement in religious Islamic duties remained independent of, and unconditioned by, dress choice – which contrasts with the working class, where women in particular are widely expected to adopt conservative Islamic clothing such as the veil. Indeed, I often observed how it would be the girl in the short skirt or excessive designer gear who would trek up to the small on-campus prayer room, cover herself in one of the body gowns provided, face Mecca and fulfil her daily prayers. According to one veiled woman, due to their authoritarian nature, working-class Egyptians have created a monopoly on religion that has led to a very narrow, yet widespread, interpretation of what *they* think it *should* mean to be a Muslim woman. It is worse being a veiled woman in Egypt, she says, as they get elevated to an unrealistic 'status of purity' which sets up too many false expectations. As 20-year-old Rasha says:

> I'm veiled and I smoke. My friend is veiled and she is in a relationship. You should see the disapproving glances we get when we are out in public. However, I refuse to give in to these people's narrow-mindedness: only God can judge what is in our souls. Look over there [pointing] at the veiled girl and her fiancé, and how romantically expressive they are being. I may not do that myself – but the point is, no one is sniggering or looking. It shows you how a lot of women here, regardless of whether or not they are veiled, have a different mentality, and they refuse to let wider society decide who they should be.

This quotation demonstrates that these young elites are not only engaging in highly classed articulations of what it means to be Egyptian, but also what it means to be Muslim and, specifically, what it means to be Muslim women. Importantly, the visibility of religious symbols in the university (veil, prayer room) is proof that subcultures are not static groups with invariable features, but involve malleable and constantly shifting social practices, often characterised by internal contradictions. Regardless of whether or not they are veiled, what unites many female students at this university in a common subversive subjectivity is their access to the same cultural and economic capital through their joint class status, and thus to frameworks of interpretation that allow them to make similar sense of the world around them. Subsequently, these women use their university campus as a space in which to endorse more liberal lifestyle choices that are normal to their parent class culture and, by doing this, they simultaneously challenge a traditional and religious dogmatism inherent in a wider Egyptian culture, which often restricts women's agency and their opportunities for expression. This is captured in the way that female students who wear revealing clothing, such as shorts and mini-skirts, were rife on campus, even though this type of dress would be unacceptable in most of Cairo's public spaces; as was the open display of physical and intimate inter-gender contact, often involving veiled women. Hana particularly caught my attention through her dynamic and unique style of dress. In one instance, she was wearing a short denim skirt and a low-cut top, exposing her chest area, while a choker with a blue-eye pendent adorned her neck. On another occasion, I glimpsed her with a crop-top (exposing the stomach) which had a large print of the Hand of Fatima (*Hamsa*): an open right hand with five protruding digits and, underneath, the well-known Egyptian proverb: 'The evil eye split the rock.' Both the *kaf* (palm) and the *a'yn* (eye) are well-known apotropaic amulets that are deeply rooted in Islamic and Arabic folkloric culture, thought to protect one against the 'evil eye' of the envious. In an interesting discussion, Hana told me that she firmly believes in the disastrous consequences of envy, as Allah warns Muslims against it in the Qur'an. However, although she considers the prevalent tradition that the palm and eye will protect one against envy to be 'superstitious' and 'uncivilised', she refers to them as 'popular symbols of our Arab heritage' that she enjoys 'experimenting with'. This reflects a clear distinction, often made by members of this class, between commitment to particular religious values and distancing from traditional practices and customs that are purely cultural. What is particularly interesting is the way that Hana takes a traditional symbol (eye, palm) out of its intended context and superimposes it on a modern form (choker, crop-top), thus (re)appropriating it in a new way that challenges a different traditional moral code relating to the covering of women's bodies in public.

Following on from the above, the university campus becomes a covert space where upper-middle-class women use their bodies in diverse ways to challenge prevalent perceptions about the 'proper' representation and conduct of the female form in Egypt. However, on leaving the campus, behaviour and appearance must be adjusted to conform to wider social expectations that shape Cairo's public spaces. Indeed, before getting into their chauffeur-driven cars to go home, I often saw Hana and other female students securing their modesty by wrapping shawls around bare shoulders or putting on long jackets to cover their exposed knees, while couples would make sure to kiss and embrace within the secure walls of the campus before walking out. One female participant informed me that the traditional lower classes are not tolerant of such behaviours, and by engaging in them publicly she would risk her personal safety. She could be perceived as a 'whore', making her an easy target for sexual harassment, verbally and often physically. Such incidents illustrate that while these young elites' subcultural practices involve performances that address and violate conventional codes of morality, they remain silent performances of discontent. They only take place within the sheltered boundaries of secure and controlled urban spaces, such as their university campus or the gated communities where they live – which are beyond the disapproving gazes of a conservative society and, most importantly, guarantee women protection from their fear of the sexually fuelled responses of working-class men. This reminds us that subcultures are complex and multifaceted constructions formed at the juxtaposition of class experiences, dominant discourses of gendered morality, and local forms of urban organisation and control.

Conclusion
Dealing with the local, imagining the global

The comparative analysis above has unearthed vital differences between the two classed groups observed, forcing us to ask what exactly makes them both subcultural, despite these disparities. What is common to both groups is that, in spite of the varying forms that their subcultural practices take, they are primarily products of their very specific and distinctive class experiences, and a route through which both groups deal with the limitations and challenges that they face in their daily lives pertaining especially to economic inequalities, an overbearing religious hegemony and the demands and expectations of a paternalistic older generation. Within this narrative the media play a prominent role as imaginative platforms that expand young Egyptians' frameworks of knowledge and cultural experience, thus allowing highly structured limits on the self to be (re)negotiated through alternative styles, leisure practices and modes of self-expression. For the working class, the economic, social and political inequalities that they are forced to deal with on a daily basis are deep-rooted and incapacitating and, sadly, an inherent reality that they have no hand in changing (or at least requiring decades of intense political and cultural reform). In this context, subcultures become spaces where these young people are able to assert some form of control over their lives and to (temporarily) regain space, identity and recognition. For the young upper-middle class, despite their protests about the restrictive nature of Egyptian culture, which limits their potential repertoire of styles and their preferred manners of expression, their class status means that they are the main beneficiaries of a dominant culture that caters largely to their interests and secures their sense of dignity and purpose. For the working class, there is a clear, consistent and tangible set of grievances emanating very specifically from their local socio-economic position, which collectively fuel the subversive acts mentioned. For the upper-middle class, it is their elite education, frequent travel and firsthand experience of distant ways of life that makes localised norms and experiences seem restrictive in the face of their broad transnational repertoire of cultural knowledge. What these young elites articulate is a heterogeneous collage of individualised expressions which adopt a varied range of aesthetic and stylising processes as a form of distinction from the broader, locally rooted, mass culture.

Furthermore, for the working class youth, as well as their subcultural acts being a statement of protest against a dominant culture that subordinates them politically, socially and economically, these acts also seek to challenge the norms of their parent class culture: specifically, the didactic ways of an older generation. Thus, as the young working class move between family, neighbourhood, educational and public spaces, there are clear boundaries that demarcate the urban enclaves where subcultural acts are or are not performed. Conversely, the upper-middle class adopt a range of youth-specific forms of expression in relation to music, fashion and technology which, although these set them apart stylistically and in terms of cultural taste from their parents, primarily represent subversive acts that seek to *assert* their minority elite status and middle-class parent culture against a more conservative dominant society. Consequently, as many of their liberal performances are to a large extent an accepted part of the lifestyle choices and socialisation roles that are inherent to their parent class – and thus predominantly tolerated by family, close community and friendship networks – they tend to merge and blur the distinctions between 'necessary' and 'free time' activities.[22] In light of these differences, it might be helpful to use Clarke et al.'s[23] term 'countercultures' to refer to the subversive movements of the middle classes, pertaining to the fact that their concerns are less a tight and collective class-driven response to named social and economic determinants, and more a diffuse milieux of alternative, culturally expressive actions. This is in no way an attempt to detract from the relevance or meaningfulness of middle-class forms of subversion, but simply to distinguish between the rich diversity of classed subcultures which, as the Egyptian case has illustrated, vary greatly in their formulation, intention and modes of expression.

An important question to end with is: how can we expect Arab and Egyptian subcultures, as we know them, to change after the 'Arab Spring'? As my research has documented, in a pre-revolutionary context subcultures provided silent and isolated means for young people to express dissent and dissatisfaction. However, as young people in Egypt now have access to new spaces of social and political engagement such as social media, political protest and grass roots activism, will subcultures become less relevant? Or, as the shackles of fear and silence have been broken, will subcultures take a new turn, adopting more defiant, daring and confident means of speaking out?

Notes

1 Anouk de Koning (2009) *Global Dreams: Class, Gender and Public Space in Cosmopolitan Cairo* (Cairo: American University in Cairo Press).
2 Stuart Hall and Tony Jefferson (1976) *Resistance Through Rituals: Youth Subcultures in Post-War Britain* (London: Routledge); Dick Hebdige (1979) *Subculture: The Meaning of Style* (London: Routledge).
3 Steve Redhead (ed.) (1997) *The Clubcultures Reader* (Oxford: John Wiley & Sons); Andy Bennett and Keith Kahn-Harris (eds) (2004) *After Subculture* (London: Palgrave Macmillan).
4 Tracy Shildrick and Robert MacDonald (2006) 'In Defence of Subculture: Young People, Leisure and Social Divisions', *Journal of Youth Studies* 9(2): 125–40, p. 126.
5 Pam Nilan and Carles Feixa (2006) 'Introduction: Youth Hybridity and Plural Worlds', in Pam Nilan and Carles Feixa (eds) *Global Youth? Hybrid Identities, Plural Worlds* (London: Routledge).
6 John Clarke, Stuart Hall, Tony Jefferson and Brian Roberts (1976) 'Subcultures, Cultures and Class: A Theoretical Overview', in Hall and Jefferson (eds) *Resistance Through Rituals*, p. 12.
7 Mona Abaza (2006) *Changing Consumer Cultures of Modern Egypt: Cairo's Urban Reshaping* (Boston, MA: Brill).
8 United Nations Development Programme (UNDP) (2010) *Egypt Human Development Report. Youth in Egypt: Building Our Future*. Available at www.undp.org.eg/Portals/0/NHDR%202010%20english.pdf (accessed 23 February 2013).

9. Al-Ahram (2012) '80% of Youth: The Revolution Did Not Fulfil Our Ambitions and Expectations for Numerous Reasons' [in Arabic] *Al-Ahram*, 12 November.
10. Sahar Al-Tawila, Barbara Ibrahim and Hind Wassef (2003) 'Social Change and Adolescent-Parent Dynamics in Egypt', in Nicholas S. Hopkins (ed.) *The New Arab Family* (Cairo: American University in Cairo Press).
11. Selim Shahine (2011) 'Youth and the Revolution in Egypt', *Anthropology Today* 27(2): 1–3, p. 2.
12. Rupa Huq (2006) *Beyond Subculture: Pop, Youth and Identity in a Postcolonial World* (New York: Routledge) p. 9.
13. Tarik Sabry (2010) *Cultural Encounters in the Arab World: On Media, the Modern and the Everyday* (London: I.B.Tauris), p. 59.
14. Pilkington, cf. Shildrick and MacDonald, 'In Defence of Subculture' p. 132.
15. Hebdige, *Subculture*.
16. Barbara Mensch, Barbara Ibrahim, Susan M. Lee and Omaima El-Gibaly (2000) 'Socialization to Gender Roles and Marriage among Egyptian Adolescents', Annual Meeting of the Population Association of America, Los Angeles, CA, 23–25 March, p. 7.
17. Sabry, *Cultural Encounters in the Arab World*, p. 60.
18. Clarke et al., 'Subcultures, Cultures and Class' p. 14.
19. Ibid.
20. Lara Deeb (2006) *An Enchanted Modern: Gender and Public Piety in Shi'i Lebanon* (Princeton, NJ: Princeton University Press), p. 103.
21. Samuli Schielke (2012) 'Surfaces of longing. Cosmopolitan aspiration and Frustration in Egypt', *City and Society* 24(1): 29–37.
22. Clarke et al., 'Subcultures, Cultures and Class', p. 60.
23. Ibid.

Bibliography

Abaza, Mona (2006) *Changing Consumer Cultures of Modern Egypt: Cairo's Urban Reshaping* (Boston, MA: Brill).

Al-Ahram (2012) '80% of Youth: The Revolution Did Not Fulfil our Ambitions and Expectations for Numerous Reasons' [in Arabic], *Al-Ahram*, 12 November.

Al-Tawila, Sahar, Ibrahim, Barbara and Wassef, Hind (2003) 'Social Change and Adolescent-Parent Dynamics in Egypt', in Nicholas S. Hopkins (ed.) *The New Arab Family* (Cairo: American University in Cairo Press).

Bennett, Andy and Kahn-Harris, Keith (eds) (2004) *After Subculture* (London: Palgrave Macmillan).

Clarke, John, Hall, Stuart, Jefferson, Tony and Roberts, Brian (1976) 'Subcultures, Cultures and Class: A Theoretical Overview', in Stuart Hall and Tony Jefferson (eds) *Resistance Through Rituals: Youth Subcultures in Post-War Britain* (London: Routledge).

Deeb, Lara (2006) *An Enchanted Modern: Gender and Public Piety in Shi'i Lebanon* (Princeton, NJ: Princeton University Press).

Hall, Stuart and Jefferson, Tony (1976) *Resistance through Rituals: Youth Subcultures in Post-War Britain* (London: Routledge).

Hebdige, Dick (1979) *Subculture: The Meaning of Style* (London: Routledge).

Huq, Rupa (2006) *Beyond Subculture: Pop, Youth and Identity in a Postcolonial World* (New York: Routledge).

de Koning, Anouk (2009) *Global Dreams: Class, Gender and Public Space in Cosmopolitan Cairo* (Cairo: American University in Cairo Press).

Mensch, Barbara, Ibrahim, Barbara, Lee, Susan M. and El-Gibaly, Omaima (2000) 'Socialization to Gender Roles and Marriage among Egyptian Adolescents', Annual Meeting of the Population Association of America, Los Angeles, CA, 23–25 March.

Nayak, Anoop (2003) *Race, Place and Globalization: Youth Cultures in a Changing World* (Oxford: Berg).

Nilan, Pam and Feixa, Carles (2006) 'Introduction: Youth Hybridity and Plural Worlds', in Pam Nilan and Carles Feixa (eds) *Global Youth? Hybrid Identities, Plural Worlds* (London: Routledge).

Redhead, Steve (ed.) (1997) *The Clubcultures Reader* (Oxford: John Wiley & Sons).

Sabry, Tarik (2010) *Cultural Encounters in the Arab World: On Media, the Modern and the Everyday* (London: I.B.Tauris).

Schielke, Samuli (2012) 'Surfaces of Longing: Cosmopolitan Aspiration and Frustration in Egypt', *City and Society* 24(1): 29–37.

Shahine, Selim (2011) 'Youth and the Revolution in Egypt', *Anthropology Today* 27(2): 1–3.

Shildrick, Tracy and MacDonald, Robert (2006) 'In Defence of Subculture: Young People, Leisure and Social Divisions', *Journal of Youth Studies* 9(2): 125–40.

United Nations Development Programme (UNDP) (2010) *Egypt Human Development Report. Youth in Egypt: Building Our Future.* Available at www.undp.org.eg/Portals/0/NHDR%202010%20english.pdf (accessed 23 February 2013).

7

Screening Everyday Violence

Youth, Globalisation and Subcultural Aesthetics in Moroccan Cinema

Jamal Bahmad

Hicham Lasri's feature film *The End* (2011) is a millennial black-and-white film set in Casablanca circa 1999. Using a dazzling combination of fast editing and visual effects that are characteristic of MTV, videogames and commercial advertising, the film tells the tale of a city on the edge through the story of M'Key (Mikhi), a disaffected youth caught between his loyalty to a ruthless police commissioner and his intoxicating love for Rita, a beauty jealously watched by her gangster brothers. The film is traversed by violent language and action to an extent unprecedented in Moroccan cinema. This begs the question of whether this visceral violence is socially meaningful or is merely pulp fiction. This question can be answered only after a thorough analysis of the film's subcultural aesthetics. *The End* is daring in its stylistic experimentation, as we will see shortly. This drive to innovation in theme and form has significant implications for the film's social vision and cognitive mapping of Casablanca, particularly when seen in the light of Fredric Jameson's conceptualisation of late modern subjectivities.[1]

This chapter examines the location and transnational circulation of youth subcultures in *The End* as an example of recent aesthetic and political trends in Moroccan cinema. Cultural globalisation in Morocco intensified in the 1990s in the wake of neoliberal market reforms, and the relative political opening up of the country brought about by social change and the end of the Cold War. Other social transformations including rapid urbanisation, demographic changes and the advent of transnational media and communication technologies have been behind the growth of new forms of youth subcultures in Morocco, particularly in large cities such as Casablanca. *The End* inscribes its aesthetic within that of the *Nayda* subcultural movement in Morocco.[2] A movie-besotted adolescent in the 1990s, Lasri came of age under the *Nayda* scene in Casablanca, where he was born in 1977. The film's deployment of what I call a 'trash aesthetic' translates, rather than imitates, global subcultures.

To this end, I will explore the representation of Casablanca's neoliberal space in *The End* with a special focus on how its exquisite attention to form affects representation of the city. Lasri's debut feature is a claustrophobic tale of the looming demise of neoliberal Casablanca in the last years of King Hassan II's absolute monarchy. This chapter aims to demonstrate how, instead of being passive consumers of global subculture, Moroccan youth have been full post-colonial agents in the translation and adaptation of global flows to their cultural heritage, consumption habits and living conditions. Moroccan cinema has engaged with the evolution of local subcultures in Moroccan urban and national space in recent times; I will examine the articulation of youth post-colonial subjectivities through subculture as a transnational economy of flows. I will also explore how *The End* is a contingent experiment in cinematic realism to render urban subjectivities and invent new cognitive maps for a post-neoliberal post-coloniality through a critical reconstruction of youth subcultures and everyday life in Casablanca. Finally, the film will be used an exemplar in relation to the gathering storm of neoliberalism's social crisis in twenty-first-century Morocco, two years after the popular uprisings across North Africa.

Youth and everyday violence

The End's opening sequence starts with upside-down shots of speeding cars in an underground tunnel. The fast, MTV-like digital filming is rendered in black and white, which confounds the low visibility of the frame constituents. The sparse opening credits are also rendered upside down on the screen, in an amusing warning to the viewers that the style of the film's form is of as much importance as its thematic content. When the procession of cars emerges into the open, we learn that it is night-time, and the vehicles belong to the police force. They have come to burn seized cannabis in a white tower. In the background, we hear an idolatrous radio report, in stately Arabic, on one of Hassan II's processions in an unnamed Moroccan city. The audience is invited to make the link between drugs, politics and the people.

The young man we had glimpsed earlier, tied to the roof of one of the vans, gets down and climbs the cylindrical tower: he looks desperate for something. He finally makes it to the roof just as the police start throwing packs of cannabis resin into the furnace. The youth atop the tower is sitting on a toilet stand when the smoke reaches him through the tower-wide chimney. When he descends and walks back into a boulevard in Casablanca, it is morning, and he looks psychedelic and unhip. A few street types, a talkative prostitute and a vagabond join him for conversation and a game of chess. He turns both offers down. Blood is flowing from a cut in the back of his head. The viewer learns through a line on the screen that it is 1 July 1999. The young man works as a parking attendant (a delicate job in Morocco because it usually comes with an acceptance of the deal of becoming a police informer). He walks into a fake classic Rolls-Royce, and discovers a beautiful girl tied to the wheel by a sturdy chain. The security alarm of a shop then goes off, and four gangsters walk back towards the Rolls-Royce. They are chased by a crowd and leave the scene, running, having robbed their way through the high street shops, from the tobacconist to the bakery and pharmacy. The police arrive and cordon off the area. Their chief, Captain Daoud Raddad, enters the scene and the film rapidly unravels into a maelstrom of tension and paranoia. He arbitrarily orders the arrest of an old skeletal baker for daring to say that the *Makhzen* (monarchical regime) must reimburse him for the items he has lost, especially now that the price of yeast has increased. Captain Daoud, as he is called by everyone, has the unmistakable aura of a Hassanain police type: godlike, he is impeccably clad and takes his time to read the scene of the heists. He summons the park attendant, Mikhi, and slaps him for alleging that he knows nothing about who is behind the robbery. He admonishes him for not being like his late father, a faithful underdog, police informer and soldier, who participated in the carnage against ordinary protesters during the 1981 bread riots in Casablanca. Mikhi walks off with Rita, the still-chained girl he has rescued from the Rolls-Royce that belongs to her four gangster brothers. Thus, the two-part opening sequence tells us enough to follow the plot, despite the unconventional filming style and perplexing visual design.

Youth living under dictatorship are never completely cut off from the wider world, even if the way that they experience it is shaped by the physical confinement and symbolic violence of their everyday lives. Mikhi and Rita walk around the city window-shopping and recycling garbage to replicate global commodity icons. With Rita still in chains, they are tracked down by her brothers in a bemused moment as they are contemplating modern objects (ticking clocks) in the windows of a high street *kissaria* (shopping arcade). The rest of the film revolves around the struggle between the System, through its self-defined pitbull, Daoud, and the social outcasts, Mikhi and the gang of four. Rita's brothers perform heists to survive as well as to undermine the economic system, which has turned them into social outcasts. They are engaged in open war with Daoud and the *Makhzen* because their father was among the thousands of the 'disappeared' during the Years of Lead (1956 to the 1990s). Desperate to be with Rita forever, Mikhi sets up the police captain. Daoud is kidnapped, beaten up and left to die in a car boot in the city's refuse landfill. The film reaches a climax when a dying Daoud is rescued by unknowns from his metal grave. After recovering in hospital and learning of the death of his disabled wife, Naima, he turns on the gangsters and manages to finish them off with harrowing brutality. These extrajudicial executions are carried out in a manner which recalls Giorgio Agamben's theory of *homo sacer*, or non-sovereign subjects, living in 'a state of exception' whereby the law is permanently suspended.[3] Whether they live or die is equally unimportant, as they are seen as being barely alive.[4] Morocco's Years of Lead were conceived as a state of exception by a regime concerned only with its survival. In the eyes of King Hassan II, most Moroccans were not *bios* (citizens and sovereign subjects), but rather *zoe* (*homo sacer*), deprived of any rights and to be killed or disposed of in camps in case of need.[5] Through the support of the capitalist West and his purging of the army during the Cold War era, the Alawite sovereign endowed himself with the 'the power of decision over life'.[6] Thus, the secret jails all over the country were camps in the Agambian sense of spaces, created 'when the state of exception begins to become the rule'.[7]

Mikhi and Rita survive Daoud's carnage. The news of King Hassan II's death is broadcast on television, and people start running in all directions. In a utopian moment that brings together the end of the political regime and the capitalist system, people do not just scatter hither and thither, but pillage commercial properties and run away with whatever commodities they can carry. Mikhi and Rita drive off in a convertible car stolen from a supermarket's parking area. The next scene is of the youth in a dark tunnel. They are sitting on a bench at the end of the tunnel facing the blinding light of the future. Can they go forward? Is it possible to go anywhere from here? If there is a post-dictatorial future or life after Hassan II, can people adjust to it after four decades lived in fear and darkness? The poetic ending leaves the future open. What is certain is that the future – if there is one – will be uncertain, and under the full force of globalisation (as the proliferation of digital icons everywhere on walls, on roads and on-screen suggests). The end is just the beginning.

The heists, as well as most of the action in the opening sequence, take place in downtown Casablanca. The black-and-white editing makes the colonial buildings look more original, with an aura of postcards and films set in Casablanca in the colonial period. However, *The End*'s events and violent outbursts betray the present-day reality of poverty and state repression under the reign of Hassan II. The background radio reports on royal affairs, in both standard Arabic and French, establish the temporal context of Casablanca in the film. The city's modernity is chained to the archaic despotism of a monarch, whose processions and fondness for byzantine traditions, such as hand-kissing (Mikhi kisses Daoud's hand in the first heist scene). The urban space is affectively intense, with violence lurking under the seemingly quiet space of a city, and a people who have accepted dictatorship and everyday surveillance as their fate. However, ordinary people are full of tactics to resist the power system's strategies of control. The quiet and estranged car park attendant, Mikhi, Rita and her gangster brothers are engaged in daily warfare for survival and subversion of control. They occupy the city from the crumbling colonial buildings and what Robert Smithson compares as 'non-sites' (vacant or half-developed plots) downtown to Casablanca's poor periphery, which houses empty factory sites abandoned under the de-industrialisation of the structural adjustment programme in the 1980s.[8] The outlaws are determined to ruin the system because their father was executed by Hassan II's regime. However, everyday tactics are not always conscious attempts at subversion, as Michel de Certeau reminds us;[9] they are the efficient arms of the daily insurrection that ordinary people resort to in the battle for survival. For example, Mikhi takes advantage of the police's nightly ritual to burn seized cannabis to get his free dose of pleasure. Thus, the neoliberal space of Casablanca is a battleground between those in control, and those who contest that control. This everyday warfare constructs a cognitive map of the city under political and market hegemony as a fraught and contested space of domination and resistance, rather than as one of full control from above.

Subcultural aesthetics

Young Moroccan filmmakers such as Lasri are no longer reluctant to source their plots and aesthetic choices in their own lives as youth or inhabitants of Casablanca. The filmic point of view becomes deliberately subjective in the process – a rare occurrence in Moroccan cinema until the late 2000s. Lasri draws on his own experience as a Casablancan who came of age in the city, and who witnessed its transformation firsthand from historical changes to the renaissance of subcultures. In consequence, *The End* is a subjective film on more than one account. As Lasri says in an interview, this is his own story as a twentysomething in Casablanca in July 1999.[10] This date is as important in recent Moroccan history as the resilient memory of the late potentate. During his reign and indeed even today, filmmakers have avoided tackling one of the oldest monarchical systems in the world. The current Alawite dynasty, which claims descent from the Prophet Muhammad, has ruled Morocco since 1631. More than any other dynasty in the country's history, the Alawites have always been adept at surviving the turmoil of history, from the decline of the Moroccan empire through colonialism and post-colonial challenges, to their power (from *coups d'état* in the 1970s, to mass social protests under globalisation). Whether one does or does not believe the official mythology of the king as the father of the nation, it is impossible to deny the strong presence of this institution in Moroccan everyday life. Public life countrywide is pervaded by the hegemony of a 'banal nationalism', to borrow Michael Billig's phrase,[11] constructed around the monarchy. Standing next to the portrait of the current monarch, King Mohammed VI, Hassan II's portrait still hangs on the walls of shops, cafes, billboards and every public building. An important scene in *The End* takes place in a Kafkaesque police station, an icon of Hassanian Morocco, where an old and emaciated baker is being tortured. He sees a portrait of King Hassan in the room and immediately clings on to it, shouting 'Long Live the King!' many times in order to seek protection from the maniac police chief, who is both an agent of the system and an allegory of it. Instead, he is knocked to the ground, with the portrait left unscathed. 'One shouldn't mess with saints,' Daoud tells the old man, who is rolling in his own blood.

However, *The End* is not about King Hassan; rather it is about a month in the life of a youth who came of age under his rule, and who witnessed the tense atmosphere in Casablanca in the days leading up to his death. The film's anti-hero, Mikhi, is one of the millions of Moroccans born and brought up under Hassan II's dictatorship (1961–99). They grew up in total fear of the brutal police regime, in an environment that vehemently discouraged them from knowing the truth. People were afraid of extrajudicial detention or 'disappearance'. The enforced silence was as violent as the reigning terror itself. This bitter truth is the subject of Faouzi Bensaïdi's landmark film *A Thousand Months* (2003), set in the Atlas mountains in 1982.[12] We lived in fear everywhere, from the cities to the remotest regions, where extreme poverty and lack of electricity and schooling made the silence a vast prison. The year of 1999 marked the end of both the Hassanian dictatorship and the silence around what he called 'his secret gardens', or detention camps.[13] As the apocalyptic and ambivalent ending of *The End* reveals, the demise of a dictator does not resolve all the problems in a people's everyday life. Instead, it throws up a series of questions: how does one react to the sudden death of a deified tyrant? Is it ever possible to come to grips with the past? Where does one begin to narrate it and heal the wounds? Finally, how can one welcome or embrace the future when one has not been brought up to expect it to arrive at all, particularly without him – as happened in July 1999?

For anyone who has lived under dictatorship, these seemingly simple questions are inevitably quintessential, even if they remain without an answer. They are unanswerable because truth is subjective. A justice and reconciliation commission was set up in 2004 to investigate the Years of Lead. It allowed thousands of Moroccans to tell their stories, or those of their tortured, assassinated or often just 'disappeared' relatives, at public hearings. Their tales of horror, torture and abuse were broadcast on public television.[14] The final public report of the state-mandated commission damned the regime's human rights violations from 1956 to 1999, yet it stopped short of naming the perpetrators, even those who are still in power.

However, public memory is something, and one's experience of both terror and truth is quite another. There is still a great desire, which seems only to grow stronger over time, for every Moroccan subject who was born under or affected by the dark decades of Hassan II's rule, to come to terms with their own truth. Cinema and literature have been at the forefront in quenching and feeding this desire for subjective truth. Despite its allegorical references, *The End* is a film about one young Casablancan's experience of a special moment in time. He suddenly found himself feeling like an orphan, having to live without the king-monster he had come to accept as being an essential element of his identity. When life leaves the idol believed to be eternal, all of a sudden Mikhi finds himself face-to-face with a present that is synonymous with nothingness. He is astride the abyss between a past imperfect and an unknown future. If dictatorship and market reforms have changed the structures of Moroccan society, Lasri's own subjective experience, projected onto Mikhi, is what matters most: through it one can glimpse the general picture of Morocco in the late twentieth century, and July 1999 in particular. The oneiric rhythm of the film is a reflection of this disaffected and drug-addicted youth, and his point of view frames both the filmed reality and our viewing experience of it. *The End* is primarily a portrait of the sudden void in Mikhi's life on that ashen day in late July 1999. The time could not have been more apocalyptic. In the film, Mikhi is living on the edge of time, just as the rest of the world is gearing up for the new millennium. For both Lasri and the lackadaisical Mekhi, the feeling was one of millennial fear and uncertainty, rather than of celebration and hope. This affective experience is projected outwards and inscribed in the present time of Casablanca, since it was being driven by spatial fragmentation, social instability and the uncertain times of globalisation. Inevitably, besides standing in for the young Lasri in July 1999, Mekhi is also an allegory of the whole of Morocco feeling confused about having to walk into the future with an unresolved past, and without its father.

It is not only the plotline of the film, which is centred on a personal story and atomic identities, that is subjective. Its aesthetic is subjective too, in the sense that *The End* embodies recent Moroccan cinema's championing of stylistic innovation in search of a language of film that is capable of telling the specific yet universal stories of Moroccan subjects today. Lasri's film is a subcultural one in both form and content. If the story is about youth and loss in urban space, the style borrows from all the media that pervade the everyday life of young people. Lasri relishes in screening a Casablancan everyday that is permeated by new media, social network technologies and commercial advertising, while avoiding a pre-digital image of the city. His filmmaking techniques rely heavily on these very digital cultures to convey on-screen a city where the everyday is already replete with cinematic potential because it is traversed by global images. There is no city outside images. Casablanca is an amalgam of images from colonial to neoliberal times, and has existed as icons and images as much as a real city. From videogames and toys, to football and trash culture, down to the new media, *The End* is made to be seen and appreciated as a filmic amalgam of all these media which have dominated the social life of youth under globalisation. Shot on digital camera and saturated with the effects of MTV video and commercials, *The End* inscribes its aesthetic within that of the *Nayda* subcultural movement, and youth cultures generally. For example, the anti-hero at its centre is named, in a typical Lasri gag, Mikhi, in parody of Mickey Mouse. Lasri does not attempt to make a sociological survey of this dominant age category; rather, he tells his own story as a Casablancan youth brought up under the dictatorship of Hassan II, and who has found escape in mainstream films, television and globalised American culture since the 1980s, which coincided with the introduction of socio-economic neoliberalisation and the zenith of political repression.

This aesthetic of subjectivism, I argue, is a reflection of the entrenchment of the neoliberal values of individualism in society. The waning of class-based and even identity-based solidarity in Casablanca has been accompanied by the ascent of capitalist social relations in everyday life. However, a close reading of *The End* and the films of Moroccan cinema's *enfants terribles* (Faouzi Bensaïdi, Mohamed Achaour, Swel and Imad Noury) reveals that the focus on minor subjectivities through unconventional film syntax is not analogous to the loss of critical totality and the potential to foreground or construct counter-archives to social and political metanarratives. Rather, their films provide cognitive maps of Casablanca and Morocco through the micro-details of individual subjectivities. Like their anti-heroic leads, the films are haunted by the quest for a new meaningful way of being Moroccan and free from domination, both in the present and the tyranny of the past. However, the experimental and sometimes outright playful styles of these filmmakers can leave the audience asking whether the violence in their films is real violence that boils over from the social and concrete structures of Casablanca under globalisation, or if it is mere spectacle. In other words, some critics may wonder if this subcultural cinema has gone mainstream and has been given over to the commodification of violence on-screen. Violence permeates recent Moroccan films so much so that it would not be beside the point to say that violence has become the most important channel in the cinematic production of subjectivity on-screen. Not only has violence become more visceral in response to changing everyday social life in the city, but also more subjective than in the 1990s.

Violence was central to colonialism and King Hassan II's post-colonial dictatorship, and the ghosts of this violent past continue to haunt contemporary Morocco. Casablanca, in *The End* and more generally in recent New Urban Cinema films, is a volcano of dark horror that lurks beneath the wholesome exterior. Take Daoud, for example: here is a man at the end of his tether. Barring his pathological love for his wife, his life is one of extreme paranoia and psychological torsion. He takes umbrage at everyone and unleashes violence at the smallest provocation, which makes the film gruelling to watch. Violent and psychotic, he is no ordinary person: his abrasive rage is historical rather than simply personal. Bearing in mind his analogy to King Hassan II, the symbol and incarnation of his country, and put into the specific context of 1999, Daoud is an allegory of a dying Morocco and of the new one that refuses to be born. For Mikhi and the youth of Morocco to come from the old womb, the ruthless, tyrannical policeman has to die – but his death is difficult. In the penultimate scene of the film, he is stripped of both his clothes and power by the crowd of ordinary people running around and robbing all of the state's and commercial institutions. They leave him stranded and naked on the tarmac. The future is opaque, with the streets of Casablanca filmed full of white fog and people running about, as if an atomic bomb had fallen from the sky and everything were about to come to an end.

The death of the 'System's Pitbull' (as Daoud calls himself in the film) unleashes great confusion in society, revealing that his reign of terror was perhaps the only thing holding it together in its fatalistic resignation. However, in another reading, the apocalyptic chaos is an expression of the repressed energy of a society that became accustomed to a certain regime in everyday life. Society's quiescence is the thing that troubled the 'Pitbull' throughout his life. Conscious of the multitude's 'sly civility' – to use John Stuart Mill's description[15] of civil disobedience masquerading as civility among dominated people – he is nervous and unleashes violence on himself and others in the face of a seemingly subservient society. Sly civility is a form of subaltern class-consciousness, or a tactic of everyday resistance used to control. According to de Certeau, everyday life is the stage for the clever tricks of the 'weak' within the order established by the 'strong', an art of putting one over on the adversary on his own turf, hunter's tricks, manoeuverable, polymorph mobilities, jubilant, poetic and warlike discoveries.[16]

Daoud's rule – or rather, the reign for which he is a vigilante – is haunted by the threat of social explosion or popular revolt at any moment. Until the end of the film, the only open threat that he faces comes from the four outlaws. For the love of Rita, Mikhi uses his sly civility to plot Daoud's kidnapping by the gangsters. Naima, Daoud's wheelchair-bound wife, dies alone and unattended at home in his absence. The four social outcasts create chaos around the city through their serious heists and cat-and-mouse games with the police. More organised forms of opposition to the regime have been decimated by the Years of Lead. However, having silenced organised opposition, the regime has to face the everyday anarchy of society's marginalised classes. Put differently, sly civility and incidents of direct engagement are the last and most insidious forms of popular resistance in urban space. Being neither fully conscious nor organised, this old/new resistance is more difficult to co-opt, control or eradicate.

In the film, the clannish outlaws live in a junkyard that is located in a wasteland that once housed factories on the outskirts of Casablanca. Abandoned under the post-Fordist de-industrialisation programme, such sites have become havens for social outcasts and outlaws. Some have turned them into hideouts from which to launch attacks on the mainstream city (the last heist of the outlaws is Frik$, a company that supplies Casablanca's financial institutions with banknotes). *The End*'s outlaws are, in Eric Hobsbawm's phrase, 'social bandits'.[17] Their activity is

> a conscious, almost a political, challenge to the prevailing social and political order and its values. [Such banditry] occurs when there is a conflict of laws, e.g. between an official and an unofficial system, or when acts of law-breaking have a distinct element of social protest in them, or when they are closely linked with the development of social and political unrest.[18]

In *The End*, Hassan II's dictatorship which, as noted previously, killed their father and the economic system and has reduced them to poverty, force the bandits into a life of robbery and plundering. They are engaged in everyday insurrection.

The End's form sticks to this subcultural vision through a trash aesthetic which both recycles and signifies through all the media that affect Mikhi's everyday life. Its counter-realism of the everyday relies on deadbeat humour, absurd violence and indexical realism to reconstruct a violent metropolis from its material trivia and the human refuse of insignificant objects and marginalised characters. Like Mikhi's life, the city is full of trash and filth. We do not see any shiny buildings, architectural wonders, upmarket estates or clean areas of town. Everything, everywhere, is a pile of garbage or painted with dirt in a graffiti of despair. Narrative dialogue intensifies the trashiness of everyday life. The characters use Rabelaisian metaphors to describe how ghastly their city and lives have become. Woven around the mouth, belly and phallus, their words and images are 'parodies that undermine officialdom' and the social order from below.[19] The street prostitute likens McDonald's logo to a backside, and their dreams and thoughts are no less excremental. After his kidnapping and torture by the outlaws, Daoud is buried under the rubbish dumps of Casablanca. *The End* hereby gears the spectatorial gaze towards seeing Casablanca from the viewpoint of its material and social waste. The rubbish dump in this scenario 'becomes a critical vantage point from which to view society as a whole'.[20] Lasri's experimental style renders this filth faithfully both through a trash aesthetic, as mentioned previously, and narrative tropes that are congruent with the gritty imagination of his characters, particularly Mikhi. Casablanca is filmed from below through the eyes of its social waste. We experience the social and urban landscapes of the city through the eyes of Mikhi, the outlaws, Rita and the prostitute. The spectator glimpses the sociospatial maps and cognitive geography of Casablanca from below, following the dominant point of view of Mikhi and the outlaws. This subalternist viewpoint and the cognitive mapping of urban space are rendered through the visual metaphor of rubbish which, as Stam points out in his influential essay on Brazilian cinema, 'reveals the social formation as seen "from below"'.[21] Meanwhile, Daoud represents the people from above. As the 'System's Pitbull', it is his job to prevent the wretched of Casablanca from rising up to reclaim their political and economic rights. He is the guardian of the temple against the 'matter out of place'.[22] On many occasions he admonishes Mikhi for stinking, and sprays cologne on him. This conflict between the System and the unwashed outcasts' 'secular defilement'[23] of its values animates the film from beginning to end.

Post-colonial subcultural politics

The End's characters' names and costumes reflect their political subjectivities as well as the penetration of global popular culture into the deepest recesses of urban space. The eldest outlaw brother wears his dead father's jail uniform throughout the film. As mentioned previously, Mikhi, who is both close to Daoud (as his informer and houseboy) and enamoured of Rita, gets his name from Mickey Mouse. His Moroccan proper name M'key (a respectable forename with a Meccan etymology) becomes Mikhi, a trashy form of both M'key and the Walt Disney character. This form of post-colonial trash culture is a recycling of globalised popular culture. Late twentieth-century Casablanca is saturated with icons of globalisation. From material culture to audiovisual trends, everything has a global provenance yet most things have been recycled to fit into a post-colonial geography. The film adopts a subcultural aesthetic that is in accord with this reality and in order to create a carnival of radical effects at the affective level. As noted previously, from MTV aesthetics to videogames, *The End* frames reality through an aesthetic that refuses to glamorise the filmed objects and subjects. Instead, it portrays them lightly by borrowing from different subcultural media. Take the soundtrack, for example. It is replete with rap and other subcultural music that comes from everywhere, from the African American inner cities of the US to Casablanca, where the *Nayda* movement revitalised marginal voices through similar strategies of vernacular speech. If Nass El Ghiwane's music was a serious response to the condition of the dispossessed in Casablanca and Morocco during the 1960s and 1970s,[24] their music is prevalent in *The End*, but has been remixed to respond to the new structures of feeling of a younger Morocco in the late twentieth century. As Dominique Caubet, who has devoted sociolinguistic studies to *Nayda* and who co-scripted Farida Benlyazid and Abderrahim Mettour's documentary film *Casanayda!* (2007), writes: 'Despite the passage of time and even if the climate is incomparable, it seems that Nass El Ghiwane music's rich poetry and imagery still speak to their Nayda offspring.'[25]

A movie-besotted adolescent in the 1990s, Lasri came of age under the *Nayda* movement in Casablanca, where he was born in 1977. In its reproduction of Nass El Ghiwane in the final soundtrack, *The End* is the product of this subcultural movement, but its use of the trash aesthetic subsumes rather than imitates protest culture. The film does not set out to outline a revolutionary programme through Casablanca's everyday space; rather, it gives an account of it through the subjective eye of a lone character, whose life and point of view are a mix of hard reality and psychedelic dreams. Between exuberantly choreographed mayhem, absurd and garrulous characters, sordid humour and flamboyant performances, *The End* is a subcultural film that parodies the culturally dominant through the original gaze and deranged imagination of a social outcast.

Lasri delights in de-iconising and re-iconising the city or deterritorialising and retrrritorialising urban space. Following in the footsteps of his film *The Iron Bone* (2007), which projects the city of Agadir through the eyes of three *hitists* (unemployed youth spending their time leaning on city walls), in *The End*, Casablanca is a ghostly landscape of icons. It is a city saturated with capitalist commodity culture. From android graffiti to Rolls-Royce and other car brands, commodity fetishism permeates the everyday life of Lasri's film characters. However, the film adapts commodity culture to suggest meanings other than just markers of presence in urban space. The commodity icons are made to signify the condition of social outcasts. For example, the Rolls-Royce is an ironic gag, not only by being out of place but also as a nod to 1950s American glamour cinema, especially to film noir and the gangster movie. The black and white editing represents the period aura in a post-colonial context. The social outcasts are immaculately dressed in the costumes of sci-fi movies, slapstick and the romantic comedy, while their everyday life involves situations and conditions of life that are far removed from their appearance. Commodity culture also can be a sign of ordinary people's imagination, rather than of alienation. They appropriate high and popular cultures in ways that serve their subjective experience. Thus the costumes and icons are political in their deployment in *The End*, an effect enhanced by the absence of a musical soundtrack.

Another satirical use of commodity culture from below concerns the cars in the film. With a heavy deployment of Hollywood tropes such as car races, violence and fast-paced, hard-hitting action, *The End* looks like a crash film at certain moments. This fits in with its representation of Casablanca as a city of youth and deadly brutality. This stylistic element leads us to seeing a city that is caught between the spectacle of globalisation and the harsh reality of its social outcasts and crime culture. Here too, Lasri embeds a level of irony through parodying a global visual culture, which only stages its incongruity with the local social reality. The violence that ensues from the car crashes is often an expression of satire, rather than of pure violence. It is shot through with the overload of cinematic references and the heavy satire of the local and the global alike. With its oneiric cinematography, refined technique and appropriation of post-modern pastiche, *The End* is replete with a 'neon' violence that is both superficial, in that it masks no pretence to depth, and ironically political, because it is an expression of youthful visions in a splintering city and a globalising world.

Melancholy characters are an essential part of *The End*'s cognitive map of Casablanca. Daoud is lonely, pensive and a man on the edge. His character and affective states come out in an aggressive idiolect that is followed by outbursts of real violence. As the film's action unfolds, we discover that the 'System's Pitbull' is an allegory of the monarchical regime. His character condenses the persona of King Hassan II, an egomaniac tyrant who lived to see Morocco and the world around him change and become out of step with his anachronistic regime. Thus, in *The End*, melancholia is a worldly condition that anchors Lasri's apocalyptic story of Casablanca in the reality of Morocco at the end of the millenium. Rather than being a mere soufflé of self-indulged experimentalism, *The End* is realistic in its filming technique and its aesthetic reconstruction of a harsh reality. Using subcultural and other hybrid aesthetics, it probes the nervous condition and state of mind of a city, a regime and a people on the edge of the millennium. A melancholic Casablanca is indicative of other psychological and political structures that are on the edge. If, in the film's allegorical tapestry, Daoud stands for a regime tormented by doubt and fear for its survival, ordinary people are also living in uncertainty under its reign and that of globalisation. All the characters are melancholic and stuck in a claustrophobic urban space. The outside world is absent on the screen, and Moroccan youths' common dreamscape of migration is passé on screen. Everyday life in Casablanca is nearing an apocalyptic end and everyone is passively waiting for death to take them away. When death comes at the end, almost everyone dies, and those left alive are at a loss about what to do with the time that remains. Daoud lies naked and passive, like a corpse, on the tarmac in the supermarket car park. This leaves the future of the city uncertain and open to new developments.

On screen, Casablanca is an open-air prison with an ashen hue. If it is often on fire in other recent Moroccan films, such as *Casanegra* (dir. Nour

Edine, 2008) and *Horses of God* (*Les chevaux de Dieu*, dir. Nabil Ayouch, 2012), in *The End*, it is a city of ashes. The black and white editing is called for by the sombre state of the city. It is a burnt metropolis on the verge of apocalypse. Here is a city devoid of life and hope. In addition to the proliferation of cemeteries and the imagery of death in the film, the characters walk like the dead in a vast graveyard of cement buildings, rundown areas and colonial ruins. Lasri's subcultural camera frames Casablanca as a necropolis (city of the dead). If Daoud is a concentrated representation of the regime, Mikhi is the incarnation of Casablanca, a dying city. He is a youth adrift in an urban wasteland with an apocalyptic aura.

The solitary figure of the Casablancan subject lost in space has been a very common type in Moroccan urban cinema since its beginnings.[26] This common type provides historical continuity and thematic coherence across the otherwise heterogeneous terrain of New Urban Cinema. From its anonymous streets to the vast wastelands in the abandoned industrial zone, Casablanca is an anonymous space of gruesome violence and extreme alienation. The ashy hue and post-apocalyptic aura make it alien, menacing and visceral, but rather than this being a purely negative vision, it is best seen as realist mobilisation of the affective energies and of the potential for decisive violence or love in urban everyday life. Lasri chooses to foreground certain aspects of the psychic ecology of the city to open new spaces for the possible that are beyond the naturalistic register of TV news and the immediacy of consumption culture. Thus, the city is filmed as a force-field of energies and potential that carry both alienation and subversion. The city is the world of the possible as much as of the gruesome. This is why everyday life in *The End*'s subcultural realism is the space of what Lefebvre calls 'an open totality' of social relations).[27] Casablanca is not just the stage for neoliberal values, but also a space for civic activism and hope for alternative futures.

Conclusion

Under globalisation, Casablanca is a city inhabited by fear, filth, ashes, melancholia and, against all odds, by dreams and hope for a better future. These phenomena are the symptoms of violence and the social and existential conditions under which post-colonial subjectivities are produced in Casablanca today. The city is strewn with both negative and affirmative violence. On the one hand, we have the state-sponsored violence that is represented by the police, with Daoud. On the other, there is the everyday violence of the social outcasts, strangers in the neoliberal 'marketplace', to borrow a term from Mike Davis.[28] This aggressivity can be directed against themselves, as in the case of Mikhi with blood streaming from his head after spending the aforementioned first night in the film at the cannabis tower. However, in a film that adopts a subcultural and subaltern point of view, violence has a critical function. It is paraded as resistance to the System (as happens when it is inflicted on Captain Daoud) or against the holders of economic power in Casablanca. Another way in which the violence from below works is as a consequence of neoliberal policies, which have created a wasteland of poverty and class alienation (as embodied by the vast urban jungle of de-industrialisation where the brutal outlaws live). Cinematic violence is a symptom of the demise of the social contract between state and society, through the transition from the developmentalist to the neoliberal state that has happened since the early 1980s. Lasri's scorched-earth approach to violence in urban space unveils the dirty side of political and economic oppression of the downtrodden, and the latter's resistance to it. At first glance it might seem that dictatorship and market reforms are two different systems with nothing in common; however, in the end, they are one regime which relies on violence for its political survival and post-Fordist control. Mikhi and the other ordinary people live under the control of both the police and commodity capital. When they rise up against systemic violence in *The End*, they pillage both in retribution for their oppression.

Notes

1 Fredric Jameson (1981) *The Political Unconscious: Narrative as a Socially Symbolic Act* (London: Methuen), p. 92.
2 *Nayda* (translation: 'It's moving!') is the common term used in Morocco to refer to the renaissance of youth cultures in Morocco at the turn of this century. Often compared to the *Movida* in post-Francoist Spain, when youth stormed the stage in cities and broke long-standing taboos about sex, nation and religion, post-colonial youth's cultural revolution in Casablanca and further afield in Morocco bears more than a superficial resemblance to that of their peers north of Gibraltar. *Nayda* is the expression of Moroccan youth's struggle for cultural change and social justice from below. The seeds of the street demonstrations led by the 20 February Movement in 2011 are to be found in this age group's cultural evolution over the last few decades.
3 Giorgio Agamben (2005) *State of Exception* (Chicago: Chicago University Press), p. 40.

4 Giorgio Agamben (1998) *Homo Sacer: Sovereign Power and Bare Life* (Stanford, CA: Stanford University Press), p. 4.
5 Gilles Perrault (1991) *Notre ami le roi*, 2nd edn (Paris: Editions Gallimard).
6 Jacques Rancière (2004) 'Who Is the Subject of the Rights of Man?', *South Atlantic Quarterly* 103(2–3), p. 300.
7 Agamben, *Homo Sacer*, pp. 168–9.
8 Robert Smithson (1996) *The Collected Writings*, ed. Jack Flam (Berkeley, CA: University of California Press), p. 249.
9 Michel de Certeau (1984) *The Practice of Everyday Life*, trans. Steven Rendall (Berkeley, CA: University of California Press), p. 40.
10 Interview with Lasri (in Arabic). Available at https://vimeo.com/41244644 (accessed 25 April 2016).
11 Michael Billig (1995) *Banal Nationalism* (London: Sage Publications).
12 The year I came into the world, and not far from two notorious desert prison camps: a truth I learned only 20 years later through the memoirs of camp survivors.
13 Perrault, *Notre ami le roi*.
14 Susan Slyomovics (2005) 'Morocco's Justice and Reconciliation Commission', *Middle East Report*, 4 April, pp. 1–13.
15 Cited in Homi Bhabha (1994) *The Location of Culture* (London: Routledge), p. 99.
16 de Certeau, *The Practice of Everyday Life*, p. 40.
17 Eric J. Hobsbawm (1972) *Primitive Rebels: Studies in Archaic Forms of Social Movement in the 19th and 20th Centuries*, 2nd edn (Manchester: Manchester University Press), p. 5.
18 Hobsbawm, *Primitive Rebels*, p. 5.
19 Achille Mbembe (2001) *Notes on the Postcolony* (Berkeley, CA: University of California Press), p. 103.
20 Robert Stam (1997) 'Beyond Third Cinema: The Aesthetics of Hybridity', in Anthony R. Guneratne and Wimal Dissanayake (eds) *Rethinking Third Cinema* (London: Routledge), p. 45.
21 Stam, 'Beyond Third Cinema', p. 45.
22 Mary Douglas (1966) *Purity and Danger: An Analysis of the Concepts of Pollution and Taboo* (London: Routledge & Kegan Paul), p. 41.
23 Douglas, *Purity and Danger*, p. 30.
24 Tarik Sabry (2010) *Cultural Encounters in the Arab World: On Media, the Modern and the Everyday* (London: I.B.Tauris), p. 43.
25 'Malgré les années, et bien que le climat ne soît pas comparable, il semble que ces textes poétiques et imagés parlent encore aux enfants de la nayda' (author's translation). Dominique Caubet (2011) 'Nayda ou les enfants des Ghiwane', in Omar Sayed (ed.) *Nass El Ghiwane* (Casablanca: Senso Unico et Sirocco Editions), p. 283.
26 Jamal Bahmad (2013) 'Casablanca Unbound: The New Urban Cinema in Morocco', *Francosphères* 2(1): 73–85.

27 Henri Lefebvre (19910 *The Production of Space*, trans. Donald Nicholson-Smith (Oxford: Blackwell) p. 11.
28 Mike Davis (2006) 'Fear and Money in Dubai', *New Left Review* 41: 114–20.

Bibliography

Agamben, Giorgio (1998) *Homo Sacer: Sovereign Power and Bare Life* (Stanford, CA: Stanford University Press).
_____ (2005) *State of Exception* (Chicago, IL: Chicago University Press).
Bahmad, Jamal (2013) 'Casablanca Unbound: The New Urban Cinema in Morocco', *Francosphères* 2(1). DOI: 10.3828/franc.2013.7.
Bhabha, Homi (1994) *The Location of Culture* (London: Routledge).
Billig, Michael (1995) *Banal Nationalism* (London: Sage Publications).
Caubet, Dominique (2011) 'Nayda ou les enfants des Ghiwane', in Omar Sayed (ed.) *Nass El Ghiwane* (Casablanca: Senso Unico et Sirocco Editions).
de Certeau, Michel (1984) *The Practice of Everyday Life*, trans. Steven Rendall (Berkeley, CA: University of California Press).
Davis, Mike (2006) 'Fear and Money in Dubai', *New Left Review* 41: 114–20.
Douglas, Mary (1966) *Purity and Danger: An Analysis of the Concepts of Pollution and Taboo* (London: Routledge and Kegan Paul).
Hobsbawm, Eric J. (1972) *Primitive Rebels: Studies in Archaic Forms of Social Movement in the 19th and 20th Centuries*, 2nd edn (Manchester: Manchester University Press).
Jameson, Fredric (1981) *The Political Unconscious: Narrative as a Socially Symbolic Act* (London: Methuen).
Lefebvre, Henri (1991) *The Production of Space*, trans. Donald Nicholson-Smith (Oxford: Blackwell).
Mbembe, Achille (2001) *Notes on the Postcolony* (Berkeley, CA: University of California Press).
Perrault, Gilles (1991) *Notre ami le roi*, 2nd edn (Paris: Editions Gallimard).
Rancière, Jacques (2004) 'Who Is the Subject of the Rights of Man?', *South Atlantic Quarterly* 103(2–3): 297–310.
Sabry, Tarik (2010) *Cultural Encounters in the Arab World: On Media, the Modern and the Everyday* (London: I.B.Tauris).
Slyomovics, Susan (2005) 'Morocco's Justice and Reconciliation Commission', *Middle East Report*, 4 April. Available at www.merip.org/mero/mero040405 (accessed 25 April 2016).
Smithson, Robert (1996) *The Collected Writings*, ed. Jack Flam (Berkeley, CA: University of California Press).
Stam, Robert (1997) 'Beyond Third Cinema: The Aesthetics of Hybridity', in Anthony R. Guneratne and Wimal Dissanayake (eds) *Rethinking Third Cinema* (London: Routledge).

8

Visualising the (In)visible

The Queer Body and the Revolving Doors of the Lebanese Queer Subculture

Nisrine Mansour

In July 2012 I was researching a documentary project on the then spiralling security, economic and social unrest in Lebanon, then one odd and brief headline stood out. The Lebanese police forces arrested 36 men at a derelict suburban porn cinema with *liwat* (sodomy) charges, and subjected them to forcible medical anal probes at police stations. The brief reporting of the incident omitted any details of the legal basis or the social circumstances surrounding the arrests, lumping detainees into an invisible group of 'sexual perverts' engaging in practices of 'deviance and prostitution'.[1] The arrests were far from the first, but not the last.[2] Yet they marked a precedent, a turn in the regulation of sexuality in Lebanon, from impromptu individual stints towards unabashed mediatisation, collectivised criminalisation and legal invasiveness. The 2012 arrests flagged the contradictions of a country that makes queerness illegal with erratic enforcement, yet has maintained a permissive outlook through a bursting queer entertainment industry since the 1990s, rebranding Lebanon as the queer playground of the Arab Middle East.

The highly mediatised operation propelled queer and human rights activists into small public protests and massive legal and virtual battles. In the following few weeks, the Lebanese police force quietly dropped the charges and released the detainees. As I frenetically scavenged through the activists' pages on social media networks, I found an avalanche of virtual condemnation, describing the arrests as a political and mediatic 'witch-hunt' against the queer community in Lebanon. I could not find much information on the individual detainees or the context in which they were engaging.

My immediate reaction was to contact allies within the Lebanese queer community – friends, family, activists, academics – in an attempt to get a non-virtual feel of the circumstances and the extent of this highly mediatised 'witch-hunt'. My contacts revealed that little was known about the detainees. The word on the street was that they were part of a long-standing, yet covert local history of men who engage in same-sex practices – paid or unpaid, with some occurring in shady public spaces – without self-identifying as queer. Thus, their practices contrasted with the political ethos of the growing queer Lebanese community that is concerned with lobbying for the legal and social recognition of a distinct queer identity.

In the last 20 years, a growing queer subculture has elbowed its way through Lebanon's postwar public mosaic. Many fashionable, queer-friendly socialising spaces hosted – apart from Arab tourists longing for a breather from more restrictive environments – many locals who, for the large part, remained closeted in their communal environments (family, work, education). Some of these locals founded or joined queer activist platforms, which mostly fight legal and social criminalisation through a handful of outspoken and visible representatives and a large base of invisible social media activists. This multilayered invisibility of queerness in Lebanon, tying in the physical with the political, resonates with a crisis that Joseph Massad attributes to a pervasive discursive exportation of a global Western 'Gay International' movement.[3] In *Desiring Arabs*, Massad exposes the centrality of culture as a colonial analytical tool that opposes the 'progressive' articulation of queerness within the identity-obsessed 'Gay International' to 'regressive' local non-heteronormative practices – often enacted, yet unnamed – within everyday lives and various social spaces across the Arab region.[4]

By incriminating culture, Massad's project was to rewind the political discourse around sexuality in the Arab region prior to that foundational moment of the colonial imposition of the Gay International. In doing this, he wanted to reclaim the aesthetics and ethics of a long, hushed, local history of non-normative, local sexual practices that, in his view, were devoid of the stigma emerging from the opposition of homosexual/heterosexual binaries. As I looked closer at the spiralling virtual debate surrounding the arrests, one issue was particularly disconcerting within Massad's thesis. As Massad grounds his analysis exclusively in the writings of Arab poets celebrating their fluid, unnamed, pederasty in their poems, I could not help but ask: whose practices and voices was he acknowledging? Also, to what extent do the writings of an elite group of cultural producers of the time reflect the experiences of everyday queerness, not least the youths, they were engaging with? While the Gay International was visible as a political project, this was not the case for the individuals conducting the practices that it upholds. The detainees, my contacts and many others tended to wrap their practices around another kind of political invisibility: one that struggles to articulate their own sexuality within the social dynamics of a country that embraces modernity and nurses its swollen conservative underbelly. Furthermore, while the Gay International was considered fixed in Massad's view, it was more ambiguous among those who upheld it in Lebanon, mainly in terms of the political visibility of the queer body.

As early sketches of these reflections brew in my mind for two intense days, I decided to modify my documentary project from political violence to queer politics. My decision related to my understanding that sociopolitical crises emanate from deeper anxieties that are often sidelined in favour of the obvious. As Vaughan contends, 'to see a film as documentary is to see its meaning as pertinent to the events and objects which passed before the camera; to see it, in a word, as signifying what it appears to record'.[5] Taken with the challenge of visualising these multiple layers of invisibility, I set to travel to Lebanon in August 2012 to film a one-crew documentary project, *Hues of Love*.

Visualising the politics of the Lebanese queer subculture

On landing in Beirut a couple of months later, my initial plan was to interview the 36 detainees, who by then were cleared of all charges and quietly released by the Lebanese police force. I thought to contextualise these interviews within the broader battle between queer activists and their public enemies, the queer-phobic police and media. My first port of call, again, was my support group of loved ones, composed of allies and self-identified queers who individually or collectively sympathise and advocate queer rights in Lebanon.

Through our conversations, the circumstances started to unfold as to the timeliness of the arrests. Some explained that the Lebanese police force used the highly mediatised arrests as a strategy of deflection from their failing efforts to contain the intensely precarious political situation in that summer, summed up with erratic bombings, collapsing infrastructure and a swollen refugee crisis caused by the neighbouring Syrian civil war. Others explained that the Lebanese police force had to act under pressure from a sensationalism-thirsty and queer-phobic media. In the year preceding the arrests, talk shows on four competing national broadcasters featured more than ten episodes on various manifestations of queerness. These shows provided the dominant broad audience platform for visualising queer bodies, either partially through pixelated appearances, or fully by hosting individuals who had no problem showing their bodies. They used these visualisations in a titillating scaremongering of queerness as a phenomenon, pushing audiences' morality buttons by exposing it as a creeping perversion, illness or deviance. The same broadcasters also hosted regular comedy shows featuring ridiculed queer characters, in addition to airing popular songs bashing the current 'unruly times' that confound women and men, and erode traditional family moralities.

The two combined narratives reflected a long tradition of hushing up non-heteronormative practices in Lebanon. Historically, the criminalisation of queerness dates back to 1943, months before Lebanon gained independence from 20 years of French colonial rule. Article 534 of the Penal Code criminalises, in one line, 'individuals who engage in unnatural sexual practices', without providing any legal definition of what is 'natural' or not.[6] While keen on regularising the body, legislators of the time were unable or unwilling to name the physical and sensual practices that bodies are supposed to perform 'naturally' or 'unnaturally'.

It is in face of this legal context that Helem crafted its reputation as the leading queer activist organisation in Lebanon. Since its foundation in 2001, Helem has become a platform for queer activism in Lebanon and grown into a volunteer-based provider of counselling and health services, legal representation and awareness campaigns. However, teaming up with leading human rights lawyers, it was less concerned with exposing the colonial straitjacketing of sexuality, or acknowledging the pre-existing local fluid sexual practices – as in the case of the 36 detainees to which Massad refers. Rather, Helem launched a multi-platform activist campaign against the 2012 arrests by legally representing detainees and organising several public protests aimed at the Ministry of Justice and the Order of Physicians, with the informal slogan 'Get off Our Asses'.[7] Within a few weeks, their efforts paid off, as both institutions issued a ban on forcible anal probes at police stations.[8]

The physical and virtual battles scored another victory against the media when two national broadcasters started a news bulletin turf war against each other over queer rights. One broadcaster, LBCI, attacked MurrTV for complying with the Lebanese police force and propagating queer-phobic sentiments by using pejorative terms such as *luti* ('faggots') and *shuthuth* ('perversion').[9] MurrTV followed with a retracting statement claiming no role in the arrests, and renewed its pledge to 'support *al-mithliyin* (homosexuals) in their fight for justice and recognition'. In this statement lay another victory. For the first time, Lebanese broadcasters invariably dropped their queer-phobic terminologies in favour of neutral ones (e.g. 'homosexuals' instead of 'faggots'), long introduced by Helem to the Lebanese public colloquialism since its establishment in 2001.

However, the front line between queer activists and queer-phobes became fuzzier as I met with more activists. Queer activists felt targeted by different media's queer demonisation campaigns. Activists explained their fury at what they perceived as the media's opportunist reporting on gay circles. Many felt betrayed by individuals within the media who were suspected of double standards and this led to divides within the activist community.

It is with this realisation that I shifted my focus from documenting activist groups to individuals who lie at the margins of queer activism stardom. The prevalence of visible over invisible bodies – both in terms of the physical and political – reflect the 'peculiar (and invisible) tensions between the film we see and the unseen film it might have been'.[10] With this choice, I sought to tie in the physical and political invisibility of the body, to convey the voices of individuals who are struggling to articulate their everyday sexuality within this charged social setting, and to convey the lived dimensions of this multilayered (in)visibility of the queer body.

Filming without a camera: experiences of queerness in Lebanon

My shift from focusing on the organised side of the Lebanese subculture was informed by Sandberg's[11] critique of earlier notions of subcultures, which solely focused on people, either groups or individuals, at the expense of the broader cultural discursive practices that bring meaning to people's experiences. As I was interested in documenting the (in)visibility of the queer body,

I found that Sandberg offered a fresh take on subcultures that locates culture, rather than people, as a central analytical unit. Sandberg's definition holds potential to understanding a subculture as an anthropologically informed

> collection of rituals, stories and symbols. They revolve around certain perceptions of the world and are often linked to general cultural currents in society. To a greater or lesser extent, people and groups internalize and embody parts of the subculture. They also exploit the subculture in creative portrayals of themselves.[12]

Locating culture at the heart of subcultures questions the delineations between filmic and social visibility and invisibility by exploring the political power lying within the physicality of the body. By unpacking culture, contributors would be more able to embody, renegotiate and reimagine subculture as a multitude of discursive practices animated by meanings.

With this new approach, I tapped into my contacts in search for individuals willing to take part in an independent documentary project. The response came before the wait. Many friends and friends of friends had stories to tell – about themselves and their friends. However, few of them wanted to talk about it in public; hardly any wanted to show their faces on camera. After meeting several potential contributors, eight agreed to participate in the film. Six out of the eight contributors were affiliated to queer activist platforms. The remaining two joined through personal contacts and did not belong to the queer activist scene. Contributors identified themselves with various orientations, including four gay men, two lesbian women, one transsexual woman (male-to-female) and one transgender man (female-to-male). They also came from various geographic, religious and socio-economic backgrounds, and enriched the discussions with varied views and experiences.

Once the filming process started, the contributors took their request for filmic invisibility to a scale beyond my expectations. Seven out of eight requested full invisibility during the filming process, rather than relying on the usual anonymising visual effects (such as blurring or pixelating) of the post-production phase. They also declined permission to film any part of their bodies or any of their actual physical and social environments on camera. Their request for filmic invisibility threw off the basic usefulness of film as visual medium. It was a challenge, both conceptually and practically, to conceive of a filmic approach to a topic that is concerned with the centrality of the queer body, yet purposefully seeking to visually make it absent. As Chanan reminds us, we need to look 'beyond the representation of the way things appear, to become a metaphor for what is going on behind and beyond the image, which the camera is unable to record'.[13] This challenge opened up new kinds of visual and narrative potentials that seek to document the interplay between political and physical (in)visibility of the Lebanese queer body.

As the contributors insisted on visually absenting the body from their narrations of everyday experiences, this yields new insights into the politics of embodying queerness and informs conceptualisations of a subculture that acknowledge the body's interconnectivity with its social environment. The contributors' concern with the (in)visibility of the queer body in this documentary project responded to Massumi's contention that the body 'doesn't just absorb pulses or discrete stimulations; it infolds contexts'.[14] Hence, as contributors tied in physical and political (in)visibility of their bodies, they were enacting Spinoza's concept of affect, articulated by Massumi as a 'prepersonal intensity corresponding to the passage from one experiential state of the body to another and implying an augmentation or diminution in that body's capacity to act'.[15]

Bearing in mind Michael Renov's warning against 'the risk of documentary being "reduced" entirely to its cognitive functions',[16] I decided to use an ethnographically informed, fluid approach to documenting the narratives of contributors. I resorted to holding free-flowing, in-depth interviews lasting between two hours and three hours each. The contributors chose the location of the interview and were comfortable lending their voices to an audio recorder, with the absence of the camera. I had given them the option to substitute their voices with written captions, but none felt the need for it.

My choice for audio recordings was obvious to compensate for the filmic absence of the contributors' bodies. As the remaining sections of this chapter will reveal, this choice did not take away from the power of their experiences; rather, it reinforced them. Endowing them with the ability to freely and fully verbally articulate their affective experiences within their narratives encapsulated the essence of affect as, in Sara Ahmed's words, 'what sticks, or what sustains or preserves the connections between ideas, values and objects' – a determination which confronts 'the messiness of the experiential, the unfolding of bodies into worlds and the drama of contingency, how we are touched by what we are near'.[17]

Thus, the interviews were led mainly by the contributors and revolved around the broad themes of the Lebanese queer context, institutional and discursive practices of discrimination (the actors, channels and moralities involved), personal experiences and reflections on the selving process, social and personal relations and future prospects. I found this way of documentation to bring out 'a specific poetics [...] requiring critical appreciation for its imaginative and often positive appeal to viewing subjectivities', opening up various possibilities of imagining characters' subjectivities beyond the linear dramatic arc.[18]

Publicness and (in)visibility of the queer body

Inevitably, the interviews started with the arrests. The contributors had heard about it on the news, or through their activist circles or social media networks. They immediately expressed their anger at the police and the media, as shown in Jamal's outburst:

> Why would they arrest them? [The police and media] have left all the problems in the country and are obsessing about how people are getting laid! [...] Which morals are they talking about? Go to poor neighbourhoods and see the misery there – incest, prostitution, drugs and crime – but no one does anything about it. They are just filling their pockets with corruption. TV stations constantly flaunt boobs and bums on our screens everyday [...] Same with [mainstream] entertainment spaces: just go and see what goes on in there, but no one dares targeting those because they have control. They are in it [*khasson*[19]], they just do it in secret and chase those wretched sods who are miserable and disgusting, and it's not their fault [...] God created them this way. They go after them because they are an easy target; they are poor and they don't have any connections.

Here, Jamal is referring to postwar (1975–90) neoliberal governments' policies and investments by the political and economic elite in Lebanon to revive Beirut as a liberal media hub and entertainment playground of the Arab Middle East. Since then – and despite a precarious political environment – the entertainment, tourism, hospitality, media and sex industries have flourished over a historically permissive social and entertainment environment traced back to Beirut's 1960s' reputation as the Paris of the Middle East. More importantly, Jamal is referring to the common same-sex practices that go on in Lebanon, which are spread across classes and remain hushed and unnamed, used as tools for political manipulation.

Joseph denounced police persecution as a broader attack on the queer community:

> It is time to speak about [police persecution]. Whatever happened in [the cinema], it was between consenting adults [...] – but things changed. Now it's our time. Now they will think twice before targeting us, they know that it is not easy to mess with us anymore.

The contributors conflated named and unnamed same-sex practices within the Queer International agenda. The successful retaliation of activists has brought political visibility and clout, especially with the successful pressure put on the police and media. While the symbolic queer body was visible and defiant, the physical visibility of the queer body remained quite dimmed, as a very small number of activists (around 30 people) joined the protests. Many activists and sympathisers – including all the contributors but one – shied away from public participation in fear of a mediatised 'self-outing'. The contributors' reluctance to mediatise visibility resonated with their choice not to show their bodies in the documentary project. While trusting my motives, they did not want to leave any visual proof of their queerness.

These reflections lead us to discuss the significance of the arrests in their everyday lives. The randomness, publicness and pervasiveness of the 2012 arrests magnified the contributors' earlier fear of exposure, and brought a generalised fear of persecution beyond direct daily experience. None of the contributors were ever arrested, and all but one had never encountered anyone who had. Only Jad recounted how the police arrested three of his friends in a trendy and queer-friendly part of central Beirut: 'They were parked in a car and they arrested them because they just because they "looked" gay.' The three friends were dragged to the police station and received the usual treatment as with similar arrests – forcible anal probes on men, or 'virginity' (hymen) checks for women. The three friends were later released without charges, because as Jad explained, they do not engage in anal sex. However, as is usually the case regardless of the outcome, detainees have to pay $80 for the coroner's probe administration fees. Jad pointed to the ironic consequences: 'So you not only get raped in prison, but you have to pay for it as well.'

Joseph did not feel as threatened by the arrests, claiming that his bodily conduct and sexual practices did not put him at risk: 'In Article 534, "unnatural sexual practices" are interpreted as engaging with anal sex. Since I don't, the Lebanese police force have no proof that I am gay.' However, it seemed that sexual practices were not enough to spare him from arrests. He quickly added, 'and anyway I don't "look" gay, so I don't think I will ever get arrested'.

The emphasis on 'looking' gay, with its elusive attributes, refers to the non-conforming affective display of the queer body that contributors feel the need to repress in certain situations. For example, Jamal makes an effort to change his bodily conduct in public:

> On the streets, I walk in a respectful manner. I don't wear loud outfits to show I am gay. At police checkpoints, I speak and interact in a poised manner to avoid any problems. Some policemen get really nasty, so you have to be careful.

Jamal explained the difference with displaying his queer body within the subculture's spaces:

> Yes, I have many gay friends and go to gay places where you can have fun and get into belly dancing, while everyone is cheering for you [...] Unlike straight places where macho men bully you, while wanting a piece of you, in [queer places] you can dance and have fun, and be yourself. That's why many straight guys are coming to queer places [...] I tell you, the other day I found half of my neighbourhood in there [...] at first I got embarrassed and hid, but then I reminded myself with a popular proverb: 'A whore sees another at a brothel and sneeringly asks her, "What are you doing here?" The other replied, "Same as you, my dear!" What are we all going to do there? [laughs] We are all going to have fun and enjoy it!'

While Jamal enjoys queer spaces, he also expressed his fear of the increasing arrests:

> Yes, there are undercover policemen who go in [queer places]. That's why one gets scared – and there are now undercover policewomen as well, snitching men and women. Yes, we have evolved my dear, gender equality in snitching.

When I asked how he was able to recognise them, he replied in a split-second:

> You can spot them easily from the way they come across. They have a too aggressive demeanour, looking around, steely, with an unwelcoming bodily expression. In contrast you can recognise someone who is coming there to have a good time. Gays would be smiling, if they don't smile, their eyes do smile'. 'Once, [laughing] we spotted [undercover cops] in a [queer-friendly] club and gave them a good beating. They asked for it, being there to spy on us.

Contributors expressed their fear of persecution not only from the police, but also from others within various public spaces. Despite his broad-shouldered and sturdy stature, Ramzi remained adamant about not showing his face on camera. When I asked him about what could possibly happen, he sounded puzzled: 'I don't know [...] there might be some macho guys who don't like it, and would decide to give me a beating or worse – stab me with a knife or something.' Frustrated with these limitations, Ramzi resorted to subtle strategies that test the limits of queer bodily display without jeopardising his safety. He started holding his boyfriend's hand on Beirut's popular seafront promenade:

> At first, we were both shy and did it sheepishly, but then we both said, let's do it in a natural way without any sexualisation – and people got used to it. Once, a bunch of young men saw us and someone snapped: 'Who is the man and who is the woman?' I looked at him calmly and said, there is no man or woman here. We are enjoying our walk. Do you want to join us? The guy looked so baffled and speechless, he dropped the conversation. People are cowards, and they shy away from confrontation.

The non-conforming gendered body is a constant cause of anxiety in public spaces. Jad, a biological woman who changed into a transgender man two years ago, did not intend to have a sex change or play the medical card. He explained:

> They don't understand how someone can look androgynous. I would be walking on the street, and people would just stare or throw slanted looks at me without saying a word. It gets irritating after a while. [...] I usually look back at them and ask them

if they want to see my ID. They immediately shy away. They are cowards.

This unease had immediate consequences for Jad's livelihood: 'I got fired from my job at a restaurant because the manager got fed up answering questions about whether I am a man or a woman.'

Sahar reflects on the fact that people generally resist non-conforming, gendered bodies. She recounts that prior to embarking on transsexual change from man to woman, she used to be harassed because her looks were 'in-between, not indicating whether I was a man or a woman – and people can't take that. All they care about are appearances'. She sensed this with her extended family, such as her grandparents, who were much more accepting of her as a transsexual than as an 'effeminate' man.

(Un)named practices and political (in)visibility of the queer body

The general anxiety of conforming to gendered practices implies certain power dynamics that underlie unnaming queer practices. Jamal recounts a conversation that he had with a neighbour. The neighbour suspected that his son was gay, and he was so devastated, he would 'kill himself' if it turned out to be the case. Jamal replied: 'Uncle, what are you talking about? When you were growing up, didn't you used to play with other boys? You know, the sorts of games of touch and feel? Getting intimate? Feeling each others' willies?' The neighbour froze and was not able to comment. Jamal continues: 'Everyone does it! They just are not honest with themselves. We all did it at one point, but then people just don't want to admit it.'

The contributors invariably explained the complexity of naming or unnaming queer feelings or practices. Ramzi recalled:

> As a child, I remember feeling butterflies in my stomach whenever I was playing with boys at school. I didn't get this feeling when playing with girls. At the time I didn't know what it meant, I initially attributed it to a sense of belonging to macho tribe, and it took me many years to allow myself to feel what it is.

Ramzi recalls a moment of duplicity, when he went out with friends one evening:

> Among the group, there was a gay friend, whom I knew for sure that he was gay because he used to trust me with his stories. The rest of the group did not know that either of us was gay. As part of the regular macho chats in such settings, our friends started bragging about their conquests with women. My gay friend joined in and he started boasting about his sexual practices with various women. I knew that he was lying, and I felt repulsed by his need to show off and conform to the macho narrative. I didn't stay for long. I left and cut off my ties with him. It's just disingenuous – but I know that many men do, like I used to. Lying to yourself to save face.

It is this duplicity that contributors opposed by upholding a well-defined queer identity, as they recognise the power bestowed within unnaming queer practices and demonising their beholders. People go to lengths to unname queer practices, as Karim recalls – an encounter while he was hitchhiking from his coastal village to Beirut:

> I just came out of the beach and wanted to hitchhike to Beirut to meet some friends. I was wearing casual beach outfits, a singlet and swimming trunks and my broad shoulders and hairy chest and legs were showing. A Muslim cleric stopped to pick me up. On the way, he told me: 'Do you know that women love hairy men? Oriental men are hairy, while Western men are patchy so women don't like them – and he felt the hair on my chest. I froze and discreetly removed it. The cleric continued: 'Did you know that women get turned on by oriental men because they are virile and satisfy them? Western men are too soft and women get bored by them – and his hand made his way up on my leg and onto my groin. I shrieked and told him to let me off the car, he reluctantly pulled over mumbling: 'What's the problem? We are only chatting.' I replied, 'I don't want to hear any of your chats' and walked away.

These unnamed, same-sex encounters not only occur with short-term hook-ups; they are an organising principle for a heteronormative affective regime that, in the contributors' view, is built around duplicity and macho-ness. Karim has a story that exemplifies this duplicity in the way his father dealt with his queerness. Karim explained that he has got a gay relative, and that they used to hang around in the village. He described his relative as a very decent young man, but his effeminate outlook labelled him of questionable ethics by fellow villagers. One day, Karim's father called him and asked him to stop hanging out with this relative, because of his ill reputation. Karim refused and asked him to gather the family – his mother and siblings – to discuss it. The following discussion ensued:

FATHER: You have to tell me now. Are you gay?
KARIM: Would it matter if I were?
FATHER: what do you mean? Are you? You have to tell me one thing. Do you fuck or do you get fucked? Are you the 'man' or the 'woman'?
KARIM: This is none of your business; I am a man whether I get to be a 'man' or a 'woman'.
FATHER: You don't need to be so strict about it. When I was your age I used to shag boys and I liked them smooth-skinned with little body hair, but then I got married to your mum and started a family, and you can do the same.
KARIM: Well, I am very different from you, I *like* men and I like them big and hairy – and that's what it is. Beyond this point, it is none of your business.

The discussion between Karim and his father reiterates Ramzi's objection to this kind of duplicity:

> Since I was a child I'd sensed that I was gay, but I was denying it. Many men do that – or at best they say they are bisexual because they feel that if they commit fully to being gay, they will have to let go of this macho-ness that we are so strictly raised to adhere to. It wasn't until I got married and lived a double life for 13 years that I realised that I could not sustain this duplicity anymore. I divorced and decided to fully embrace my homosexuality. It was only when I got rid of my attachment to the macho culture that I could be myself.

It is with these examples that Massad's premise is challenged. Massad's claims of more fluid local sexual practices in the Arab region fail to account for the stigma around the queer body. While Karim's father and many other men like him accept unnamed same-sex relations as part of everyday life, they displayed anxiety about the 'macho' meanings attached to queer bodily practices. Local practices in history and current times revolve around the taboo of penetrating the anus. Hence, 'active' partners of same-sex practices are not stigmatised, only those at the receiving end are. It is these power dynamics that Massad missed in his analysis of historical queerness in the region[20] – power dynamics that oppressed 'passive' queer actors long before Western colonialism crystallised heterosexuality as a marker of civilisation, and which are perpetuated until our current time.

Queer desires and the performativity of queer (in)visibility

The confrontation between Karim and his father is an example of many instances that tested the contributors' ability to acknowledge their queer selves and lead a fulfilling queer existence, while manoeuvring the extent and quality of their physical and political visibility. Ramzi recalls:

> My biggest worry was: what would my parents think of me, how I failed them by being their gay son [...] I was feeling guilty because the shame they could feel because of me – before their own selves and before their environment – would be devastating for them.

It is this worry that preoccupied the documentary contributors: whether, to what extent . how they would reconcile their parents' expectations with their own queer selves. Ramzi continues:

> Since we are children, we are raised on the myth that a man marries a woman, and they have children, and they live happily ever after. I went through this: I got married for 13 years while knowing that I was attracted to men.

For Ramzi, it was not easy breaking it to his parents, but it came at a time while he was working abroad and fully independent financially. His mother reluctantly came to terms with it by avoiding the discussion. His father's initial reaction was to question him about whether he was a 'top' or a 'bottom'. Following a heated argument, Ramzi's father blocked any attempt at discussing it. A couple of years later, he fell severely ill and Ramzi managed to introduce him to his boyfriend, days before he passed away. Ramzi remembers going with his boyfriend to issue his father's death certificate. When the clerk asked for two witnesses, Ramzi and his boyfriend signed it together:

> Of course I was devastated by my father's death, but for me this certificate was the proof that nothing can make it go away. No matter how averse my father was to my sexuality, his departure from this world was sealed with it.

This was the symbolic closure that Ramzi found solace in, to acknowledge his queer self and reconcile with it.

For Karim, the confrontation with his family did not deter his father's constant pressure on him to 'fix his problem' and get married. Karim felt this pressure, so he decided to get engaged in order to get his father off his case; however, knowing full well that it would be hard for him because he felt physically repulsed by the female body:

> My father was over the moon and he chose the bride for me – the daughter of a family friend. The girl was all right, but when she came near me, my hair stood up on my skin and I couldn't even hold her hand. As the wedding was getting nearer, I became worried that I would not be able to sleep with her. So I went to my cousin who knows about me and supports me. She came up with the solution: to ask her husband to hire me a hooker from a brothel, so that I could go and practice with her for a few days in a hotel.

Karim then describes this agonising week, where his best intentions to have sex with a woman did not materialise. He confessed to his cousin that he would not be able to get married. She respected his decision and promised to help him stand up to his father and break off the engagement. Karim's father was furious, and asked him to go and visit a psychiatrist. Karim went with it, and he visited three:

> The first one asked me to work on my imagination and try to grow my fantasies for women by watching straight porn, something that I couldn't do because I always felt physically repulsed by the female body. The second one suggested for me to sleep

with women from behind and imagine that I am shagging a man, which basically meant that I would lie to myself [...] The third one prescribed me a course of antidepressants to get me to cope with the depression resulting from my homosexuality. He also warned me that these pills would weaken my sex drive [...] I thought to myself, why reduce my sexual drive and be miserable? I decided to drop the whole thing and enjoy my sex drive and my preference for men.

Sahar, on the other hand, found in psychological counselling a useful resort to come to terms with her situation. She recounts:

> There is a video recording of me at the wedding of one relative [...] I was two years old, so before I could even speak let alone understand the difference between boys and girls [...] In the video, I had made and worn a makeshift bride's tiara and I was dancing to the bridal tunes, like in trance. I so wanted to be that bride [...] as I became a bit older, I used to hide in the toilet at weddings and cry my eyes out, asking God to turn me into a girl so that I could get to be a bride.

The psychologist explained to Sahar about transsexuality, and it made sense to her. She also helped her break it to her parents by holding a joint meeting with them. Through the process of self-acceptance, Sahar turned to science and God, which facilitated her parents' acceptance of her situation:

> Before my treatment, I felt dead. I didn't feel my body. Once the treatment kicked in, I became very conservative, obsessed with protecting my body. As you see, I hardly put on any make up and wear unrevealing clothes [...] I explained to my mother that it is a biological condition. I read about it, it happens during pregnancy. If the mother receives a shock, the hormonal balance in the foetus' brain changes, and it starts there – and this is why in Shi'a Islam, transsexuality is accepted and there are *fatwas* from Iran that allow it. So I don't have any [ethical] problems with it. I told this to my mother and she accepted it [...] I pray and fast and embrace other faiths as well, so I have the cross and a statue of Virgin Mary by my bedside. As a man I was very promiscuous because I didn't care – now I am not. My mother tells me 'Be careful, don't be loose now that you are a girl' and

> I agree – I want to preserve myself for a man whom I love. I am a conservative trans and I am proud of it.

Sahar is not the only one to turn to religion for self-acceptance. Maya, a devout Catholic, struggled with her mother's fierce opposition to her lesbian preference. Maya's mother also adheres to Catholicism. Raised at a convent school and adhering to strict Catholic teachings, she considered queerness a deadly sin. Once suspicions crept in, she hacked into Maya's email and started watching her every move. Maya's queerness brought her into conflict with her faith and her family. She was soul searching for a way to reconcile her faith with her sexuality. One day her mother asked her to visit a priest, claiming that he was open-minded and approachable. Maya agreed, in an attempt to appease her mother.

> Once there, he called me to his office and asked another priest for assistance [...] It was a hot summer day and the room was stuffy with incense. Suddenly, he turns to me and shouts: 'Don't you know what Jesus had to go through to erase your sins?' Then he brought his cross close to my face and shouted 'Where are you? Get out of her!'

Maya found herself in an exorcism arranged by her mother. In order to avoid a clash with her mother, she carried on with it, in frozen bewilderment:

> 'How many are you in there? How many are you? Surely, surely, there is more than one demon inside her.' So the conclusion was that I was possessed by many demons because I liked sleeping with girls.

This incident drove Maya away from her faith, for rejecting both herself and her body. It was not until a couple of years later that she met a French priest and asked him for guidance:

> He told me: 'Pray and listen to what your heart tells you.' I told him, when I pray, my heart tells me that I am not doing anything wrong. He replied: 'Then you should trust your heart.'

Since then, Maya has reconciled her queerness with her faith through listening to her body, as she expressed it: 'Something inside me felt very right, I cannot identify what it is, it's more than a feeling. I don't know.' Maya re-engaged with her faith, tracing Catholic rejection of queerness to historical queerphobic translations of the Bible. She took upon herself to retranslate the Bible into Arabic and include the long missing queer-friendly passages.

The contributors' strategies for reconciling queerness with their immediate environment also revolved around manoeuvring the extent to which they are willing to reveal or absent their queer bodies in their future lives. When asked about their dreams, they all mentioned firm plans to get married to their present or future partners and have children with them. The process of reaching this dream took a convoluted route for each of the contributors. Some found that since their parents would never accept their queerness, they were left with the only option to emigrate to queer-friendly countries. Beyond the financial and relocation hurdles tied to immigration, some contributors worried that their partners would not want to leave Lebanon. Another option for gay and lesbian contributors was to team up with same-sex couples from the opposite sex and contract a 'cover' marriage, in order to be publicly accepted by their families and wider social circles. Since then, their plans have not yet materialised. Perhaps what transpires most from this project is the contributors' willingness to absent their public queer self by conducting a heteronormative social bodily performativity, while being adamant to nurture their queer selves in their intimate circles of existence rather than denying it.

Conclusion

This chapter has reflected on the process of understanding queer existence and subculture in Lebanon through the medium of documentary filmmaking. The documentary project *Hues of Love* sought to document the experiences of many individuals who embody queerness in various ways and enact it selectively within various social spaces. The characters represented a growing community that lies between the few who have gone public with their sexuality, on the one hand, and others who engage with non-heteronormative sex practices without identifying as queer, on the other.

My interest in the topic began with the news of the arrests of 36 men in a derelict adult cinema in 2012, which exposed a range of manifestations of queerness within Lebanese society. Despite legal and political hostility and random persecution of queerness, queer entertainment and socialising spaces have operated publicly, with a clear policy bias favouring the upper end of the queer consumption range. These spaces are public yet contained geographically within a few trendy neighbourhoods in Beirut, or tucked away in the seedy alleys of the swollen Lebanese marginal underbelly. These manifestations sketch a multifaceted mosaic of queer existence and enactment that is yet to be thoroughly explored both at epistemological and filmic levels.[21] This mosaic is discursively, spatially and temporally mediated, juxtaposing an eclectic local historio-cultural repertoire on sexuality with a Western conceptual imposition of fixed sexual identities.

Gradually, the research and filming process took me away from popular classical views of documentary-as-testimony, or reality-as-truth. At the starting point were assumptions about a unified queer identity derived from Western conceptualisations in the field. In addition, I initially approached the Lebanese queer subculture with classical Marxist definitions concerned with solidarity within fixed groups of people in face of a hegemonic heteronormative regime.[22] Halfway through the filming process, it became clear that the main intersections between characters related less to a unified understanding of queerness, or blanket solidarity. As Gagné sharply points out, the convoluted enactment of individual queer existence in Lebanon stands out amid the dual permissive and restrictive cultural, sociopolitical and legal context.[23] In order to explain these variations, I turned to critiques of these classical views at the filmic and analytical levels, and was reminded of Grierson's assertion that documentary is 'the creative treatment of actuality'.[24] I also considered Massad's rejection of queerness as a Western colonial imposition of a fixed queer identity that shadows more fluid, and less stigmatising, local historical queer practices. The contrasting contributors' narratives alluded to a post-modern take on subcultures: one that refutes the concept on the basis of the individualistic fragmentation that sums up the post-modern condition.

The filming process was a revelation that contested the classical views and their critiques. In the dual restrictive and permissive Lebanese context, the contributors – and many others expressing interest in participating in the project – categorically refused to be filmed on camera. Here was a clear request to absent the queer body from visualisation. This request threw off the usefulness of the documentary genre as a visual medium, and tested the limits of Grierson's apolitical view of 'creative treatment'. It drew my attention to Kaminsky's[25] rebuttal of reality as 'mediated, politically influenced and subjective', which is bound to bring up 'peculiar (and invisible) tensions between the film we see and the unseen film it might have been'.[26] The contributors' urge to participate in the film, and their request to visually absent their queer bodies, was a metaphor for the broader intricate politics of individual and collective queer existence in this dual context. My challenge was how to make sense of the Lebanese subculture beyond the classical and critical conceptions of documentary visualisation, queerness and subculture theory.

At a filmic level, visually absenting the queer body liberated the project from two well-established aesthetic modes of documentary analysis identified by Corner.[27] Pictorialism – the creative 'organization of [documentary]'s visual design and the "offer of seeing" it variously makes to audiences' – has been widely used in documentary, serving either as an observational gaze or an illustrative function.[28] Similarly, the popular blueprint of structured narratives, or 'fictional models produced in full dramatization' position characters within binaries of victimisation and agency.[29] As Panse contends, these narratives are emotionally wired to evoke patronising and distant sympathy, only asserting the superiority of the audience.[30] Doing away with both fetishes of documentary – pictorialism and linear storytelling – has allowed for a transcendental approach in perceiving life: one which captures the deep existential workings of subjectivities and their fluid formation.[31]

Here, the absence of the audience's gaze switched emphasis from the common reactionary emotional accounts that entrench active differentiation between the subject and their social environment. It allowed for in-depth articulation of the characters' feelings, which are key to understanding the offerings of a transcendental lens.[32] Feelings tap into a deeper reflection of the existential condition and bring further connectivity between the characters' situation and the world in which they live. Combined with an ethnographic approach to interviewing, the characters amply made sense of their experiences and reflected on the absenting of their queer bodies. Capturing the transcendental power of feelings proved as crucial as elusive to documentary film.

Throughout the accounts, the absence of the queer body revealed its centrality in the characters' navigation in and out of the queer subculture. As the contributors' feelings about queerness unfolded, they pointed to specific politics behind their reluctance to expose their bodies filmically and socially. These politics revolved around the affective display of the queer body (legal, social, media, public). For, as Damasio reminds us, feelings are structured through affect and without affect, 'feelings don't "feel"'.[33] So, the affective embodiment of queerness became the contact point between various clashing discourses on the Lebanese subculture.

Positioning affect at the centre of the filmic and analytical lenses emerged both as filmic and conceptual 'glue' that sticks together various discursive and experiential components of documenting queer subculture.[34] As the contributors articulated the affective politics of queer embodiment, they allowed for a reconceptualisation of subcultures and documentary away from victim/rebel binaries or fragmented individuality.

Sandberg's reconceptualisation of subcultures away from unitary and pulverised notions allows for accounting for the post-modern condition of fluid temporality and subjectivity, rather than negating it.[35] In particular, reinstating culture instead of people as an analytical unit redefines subculture as a fluid weaving of meaningful symbols, rituals and stories. In the case of Lebanon, the contributors' accounts helped to position affect at the heart of this cultural definition, and illuminated avenues for exploring the elusive interconnectivity noted within the Lebanese queer subculture. In doing so, affect animated the politics of the (in)visibility of the queer body, and articulated stories, symbols and rituals meaningfully as an intermittent process of revoking and evoking the queer body, through the revolving doors between the Lebanese queer subculture and the broader heteronormative context.

Notes

1 Murr TV News (2012) 'Daara wa shuthuth fi al-sinama' ['Prostitution and Perversion in Cinemas], 28 July. Available at http://mtv.com.lb/News/108657 (accessed 15 July 2014).
2 At the time of writing, the Lebanese police force conducted another raid, arresting 45 men in a hammam in Beirut on the same charges. Colin Stewart (2014) 'Report: Lebanon Targets Gay Men in 3 Raids, 45 Arrests', *Erasing 76 Crimes*, 15 August. Available at http://76crimes.com/2014/08/15/report-lebanon-targets-gay-men-in-3-raids-45-arrests/.
3 In the chapter, I use the term 'queer' rather than 'gay' or lesbian, gay, bisexual and transgender (LGBT), as it acknowledges the varying manifestations of sexuality.
4 Joseph Massad (2007) *Desiring Arabs* (Chicago, IL: University of Chicago Press).

5. Dai Vaughan (1999) *For Documentary: Twelve Essays (Berkeley, CA:* University of California Press), pp. 84–5.
6. Prior to the French Mandate, various parts of Lebanon were ruled by the Ottoman Empire for 400 years. In 1858, the Empire sought bureaucratic modernisation and decriminalised homosexuality.
7. Official Facebook page for Helem: https://www.facebook.com/Official-Page-for-Helem-Lebanon-133916233311662/.
8. Helem registered a legal precedent at the Court of Appeals in 2011: kudos to the judge who legally interpreted the infamous legal category of 'natural sexual relations' beyond heteronormative monogamous sexual practices to include any 'consensual sexual acts between adults'. However, this precedent was not upheld by the Lebanese police force, as it has carried out several group arrests including the 36 detainees since then. Lebanese Medical Association for Sexual Health (n.d.) 'Order of Physicians Response/Ban on Anal Probes'. Available at https://lebmash.wordpress.com/2014/07/07/الشرجية-الفحوصات/ (accessed 25 April 2016).
9. One of Helem's contributions includes introducing neutral, Arabic queer-related terminologies such as *mithliyin/at* (gay and lesbian), *mutahawilin/at* (transsexuals) and *mutahayirin/at* (intersex) into public discourse. As discussed above, these terms gradually replaced the common pejorative term of *luti*, which derives from the Abrahamic religions' curse of Lot's people for practising sodomy. On media outlets, war and apology: LBCI (2012) 'News Bulletin', 31 July. Available at www.youtube.com/watch?v=iOqMhTfutjY (accessed 25 April 2016).
10. Michael Chanan (2008) *'Filming "the Invisible", in* Thomas Austin and Wilma de Jong (eds) *Rethinking Documentary: New Perspectives, New Practices* (Maidenhead: McGraw-Hill/Open University Press), p. 125.
11. Sveinung Sandberg (2012) 'Cannabis Culture: A Stable Subculture in a Changing World', *Criminology and Criminal Justice* 13(1): 63–79.
12. Sandberg, 'Cannabis Culture', p. 6.
13. Chanan, *'Filming "the Invisible"', p.* 126.
14. Brian Massumi (2002) *Parables for the Virtual: Movement, Affect, Sensation* (Durham, NC: Duke University Press), p. 30.
15. Brian Massumi (1987) 'Notes on the Translation and Acknowledgements', in Gilles Deleuze and Félix Guattari, *A Thousand Plateaus* (Minneapolis, MN: University of Minnesota Press), p. xvi.
16. John Corner (2008) *'Documentary Studies: Dimensions of Transition and Continuity', in* Thomas Austin and Wilma de Jong (eds) *Rethinking Documentary: New Perspectives, New Practices* (Maidenhead: McGraw-Hill/Open University Press), p. 22. See for example, Michael Renov (ed.) (1993) *Theorizing Documentary* (New York: Routledge); (2004) *The Subject of Documentary* (Minneapolis, MN: University of Minnesota Press).
17. Sara Ahmed (2010) *The Promise of Happiness* (Durham, NC: Duke University Press), pp. 29, 30.
18. Corner, 'Documentary Studies', p. 22.

19 *Khasson* is a colloquial expression referring to people who are into non-heteronormative sexuality without identifying with queerness.
20 Massad, *Desiring Arabs*.
21 With few exceptions such as Sofian Merabet (2014) *Queer Beirut* (Austin, TX: University of Texas Press).
22 By 'classical subculture views', Sandberg refers to the Centre for Contemporary Cultural Studies (CCCS) at the University of Birmingham, led by Stuart Hall, Phil Cohen and Paul Willis.
23 Mathew Gagné and Adriana Qubaia (2013) 'The Delusions of Representing Male Homosexuality in Beirut' *Jadaliyya*, 30 December. Available at www.jadaliyya.com/pages/index/15807/the-delusions-of-representing-male-homosexuality-i (accessed 13 July 2014).
24 John Grierson (1966) 'The First Principles of Documentary', in *Grierson on Documentary*, ed. Forsyth Hardy (London: Faber & Faber), p. 147.
25 Kaminsky, in Gunthar Hartwig (2001) 'New Media Documentary: Explorations of the Changing Form, Theory and Practice and Documentary', 12 December. Available at www.gunthar.com/gatech/digital_documentary/Database_Documentary.pdf (accessed 25 April 2016).
26 Chanan, *'Filming "the Invisible"'*, p. 125.
27 John Corner (2008) *'Documentary Studies: Dimensions of Transition and Continuity'*, in Austin and de Jong, *Rethinking Documentary*, p. 22.
28 Ibid.
29 Ibid.
30 Silke Panse (2008) 'Collective Subjectivity in the Children of Golzow vs. Alienation in "Western" Interview Documentary', in Austin and de Jong, *Rethinking Documentary*.
31 Erik Knudsen (2008) *'Transcendental Realism in Documentary'*, *in* Austin and de Jong *Rethinking Documentary*.
32 Ibid.
33 António Damasio (1994) *Descartes' Error: Emotion, Reason and the Human Brain* (New York: Putnam Publishing), pp. 204–22.
34 Ahmed, *The Promise of Happiness*, pp. 29, 30.
35 Sandberg, 'Cannabis Culture'.

Bibliography

Ahmed, Sara (2010) *The Promise of Happiness* (Durham, NC: Duke University Press).
Chanan, Michael (2008) 'Filming "the Invisible"', in Thomas Austin and Wilma de Jong (eds) *Rethinking Documentary: New Perspectives, New Practices* (Maidenhead: McGraw-Hill/Open University Press).
Corner, John (2008) 'Documentary Studies: Dimensions of Transition and Continuity', in Thomas Austin and Wilma de Jong (eds) *Rethinking

Documentary: New Perspectives, New Practices (Maidenhead: McGraw-Hill/Open University Press).

Damasio, António (1994) *Descartes' Error: Emotion, Reason and the Human Brain* (New York: Putnam Publishing).

Gagné, Mathew and Qubaia, Adriana (2013) 'The Delusions of Representing Male Homosexuality in Beirut' *Jadaliyya*, 30 December. Available at www.jadaliyya.com/pages/index/15807/the-delusions-of-representing-male-homosexuality-i (accessed 13 July 2014).

Grierson, John (1966) 'The First Principles of Documentary', in *Grierson on Documentary*, ed. Forsyth Hardy (London: Faber & Faber).

Hartwig, Gunthar (2001) 'New Media Documentary: Explorations of the Changing Form, Theory and Practice and Documentary', 12 December. Available at www.gunthar.com/gatech/digital_documentary/Database_Documentary.pdf (accessed 25 April 2016).

Knudsen, Erik (2008) 'Transcendental Realism in Documentary', in Thomas Austin and Wilma de Jong (eds) *Rethinking Documentary: New Perspectives, New Practices* (Maidenhead: McGraw-Hill/Open University Press).

Lebanese Medical Association for Sexual Health (n.d.) 'Order of Physicians Response/Ban on Anal Probes'. Available at https://lebmash.wordpress.com/2014/07/07/الفحوصات-الشرجية/ (accessed 25 April 2016).LBCI (2012) 'News Bulletin', 31 July. Available at www.youtube.com/watch?v=iOqMhTfutjY (accessed 25 April 2016).

Massad, Joseph (2007) *Desiring Arabs* (Chicago, IL: University of Chicago Press).

Massumi, Brian (1987) 'Notes on the Translation and Acknowledgements', in Gilles Deleuze and Félix Guattari, *A Thousand Plateaus* (Minneapolis, MN: University of Minnesota Press).

_____ (2002) *Parables for the Virtual: Movement, Affect, Sensation* (Durham, NC: Duke University Press).

Merabet, Sofian (2014) *Queer Beirut* (Austin, TX: University of Texas Press).

Murr TV News (2012) 'Daara wa shuthuth fi al-sinama' ['Prostitution and Perversion in Cinemas'], 28 July. Available at http://mtv.com.lb/News/108657 (accessed 15 July 2014).

Panse, Silke (2008) 'Collective Subjectivity in the Children of Golzow vs. Alienation in "Western" Interview Documentary', in Thomas Austin and Wilma de Jong (eds) *Rethinking Documentary: New Perspectives, New Practices* (Maidenhead: McGraw-Hill/Open University Press).

Renov, Michael (ed.) (1993) *Theorizing Documentary* (New York: Routledge).

_____ (2004) *The Subject of Documentary* (Minneapolis, MN: University of Minnesota Press).

Sandberg, Sveinung (2012) 'Cannabis Culture: A Stable Subculture in a Changing World', *Criminology and Criminal Justice* 13(1): 63–79.

Stewart, Colin (2014) 'Report: Lebanon Targets Gay Men in 3 Raids, 45 Arrests', *Erasing 76 Crimes*, 15 August. Available at http://76crimes.com/2014/08/15/report-lebanon-targets-gay-men-in-3-raids-45-arrests/ (accessed ????).

Vaughan, Dai (1999) *For Documentary: Twelve Essays*. (Berkeley, CA: University of California Press).

9

Web-based Identity Discourse from the Maghreb

The Case of *Mithly.net*, 2010–11

Justin McGuinness

What opportunities does the web offer for communitarian organisation and minority group expression in countries such as Morocco, now emerging from authoritarian rule? What, in particular, do web platforms have to offer to young people in south-shore Mediterranean states, as they explore new forms of identity that are made available thanks to digital and portable communications technologies? This article analyses a particular form of digital discourse: that of a website created in 2010 for an imagined public of Moroccan gay people (mainly Arabic readers), but also partly francophone. Like many a community magazine or fan publication, the site, *Mithly.net*, was short-lived, running for just six issues in its first incarnation in 2010 and 2011. The second, more sophisticated version of the site, ran for a further handful of issues before disappearing in 2012. Today, to the best of my knowledge, there is no trace of *Mithly.net* on the web, and no major active site addressing the interests of Moroccans whose interests lie in same-sex relationships.

A starting point for our discussion of *Mithly.net* could be a moment in Daoud Aoulad Syad's 2010 film *A Jamaâ* (*The Mosque*), which is set in a remote Moroccan community. The *muqaddim* (local headman) says to one of the villagers: 'We know what you are thinking, even before you thought it.'

In a phrase, Aoulad Syad sums up the nature of the relationship between the rulers (*Makhzen*) and the ruled (*shaâb*), at the beginning of the twenty-first century. This is – or was – a relationship based on a mixture of fear, worry and mutual mistrust. However, this is a relationship that seems set to change, notably given the nature of the Arab uprisings of early 2011. As numerous commentators and academics have written, mobile digital devices played a major role in developing anti-authoritarian discourse and action in the Arab states. In Morocco, the desire for freedom of expression, civil liberties and responsible, open government found expression in the Mouvement du 20 Février 2011 (M20) and later in related collectives such as Mamfakinch (2012) and Free Koulchi (2013). Partly in reaction to M20's demands, the Moroccan leadership produced a new constitution and held elections which led to a government headed by the religiously-minded right-wing. Nevertheless, although much of Morocco's population has a broadly conservative mindset, the country is now open to varied political and identitarian discourses that are just a click away in the global souk of mediated communication. In terms of intimate relationships, the focus of the website analysed in the present chapter, Morocco might be said to be entering a period of 'sexual transition' – to use a term that has been foregrounded by the sociologist Abdessamad Dialmy (2014).[1]

The website discussed in this chapter was founded prior to the constitutional changes of 2011. Despite its brief existence, *Mithly.net* can be seen as being emblematic of a longer-term shift in modes of everyday life in Morocco. For the first time, here was a medium transmitting the attitudes and demands of a gender minority which, until then, had almost no positive presence in the Moroccan public sphere – except perhaps for the odd *fait divers* or feature article in a francophone weekly.

My aim in this piece is to trace the contours of an emergent Moroccan discourse both for, and partly by, people who prefer intimate relations with others of the same gender. How do the creators and contributors to *Mithly.net* situate themselves with respect to the Moroccan nation state? How do they see themselves in relation to communitarian expressions of gay identity, and the question of the global discourse of minority rights? How does *Mithly.net* use the opportunities offered by digital technology? Is it possible to see the emergence of a new form of gay communitarianism emerging in Morocco thanks to Web 2.0 and, in particular, thanks to sites such as *Mithly.net*? The interest of this chapter lies in its exploration of an area where different ways of envisaging living together both meet and criticise each other. This chapter also aims to make a small contribution to the debate on individual freedoms at a time when they are being demanded as never before in both Morocco and across the Arab and Arabo-Amazigh states. For the first time perhaps, both in the great coastal cities and in the settlements of the interior, the *muqaddim* is no longer fully aware of what exactly it is that the individual is thinking.

The theoretical frame: global and local

The present analysis of a specific website targeting a public of younger Moroccans is to be situated in the wider framework of studies on the development of communitarian – and more specifically, the creation and use of digital – media by gay people across the global South. The analysis questions the diffusion of North America and parts of Western Europe to societies in the global South, where religious references frame social life. Underpinning this chapter is something of a militant logic. The situation of people whose cultural and sexual intimacy is oriented towards people of the same sex is difficult in many parts of the world. For example, note the legislation in force in many Commonwealth countries, and the systematic persecution that gay people face in countries such as Cameroon, Uganda and Iran.[2] With respect to that diverse entity 'the Arab world', the heavily homophobic trials which followed the arrest of young men in the Queenboat nightclub in Cairo[3] in 2000 remains, for the moment, an Egyptian exception.[4]

Reference to this appalling case allows me to link to one particular academic debate around issues of gender identities and their circulation that was raised by the Columbia University academic Joseph Massad, in his 2007 book *Desiring Arabs*. With reference to the events surrounding the *Queenboat* trials, Massad argues that 'The Gay International and its activities are largely responsible for the intensity of this repressive campaign'.[5] At the time of publication, *Desiring Arabs* raised a lot of discussion due to such lines. However, simplifying heavily for reasons of space, Massad had produced an effective critique of how Western sexual categories (hetero and homo) had gone global, with often unfortunate consequences. Nonetheless, Massad was more than just unhappy with this globalised dual taxonomy. More interestingly, he was arguing that, in any case, thinking of sexuality as a category is borne of a particular regime in a particular sociocultural context. Subsequently, the hetero/homo binary was imposed by the politics of imperialism and the capitalist mode of production. In this context, North Atlantic homophobia (among other attitudes to sexuality) was exported across the world in the nineteenth century. In the 1990s, still *pace* Massad, a new global solidarity ('the Gay International'), led by people in the West who thought they knew best, tried to reverse the situation – notably through the work of independent organisations. Despite the scope of his intellectual history of certain desires, Massad has taken flack from gay people, both of Arab and other backgrounds, and from non-governmental organisation members who see themselves as being unjustly portrayed as imperialist agents of the West. Obviously his position is far more complex, although it does not leave much room for a liberatory politics of sexual identity, as per the quote relative to the Queenboat affair. (However, note that there has been much research on same-sex relationships in the global South outside the Arab countries, as will be discussed later in this chapter.)

In Morocco, university research into sexuality first began to reach a broad readership in the late 1990s, as the regime began to 'unfreeze' at the end of King Hassan II's reign. In 1997, the sociologist Soumaya Naâmane Guessous published her *Au-delà de toute pudeur: La sexualité féminine au Maroc*,[6] based on a survey of women in Casablanca. It was the first publication of its kind, and so popular that it went to a tenth reprint. In the same year, Abdessamad Dialmy's report for the Ford Foundation, *Jeunesse, SIDA et Islam au Maroc: Les comportements sexuels*,[7] was released. In pre-internet days it could only reach a restricted audience, but its content was still picked up by the press, which was then beginning to talk more freely on sexual matters. Completing a trio of Moroccan academic work on sexuality from the late 1990s is El Harras' 1998 study, *Facteurs socio-culturels affectant les comportements en matière de démographie*,[8] which was researched under the aegis of UNESCO and Fonds des Nations Unies pour la Population (FNUAP). Same-sex relations were essentially outside the scope of these reports. Nevertheless, some five years later, a workshop held in Malta, with participants drawn from non-governmental organisations in most of the Middle Eastern and North African (MENA) region countries, raised the question of sexual orientation: notably, what strategies might be developed to promote civil rights in this area. Projects underway in Lebanon, Tunisia and Turkey were mentioned. However, deep-rooted prejudices – that women working on sexuality are promoting lesbianism, or that any talk of sexuality is akin to blasphemy – were seen as being significant obstacles, wrote Liz Amado in a report on the meeting.⁹ Such prejudices are still present today.

Without wishing to argue for some inevitable extension of Massad's hetero/homo binary, there are other discursive sites where an evolution in intimate practices is being portrayed. In Morocco, as elsewhere, literature and film (and of course, the internet), have moved in to provide representations where researchers have left off. The novels of francograph authors such as Mehdi Binebine and Mohamed Nedali contain characters whose sexual needs and desires are portrayed in a frank and realistic way.[10] The same repositioning is true of film, in works such as *Sur la planche* (dir. Leïla Kilani, 2012) and *L'amante du Rif* (dir. Narjiss Nejjar, 2011), to name but two. Such works show the flipside of an inegalitarian system which, in the words of Makhlouf-Obermeyer, works through 'restricting women's autonomy and privileging male satisfaction'.[11] In the artistic representations of society that appeared in the 2000s, sexual and other individual freedoms are neither condemned as a Western import, nor are they shown as being particularly immoral. Often they show, to return to Makhlouf-Obermeyer's words, that there is 'a keen awareness among women of the connections between sexual exchange and power relationships'.[12]

This chapter represents a small contribution to the academic work on youth, identity choices and personal intimacy in the Maghreb, opening a window onto the 'sexual transition' and the new identity politics of the individual, now much discussed in Morocco's media. The chapter does not argue about how something called 'sexuality' operates within a general sphere, like 'Islam'. Rather, it looks at the workings of specific discourse on sexuality that are produced by activists, journalists and other writers for what was, in 2010–11, the relatively new medium of the internet.

The appearance of *Mithly.net*: names and content

How and when did *Mithly* first appear? Put online in 2010, the magazine was quickly dubbed 'the first gay site in the Arab world' by foreign francophone media. Initially, it seemed to be a continuation of a blog run by the Moroccan gay association KifKif (approximate translation: 'All the same', http://kifkifweb.blogspot.com), which ceased publication in March 2009. Optimistic articles hailed the new site. Its founder, Samir Bargachi, was widely interviewed.[13] The name of the site, *Mithly*, was carefully explained: the term *mithly* signifies 'like me' in Arabic, and was coined to avoid usage of the highly pejorative terms existing in that language's formal and informal registers to denote 'homosexual', the terms 'gay' and 'queer' having no widespread currency (this root term gives *mithliya* for 'homosexuality'.) Initially designed as the digital version of a print magazine, *Mithly* quickly gained a certain visibility. Every two or three months in 2010 and 2011, new issues appeared on the web. With the exception of the generalist weekly *Tel Quel*, known for the quality of its socio-economic reporting and political commentary, the Moroccan press ignored the new publication.[14] The only coverage was brief and slightly sensationalist, recounting the negative reactions of the Islamist Right, always ready to reinforce its moral capital with a conservative electorate. In March 2011, after six issues, *Mithly* abandoned the original A4 printer-friendly format and adopted a dynamic, purely web-based style, including links to Facebook. In summer 2011, the first six issues were removed from the online archive. The new format *Mithly* was not to last for long, disappearing from the web in 2012. The last issue featured an interview with celebrity Red One (Nadir Khayat), the producer of singer Lady Gaga, among others. At the time of writing, the magazine seems to have completely disappeared from cyberspace: typing in *mithly.net*, the surfer is directed to a page in a Far Eastern script.

This chapter examines the first six hybrid-format issues of *Mithly*. The original home page was composed of a banner headline and a chequer board of rectangles, each containing the title of a news piece accompanied by its first phrase. At the top of the page was a vignette featuring the cover of the printable version of the magazine, usually a strong image, with the word *mithly* and the titles of the main articles. Access to content was achieved by clicking on a title. Articles were generally short, rarely more than three or four paragraphs. In the first two issues, content was solely in Arabic; subsequently, there was a mix of material in Arabic and French, with the majority of articles in the former language. There were few images. Content in Arabic took the form of editorials, short essays written in reaction to current events and interviews with singers and writers. Content in French consisted of short pieces taken from francophone gay media, with sources generally attributed. Broadly speaking, the editors were writing for a youth audience concerned with the problems facing an emerging gay community. Given that *Mithly* was published every two months and clearly operating with a tiny team and small budget, there was no up-to-the-minute news coverage.

Even when the magazine adopted a fully web-based format, updates were few and untimely.

Mithly.net in the Moroccan context

Before moving to the content of *Mithly.net*, it is important to situate our analysis further with respect to the extensive body of work on the emergence of gay audiences outside the Anglo-European and Western European contexts, as well as to provide some background on the Moroccan context. *Mithly* is the product of a specific culture, shaped by Islam and proximity to Europe and the Middle East. This culture, rooted in the Amazigh and Arab linguistic areas, was reshaped through colonialism, the spread of capitalism and the formation of the Moroccan nation state. At the end of the twentieth century, Morocco emerged from a long period of authoritarian rule. The so-called 'Arab Spring' of 2011 has accelerated the process of administrative and political reforms, notably by the adoption of a new constitution in July 2011; however, the sociopolitical context remains highly conservative.[15] The monarch and politicians regularly make use of religious references in their pronouncements, an element which makes the analysis of a digital medium such as *Mithly.net* particularly interesting. Another contextual factor which makes the study of a counter-hegemonic medium such as *Mithly* important, is the populist turn taken by a number of Moroccan newspapers since the mid-2000s. Although the topic of same-sex intimate relations may be covered in a fairly balanced way by certain media – the special *dossiers* in the news magazine *Tel Quel* are one example – the tone of most other news outlets is frankly homophobic.[16]

Same-sex relations between two people are a criminal offence in Morocco, punishable by up to three months in prison, under Article 489 of the Penal Code. In practice this article is very rarely applied, and those who prefer homosexual relations – to use a term with a somewhat medical ring – are rarely bothered by the authorities. That said, when charges are brought by the police, as happened in spring 2013, the case is exploited to make 'good' media copy.[17] The weight of tradition is strong, expressed in Moroccan dialect by the terms *hchouma* (shame)[18] and *chouha* (scandal), words which condemn any form of behaviour that breaks away from good manners and established tradition. With respect to sexual relations between men, these are feasible as long as scandal is avoided. Experimentation and long-term relations are possible, as long as those involved ensure that shame is not brought on their families and immediate circle. Apart from a small number of individuals born in the *bourgeoisie éclairée* and the much trumpeted case of francograph author Abdellah Taïa,[19] 'coming out' is far from being the norm in Morocco. Of course, thanks to satellite media, large segments of the population are highly aware that other modes of family life and cultural intimacy function elsewhere. In major centres such as Casablanca, Rabat and even Marrakech –cities sufficiently large for anonymity to be possible – an urban gay life exists, articulated around cafes, parks, nightclubs, sports centres and hammams, as well as the homes of friends and global virtual spaces such as Gaydar, Manjam and GayRomeo. In the provinces, these spaces provide a welcome outlet for gay people unable to make it to 'Casa-Rabat' or Marrakech for an occasional weekend. In all areas of the country, individuals devote time to creating avatars on several sites, surfing the web, according to their means either in cybercafes (preferably not in one's neighbourhood) or at home. This was particularity noted by the authors of a 2006 enquiry into the social changes brought about by the web in Morocco:

> Homosexuals, largely marginalized in Morocco, create new social links for themselves via on-line discussions. The Net has given them the opportunity to express themselves and affirm their existence under the cover of anonymity.[20]

For some gay people, dreaming of 'elsewhere' provides romantic focus:[21] a meeting with a foreigner can be the determining factor in moving into life as part of a couple. For others, a period of gay freedom in youth or early adulthood is quickly followed by heterosexual marriage and settling down into the everyday life of a hetero-normed society. Until the arrival of *Mithly* in 2010, no group in Morocco had publicly expressed a desire to see positive changes in the status of homosexuals and lesbians (or rather of *mithliyine* and *mithliyat*, to use the terms preferred by the site).

It could be argued that the spread of both portable, easy-to-use digital devices in the mid-2000s and the arrival of Web 2.0 enabled the creation of *Mithly*, and hence the beginning of a new, more public, gay youth culture. However, these technologies were not without their disadvantages for gay people and other outsider groups (as will be seen below). Around 2005, the Moroccan media, and in particular the press, became bolder in publishing all sorts of scandals. Almost everything seemed publishable, provided that three invisible but very real red lines were not crossed: criticism of the Islamic religion, the person of the king and 'the kingdom's territorial integrity'.[22] From the mid-2000s, both the gutter press and certain serious news outlets treated stories with a homosexual component as scandals. Two examples will suffice: the case of a party in the northern city of Tétouan in summer 2004, dubbed a 'gay wedding' by the press,[23] and the case of a student at the Dhar Mehrez campus of the University of Fès, who was 'accused of homosexuality' by a self-styled court of law set up by radical Islamist students. However, these pieces tend to be quickly swallowed up in the sheer mass of stories dealing with celebrities, politicians, private catastrophe, public corruption and vice. Note too that the television, which remains under strict state control, and private FM radio stations rarely discuss sexual scandals openly. When a private radio station goes beyond the unspoken limits in this area, it is quickly called to order by Haute Autorité de la Communication Audiovisuelle (HACA, established in 2002), the public body responsible for overseeing the content of radio and TV programming.

In 2007, a storm broke around another supposed 'gay marriage': this time in Ksar el Kébir, a sleepy town in the north-western Gharb region. On 18 November, friends had gathered for what turned out to be a boozy evening of the sort that takes place regularly across Morocco. The only unusual feature of the evening was that a number of the male guests were dressed up as women. In short, this was a private party attended by friends – gay, queeny, straight-acting and straight – to use an Anglo-classification. Unfortunately, one guest, who filmed at the party with his mobile phone, had the bad idea of posting the video on YouTube. In certain sequences, effeminate young men having a laugh and playing up to the cameraphone, along with guests drinking alcohol, are clearly visible. Magnified, as it were, by digital technology, given excessive attention by the media, these unexpected images allowed a latent homophobia to express itself all too vehemently in real public space. A demonstration was held against the 'immoral' men who had sullied the name of Ksar el Kébir. Liberal-minded journalists were to debate the degree to which the local branch of the Parti de la Justice et du Développement was involved in rousing righteous public opinion and transforming the demonstration into a man-hunt.

The Ksar el Kébir affair and that of the so-called gay weddings at Sidi Ali, studied by sociologists Florence Bergeaud-Blackler and Victor Eck,[24] were transformed into national scandals thanks to the power of Web 2.0 and the mastery of digital media. Both in legal and personal terms, the consequences of Ksar el Kébir were harsh for a number of guests. Legal action was taken against eight partygoers for 'acts against the Law' (but not for committing 'an indecent act or an act against nature with an individual of the same sex' under the terms of Article 498 of the Moroccan Penal Code.[25] At the time of writing (summer 2013), certain extracts from the unfortunate video were still visible on Moroccan news outlets, often followed by threads of aggressive and homophobic comment. At the time of the incident, representatives of a major Moroccan human rights organisation, the Association Marocaine des Droits de l'Homme (AMDH), travelled to Ksar el Kébir to show solidarity with the victims. Four years after the event in 2010, the web magazine analysed in this chapter was created to promote the civic rights of those who were not yet called *mithliyine* and *mithliyat*.

This brief contextualisation also requires a word on the people behind the creation of *Mithly* and those writing for it. Samir Bargachi, an openly gay Moroccan in his early twenties at the time of the site's launch, was the key actor. Resident in Spain, Bargachi was a founder member of the KifKif collective, established to defend and promote the interests of lesbian, gay, bisexual and transgender (LGBT) individuals in Morocco. The people writing for *Mithly*, both men and women, were Moroccan and worked from Morocco. Some prefer to write under pseudonyms or anonymously, while others publish under their real names. Unlike Bargachi, none of the magazine's collaborators working in Morocco were 'out'. These individuals, courageous in their open tackling of sensitive questions of gender identity and civic rights, did not appear on Moroccan TV, for example, to talk about the magazine and *mithly* culture. For the first six issues, the civil rights aspect of *Mithly*'s discourse remained confined to virtual space. (A very small number of printed copies of the first issue was distributed in Casa-Rabat.)

Development of individual access to the internet in Morocco

With *Mithly*'s position regarding same-sex intimate relations in Morocco now established, it is time to move to a second contextualisation, situating the magazine in respect to the expansion of web access in Morocco. The impact of digital technologies has featured in numerous articles and talk shows in both the Arabic and French-language media. By the mid-2000s, practically every urban neighbourhood had a cybercafe. For the relatively small sum of 5 to 10 dirhams an hour (approximately 35p to 75p in English money), depending on the area and the nature of the services, one could surf the web. The '*cybers*', as they were called, sometimes tacked onto an existing *téléboutique* (phone shop), tended to be housed in converted ground-floor shops or apartments. They quickly became a social phenomenon. In the close proximity created by the cramped premises, the clients – mainly adolescents and young adults – communicated with friends, family and unknowns across the country and the world. However, in mid-2010 the situation changed, as cheap secondhand portable computers came on to the market, and the main telecom companies (Maroc Télécom, Méditel, Inwi) launched pay-as-you-go WiFi services, accessed via own-brand USB devices (monthly cost 200 dirhams, little more than £14). The new system was extremely successful, as henceforth one could surf from home or a cafe without needing to take out a costly telecom subscription or handle the constraints of the *cyber* (who is looking over my shoulder at my screen?). Gradually, the *cybers* changed to other services, generally videogames for children and adolescent boys. Given the intimacy offered by the new WiFi service, the time was right for the launch of an online magazine such as *Mithly*.

Research into the expansion of gay discourse in the South

The last four decades of the twentieth century saw radical change in social practices, styles of belonging and notably in what Foucault calls 'technologies of the self'.[26] Essentially, with the expansion of individualist consumer society and the rise of mass-media, intimate desires and practices were reframed. New identity forms that were articulated around sexuality emerged, often focused around emergent feminist and LGBT movements. The body became politicised as the locus of personal choice (the right to manage one's fertility, for example). New forms of activism developed, creating new identity positions which gained considerable visibility wherever socio-economic change was widespread. Of course, there is a considerable academic literature on these phenomena including, for example, a large body of work on the emergence of the gay and lesbian movements in the historically central countries of the English-speaking world. By way of a theoretical anchor for the present chapter, a 1998 article by Bluthenthal[27] provides a useful definition of a social movement, described as one which represents rational attempts by excluded groups to mobilise enough political influence to advance collective interests by non-institutional means. Without making any value judgements, the central question could be: how far does *Mithly.net* represent just such an attempt at group mobilisation?

With respect to the emergence of LGBT movements, places and practices outside Protestant North America and Europe, academic studies reach publication from the mid-1990s onwards. Nardi explored the Italian case in 1998,[28] providing a concise overview of the expansion of global gay discourse and taking a theorisation of social movements as a base. In 2002, Brown traced the rise of the gay and lesbian movement in Argentina,[29] describing its organisation and stressing how a grasp of its identity politics allows for a proper understanding of its strategies. For South and East Asia, the collective volume, *Mobile Cultures: New Media in Queer Asia*, constituted a key advance.[30] Focusing on Indonesia, Tom Boellstorff's work is central: his 2004 article[31] on zines – a form of identitarian micro-publishing for like-minded groups of friends and individuals – was influential in the research for this chapter, in that it analyses the interface between a technology, communication practices and the discourse of a stigmatised minority in the global South. A collective volume exploring the circulation of different forms of gay linguistic expression across the world was also important.[32] Following Boellstorff, the present author rejects the idea that the 'global gay discourse' necessarily brings salvation for isolated communities in its wake. As Vidal remarks, following authors such as Lila Abu-Lughod[33] and Saba Mahmood,[34] the discourse of individual emancipation, born in heavily industrialsed societies,

> can lead us to perceive as 'illusionary' or 'backward', the expressions of an alienated and dominated form of life, [which] can also actually be a resource on which the agency of those concerned and targeted by this disqualification can draw.[35]

Thus, our analysis of a fragment of gay discourse, produced on the periphery of global gay culture, will attempt to follow the contours of a local sensitivity and consider its nuances closely. Following McLelland in his 2000 study on homosexuality in Japan,[36] there is no question of considering that the homosexuals (or rather, the *mithliyine* and *mithliyat* of Morocco), should obligatorily follow the highly consumerist gay identitarian model of the global North. Although it is highly probable that this model will continue to expand across the planet through the diffusion of certain cultural forms, tourism and migration, both chosen and forced and the likely development of global citizenship, the extension of gay discourse and practice necessarily will produce hybrid types of meaning-making and social life.

Analysing an emergent identity discourse: terms and linguistic context

Underpinning the *Mithly* project – as the very name of the site indicates – is a will to establish a new identity profile for people who choose sexual and affectionate practices that are stigmatised by Moroccan society. Thanks to the site, *mithliyine* and *mithliyat* will be worthy of consideration as members of a new social category. The term *mithly*, as indicated earlier, denotes likeness and exemplarity. The site does not use the global term 'gay' in articles in Arabic. The term 'lesbian' does not figure either, with writers preferring to use *mithliya* (intimate relations and partnerships between women are rarely discussed on the site).

Nonetheless, the terminology used in the Arabic articles takes up certain tropes and metaphors that are common to the global discourse of gay and lesbian awakening. The expression 'coming out of the closet' is used, for example. The people interviewed by *Mithly* – emerging figures on the North African cultural scene, such as the writer Abdellah Taïa and the Tunisian filmmaker Mehdi Attia, as well as those interviewed in articles taken from other publications, reveal that they realised their sexual difference at an early age. These figures are seen as developing a more acute sense of self thanks to an individual life project. Unlike the Indonesian gay publications analysed by Boelstorff,[37] *Mithly* has little content that is directly contributed by readers.

Nevertheless, the global term 'gay' is known to many Moroccans who spend time surfing international gay meeting sites. (In Moroccan dialect the term *gay*, as used by young adults, seems generally to denote an effeminate man or the passive partner in a sexual relationship between men. It does not have positive connotations.) The use of the term *mithly* by contributors can be seen as a small attempt to get the formal Arabic neologism accepted – and used – in the different discursive registers that are present in Moroccan society. These writers are also attempting to gain recognition for other concepts that are central to equal rights and the recognition of gay people by using terms for homophobia, for example, in standard Arabic. In *Mithly*'s third issue, the editorial writer Karim Samti expresses the site's position with respect to terminology: 'We think that all the terms used [in Arabic at the present time] to denote this 'relationship' or 'behaviour form' have not been able to reduce their sexual or defamatory charge.'[38] Later in the same article, Samti writes:

> The fact that Arab intellectuals have not been able to examine 'the *mithliya* question' has led necessarily to the spread and consecration of terms which do not express the deeper meaning of the phenomenon and are filled with embarrassment, bitterness and linguistic violence.[39]

Samti concludes his analysis of the terms available in Arabic to designate the homosexual person by calling on all those concerned with *mithliya* 'to try and develop a term which will be more faithful and expressive'[40] than the negatively connoted words that are used currently. This discussion of terminology recalls the debates in academia and civil society in France in the 1960s and 1970s, when terms such as *homophile* – preferred by the Arcadie movement – gave way to the global word 'gay'. However, in the 1990s in the French-speaking world, the term 'queer' was to spread in university circles and among members of certain voluntary organisations without gaining common currency.

Thus, the writers of *Mithly.net* situated themselves at the heart of a debate about politically correct language which goes back to the 1960s. The linguistic situation in Morocco has been the topic of numerous articles: for example, recent work by Catherine Miller, among others.[41] Right from the beginning, *Mithly* essentially opted to publish content in modern standard Arabic: an editorial decision that fitted perfectly with the project of speaking to as large an audience as possible in an attempt to change attitudes to same-sex relations. The hope, no doubt, was that accepting attitudes would take hold gradually. However, *Mithly* also published content in French. The fourth issue (August 2010) had four articles out of 11 in French, while the fifth issue (February 2011) contained five, with several taken directly from global francophone gay media, including the gay leisure magazine *Têtu* and the site *yagg.com*.[42] Issue six saw a return to content solely in Arabic.

By using modern written Arabic, *Mithly* is positioning itself on the symbolic territory of the Moroccan nation state. Note that Moroccans of the country's wealthy elite – a tiny minority with enormous influence in the country – often have difficulties in reading the standard Arabic of the media as a result of secondary education in the private sector that is principally delivered in French. However, political discourse runs chiefly in Arabic, and it may well be for this reason that the site's creators opted for Arabic as its main language. The editorial team also chose to keep away from the treacherous terrain of publishing in a form of Moroccan dialect, *darija*, which a handful of journalists and political activists would like to see transformed into a national language with a standardised written form.[43] The most read newspapers in Morocco – *Al-Massae, Al-Ahdath Al-Maghribiya, Akhbar al-Yawm* and *Al-Sabah* – are in ordinary modern Arabic. With the growth in the number of satellite channels broadcasting in Arabic, and in particular with the huge mass of news linked to the Arab uprisings from January 2011, this language is once more a vehicle for political discussion. It is in standard Arabic that crucial debates regarding the future of the whole region are taking place.[44]

Debates and demands

Moving on from questions of terminology and language, we now turn to content by examining the nature and tone of the debates on *Mithly.net*. The site essentially functioned as a space where the injustices of which *mithliyine* and *mithliyat* could be discussed, and their sociolegal roots debated. The site's activist stance was based on a critique of instances of oppression, stressing the need for resistance to stereotypes. Examples of such resistance from elsewhere in the world were presented in brief news pieces. As noted previously, current Moroccan legislation criminalises sexual relationships between persons of the same sex according to Article 489 of the Penal Code. The need to abolish this article was raised several times in *Mithly*, alongside other questions regarding civil rights that notably includedy the position taken by the Mouvement Autonome pour les Libertés Individuelles (MALI) in 2010 with respect to the freedom to fast or not during Ramadan.

Issue 3 of *Mithly* featured a short piece on a petition that was circulating via Facebook that called for the abolition of Article 489.[45] A link was provided to the petition, mentioning that it called specifically for 'the inclusion of the rights of *mithliyine* and *mithliyat* to express their sexual orientation freely'; there was no demand for this right to be constitutionalised. The article considered that Article 489 is used not only to criminalise *mithliya*, but also to 'encourage the public expression of hatred towards *mithlyine* and *mithliyat*'. The petition's objective was to collect thousands of signatures which the organisers could then forward 'to all those in public office to push them to abrogate Article 489'.[46] Unfortunately, the petition was never mentioned in subsequent issues of *Mithly*, so it seems unlikely that it ever reached the desks and computer screens of Morocco's politicians and senior civil servants.

To move to the activities of the MALI collective, a piece entitled 'Clause 222', by Mohamed Sassi, raises the question of an article in the Penal Code which specifies the penalties facing 'all those who are known to embrace the Islamic religion' if they break the fast in daylight hours during Ramadan.[47] Without going into the details of the argument, Sassi notes that this clause contradicts international human rights conventions, adding that if one has the right to practise a religion, logically one also should have the right not to practise it. To give more weight to his argument, Sassi adds Qur'anic references to underscore the fact that individuals must be able to choose their religion:

> For us as Muslims, the right to choose a religion and to make known this choice may be built on significant pillars in our sublime Sharia, that is to say 'there is no obligation in terms of religion' and 'We have given [capacities] to the sons of Adam'. It can thus be seen that Islam is on the side of freedom and human rights as a general principle.[48]

As a result, according to Sassi, the young people of the MALI collective were not acting against the main principles of Islam when they broke their fast with an afternoon picnic in the woods near Mohammedia. After all, their objective was not to provoke the pious majority of the Moroccan people, but:

> to raise the awareness of people [*al-jumhur*, literally, 'the masses'] on the need for a calm debate between fasters and non-fasters so that the serious implications of forbidding non-fasters from practising their natural right to not fast openly during Ramadhan might be studied, taking as a basis Article 8 of the International Convention on Human Rights.[49]

In putting forward this question for debate so clearly, Sassi can be seen to be suggesting that parallels should be drawn with respect to the treatment of other minorities in Morocco, whose beliefs and practices are situated outside the general religious consensus.

Representing difference

Thus as a collective actor, *Mithly* seeks to reshape the vision held by Moroccan society – and its official instances – of a certain social category. How is resistance to the dominant discourse articulated in this medium? How, at both individual and collective levels, can gay difference be expressed in a largely homophobic context? What repertoire of cultural symbols do *Mithly*'s collaborators draw on to give positive value to the identity positions advanced by the site? As in any gay medium, there are various sorts of content: editorials, personal essays, interviews with figures important to gay culture, which construct meanings around what it means to grow up, live and identify oneself as *mithly* in contemporary Morocco.

In the editorials and personal essays, the authors reflect with critical distance on being *mithly*. The very first issue in April 2010 contained a number of pieces which can be taken as representative: an editorial by Samir Bargachi, entitled 'Useless prattle', an essay entitled '*Al-Mithliya*, natural or not?' and a piece by Karim Ziyad entitled 'Coming out'. Note that *Mithly.net* was lucky to be launched at a point in time when there was a polemical debate in the Moroccan media marked by much homophobia. As will be seen, this debate gave writers the opportunity to leap straight into a current public issue.

One might have expected that the first editorial of April 2010 would be used to review the situation of gay people in Morocco, perhaps accompanied by an analysis of the legal changes that the magazine felt to be desirable. Instead, it was devoted to a detailed analysis of the protests by leading Islamist politician Abdellah Baha against a concert to be given by Elton John during the June 2010 Mawazine Festival in Rabat. Baha, the Secretary-General of the Parti de la Justice et du Développement (religious-minded conservative Right), had made some extremely homophobic remarks to the weekly paper *Aujourd'hui le Maroc*.[50]

Bargachi adopts an ironic tone to refute Baha's argument, suggesting that perhaps it would be a good idea to stop Christian singers and musicians from participating in festivals because there would be a risk of Moroccans being Christianised. Bargachi stressed that Elton John must be appreciated for his qualities as a great musician, adding by way of conclusion that according to Baha:

> It is as though Morocco's youth lived a form of emotional homosexuality and were just waiting for someone to push them to

practise it. This accusation is dangerous, polemical, political and nasty, a form of stupid demagogy [...] and in any case, aren't Morocco's youth already aware of Elton John thanks to internet and audio-cassettes? These little politicians are very strange![51]

In this first issue, resistance to the current order of things is expressed in an article entitled 'Al-Mithliya, natural or not?'[52] written by an author who takes as a pseudonym 'Ghulam (servant, page) of Abu Nuwas', in reference to the great Arab poet of the Abbasid period, known for his verses celebrating wine, music and the beauty of young men and women. This article focuses on the hypocrisies surrounding the term 'natural' and criticises the exclusionary practices in the chic nightclubs of Beirut, access to these places being limited on the basis of wealth rather than sexual orientation, and this selection by wealth being considered entirely normal. Ghulam Abu Nuwas suggests that 'when normality takes first place on the agenda of the *mithliya* movement, something is clearly wrong'.[53] In the final analysis, the essence of the article is that the importance given to the need to belong to a supposed natural order is repressive, even though it is not put exactly this way. Citing the Moroccan fable 'The Crow who tried to walk like a Peacock', the author concludes by stressing the dangers of trying too hard to fit in with heterosexual norms (the crow broke its neck).

A similarly critical, but more militant, tone can be seen when an author has a dialogue with religious discourses on *mithliya*. In February 2011, his article 'I'm *mithly* [...] and I'm Syrian', Sami Hamaoui[54] takes as a starting point the idea that Syria is representative of all the Arab countries, given that the Syrian mosaic is *muta'adid al-atraf*, containing samples of all the different social elements that are present in the other states in one way or another. (Remember that this was written before the Syrian uprising.) Syrian society is saturated by the religious gaze: that is to say, a gaze that forbids and criminalises *mithliya*. While the religious authorities, both Christian and Muslim, agree that it is 'against nature', members of the various secular-minded groups, nationalists, communists and atheists are just as ready to instrumentalise the concept of *haram* (forbidden) to counter and condemn any way of thinking which goes against their positions. Hamaoui considers that there is a collective Arab spirit that is deeply religious, and that 'the arm of religion' is used 'in attempts to repress any issue'.[55]

What, then, is the situation of the *mithliyine* and other elements who are ready to challenge the system? According to Hamaoui, in a country such as Syria, 'it is impossible to eliminate religion as one of the factors [underpinning] the fear and lack of stability felt by Arab *mithliyine*'.[56] It is also futile to launch a full-on attack against religion:

> Whatever the geographic space we belong to may be, whatever the period, we human beings need a credo and a model to follow, on which we may call, whether it be divine or imagined by an individual.[57]

Hamaoui's pragmatic position concerning how *mithliyine* should operate in societies structured essentially by monotheistic religion can be taken as representative of the line that was proposed by *Mithly* in its first issues. The demythologisation of the world is not for now. As Nietzsche argued in *Le Gai savoir*, we must know that society is dreaming – and will continue to dream.[58]

Despite its problematic character, resistance to dominant social models is expressed in other articles telling of the *mithly* experience, of what it is to grow up with socially unacceptable feelings in a patriarchal society. The following five articles are representative of this type of discourse: 'Coming out' by Karim Ziyad,[59] 'I am *mithly* and I exist' (Anonymous),[60] 'My wedding, my tears and my smile' by Zayra,[61] 'The smell of men' by Ayman,[62] and 'Love in the world of the forbidden', again by an anonymous author.[63]

The article 'Coming out' is written in the register of psychological advice. Like a close friend, Ziyad dispenses advice to those growing up with feelings of emotional attraction to people of the same sex 'in a society like ours'. He reveals that he does not yet feel ready to reveal his nature completely. Whether he likes this situation or not, he will remain an individual, adding:

> [W]hatever my attempts may be to rebel against some of these ideas and beliefs which I consider wrong, touching as they do on my personal dignity and freedom, I do not wish to throw myself into a war which I would lose. Nevertheless, this does not mean that I am going to surrender to oppression and hypocrisy.[64]

Ziyad wishes to resist as he reflects and sorts out his ideas, all the better to defend them, provided that they do not harm the freedom of others. This personal reflection will be the second part of a 'coming out'. In this process, he tells the readers that his blog (*mudawanna*) has been extremely useful.

Elsewhere in the personal essays, the authors recount initiatory moments (time spent with the local barber in 'The smell of men', or the difficult acceptance of one's desires in 'I am *mithly* and I exist'. In this latter article, the anonymous author describes an interior struggle between the emotions of love and desire, 'in a context in which all those who have feelings like this are designated by a range of defamatory terms like *zwamil* or *mukhanathine* or *mbanetine* [girly] or *qawada* [snitches]'. For this anonymous writer, society does not understand him, leaving him – at least for part of his life – with a single option: self-repression. In this piece, as in several others, the author reflects on the nature of the religious referent:

> [Moroccan society] lives mentally in the Palaeolithic Age and materially in the twenty-first century. This is a society which forbids individuals to engage with all that development and comfort naturally offer them in terms of a better future, sometimes in the name of religion – and religion is as innocent of oppressing an individual in his existence and freedom as the wolf was of the blood of Joseph.[65]

The author concludes that it is the human race that corrupts and interprets religion in a given place and time – in its own interests, of course.

The religious referent comes up in other articles and is used to argue against the oppression of *mithliyine*. For example, it would be impossible for God to have created a being so that it might experience such suffering.[66] As we have already seen in the article on Article 489, Mohamed Sassi underlines how Islam is tolerant in its very essence, citing two *hadith* (sayings or teachings of the Prophet Muhammad) in support of this position. This writer adopts the well-honed argument that Islam is a religion that freed humankind.

Mithly's identitarian discourse is also elaborated in a third way, through a series of interviews with individuals from the world of culture and showbusiness who are important in Morocco and, to a lesser degree, the Maghreb.[67] The singer Hakim made the cover of issue 3, while other celebrities featured include the singer Halim Corto, issue 5), the writer Abdellah Taïa (issue 6) and the Tunisian film director Mehdi Ben Attia (issue 6). The second issue included an interview with El Rubio, an old friend of the distinguished Tangiers author Mohamed Choukri. There is no question in these interviews that anyone is making stand-up confessions of their sexual preferences – except in the case of Corto, the Franco-Moroccan singer, resident in France and interviewed on the subject of his song 'Juste par amour', written in homage to Mahmoud Asgari and Ayaz Marhoni, two young men executed by hanging in Iran in summer 2005. They were sentenced on the basis of accusations that were related to their sexual preferences. On this question, Corto remarks: 'I target Iran in my song, but I keep in mind too all the taboos present in our housing estates, even here in France, the suicide rates among young men who discover their different sexuality.'[68]

How do the celebrities interviewed actually consider the nature of gay life in Morocco – or the Maghreb, for that matter? Although the sample is vanishingly small – five interviews – it does seem representative of attitudes to the public expression of homosexuality. On the one hand, there are the singer Hakim and the writer Taïa, both figures with a certain public profile. Resident in Spain, Hakim was decorated by King Mohamed VI during the monarch's visit to that country. He remarks to the journalist, Mourad Haddad: 'My sexual orientation is a private affair and I am very relaxed on this question.'[69] Taïa, interviewed by Omar Brouksy for Agence France Presse, explains that: 'For me homosexuality is not a cause but an individual freedom. Evidently, my status as a writer with major [French] publishing houses protects me.'[70] From what sort of dangers, Taïa does not say. Essentially, both these figures live and work in the European Union, benefiting from the freedoms that it offers, even though Taïa, in particular, returns frequently to Morocco.

Both Taïa talking about Morocco, and Ben Attia discussing the Tunisian case – prior to the January 2011 revolution – indicate that there have been significant gains in the last decade in terms of individual freedoms. For Taïa, 'there have been [...] extraordinary things in terms of the proclamation of individual freedoms by a number of elements in Moroccan society, supported by the independent press',[71] while in Tunisia, 'there are pockets of tolerance in the artistic and cultural spaces in a number of cities'.[72] However, an openly gay Maghrebi youth culture is not about to emerge, it seems.

Another nuance can be seen in the article about the writer Mohamed Choukri, as well as in the interview with Ben Attia, although to a lesser degree in the latter case. Choukri represents the archetype of the creative homosexual, living on the bohemian edges of society, doubly marginal because of his poor origins and sexuality. Like Taïa at the beginning of the

2000s, Choukri initially gained some recognition of his artistic worth thanks to the assistance of foreigners. Unlike Taïa, he was never absorbed by the cultural establishment, keeping certain *zones d'ombre* in his life. El Rubio, Choukri's old friend, notes in regard to the writer's private life: 'There are things which we cannot talk about publicly in Morocco.'[73] This phrase is echoed by Ben Attia, who intelligently remarks that: 'To a certain extent, we are told "do what you like but don't disturb us." It is not really forbidden to be involved in homosexual practices. It is forbidden to say one is homo.'[74] Thus, in the final analysis, not one of the celebrities considers themselves able to come out and take a public position with respect to the status of *mithliyine* and *mithliyat* before the law.

Conclusion
Digital spaces and minority cultures

Here and there in the texts published by *Mithly*, individuals stress the importance of the internet as the place where they are able to gain access to global gay culture. By way of example, Ziyad refers to his blog which 'opened a vast field to me [...] by this *mudawwana* I was able to build links with people all across the world and I have been able to look at many different *mithly* experiences'.[75] The very magazine itself, *Mithly*, would have been impossible without the internet, although numerous opposition newssheets circulated in Morocco during the 1960s and 1970s, often at a very high personal cost to their producers and readers. Thanks to digital dissemination from a distance, risk is transformed and, in many cases, lessened.

At an aesthetic level – layout, choice of colours and images – *Mithly* was transformed after its sixth issue. The original concept, a *samizdat*-type news bulletin which also had a website, was outdated. In summer 2011, it gave way to a well-produced site with rotating images and a tickertape banner. Access to content was improved with new search options. However, in terms of quantity, the number of articles actually written by Moroccan contributors remained limited, and material continued to be imported from global gay websites. The new *Mithly* continued with something of a do-it-yourself ethos, only to disappear completely at some point in 2012.

To return to our focus, in the six issues of 2010 and 2011, it might have been expected that a clearer position would be taken with respect to local issues. Some writers did try to reverse or transform commonly held definitions and suppositions – their comment pieces on labelling and the possibility of a valid gay life are two examples. However, broadly speaking, *Mithly* remains conventional, both in visual terms (there is nothing to shock, no experimental aesthetic) and on the linguistic level. The most used language is the standard Arabic of the education system and media. A more radical medium might have opted to publish pieces in *darija* (Moroccan dialect). However, this strategy would have had the disadvantage of making content inaccessible to readers from outside Morocco. Thus, although exploring a globalised sexual identity, the review situates itself on the symbolic terrain of the Moroccan nation state, the guarantor of the country's linguistic purity. Was it the case that *Mithly*'s founders considered that the use of dialect to express the site's objectives would have been harmful to the collective identity of an emerging gay movement? Whatever the case may be, the mixture of languages, images and identity positions gives the magazine a hybrid character.

As we have already noted, *Mithly* must be taken in its sociocultural context. In one of the first editorials (issue 2, June 2010), Bargachi remarks that there are people who consider the very existence of a medium through which 'we can express our concerns and demand our legal rights as being a menace for society's values'.[76] He mentions the comments made by one Omar Ben Hammad, Vice-President of the Islamo-Conservative Mouvement pour l'Unicité et la Réforme (MUR), at the time of the magazine's launch:

> When the *shuwwadh* [perverts] transmit their ideas to individuals via the propaganda of a magazine, it is either a practical joke or something very serious. At this point, the competent authorities must show themselves responsible and isolate the active cells – as they have already done in the case of dormant terrorist cells [...] all those who touch Moroccans' values also touch their land and their security.[77]

Mithly was first produced in a highly conservative social context where numerous public figures, both political and politico-religious, were all too ready to make capital by defending the eternal values of the nation state. It is clear that although the magazine may be a vehicle for meaning in one way for a gay or open-minded reader, it will be read and discussed very differently by other audiences. The attempt to construct an affirmative social presence can be seen as the beginning of a long and difficult struggle. For the moment, the clichés (and not just about outgroups, such as the *mithliyine*) which support much of Moroccan official discourse, rooted in a pietist, neo-liberal vision of the world, are created and maintained at the political centre. However, counter-discourses are emerging thanks to digital technologies. As a specific symbolic environment, allowing for the expression of a new vision of individuals and their rights, *Mithly.net* will not be able to transform structures of belonging and feeling alone. Its discourse is pragmatic, recognising both the shifting and the constant elements of the Moroccan context, suggesting that a certain form of do-it-yourself identity is the best way forward. The site's contributors implicitly recognise that the restricted quality of the media is such that populist narratives will continue to run for many more years – as Edward Said described so well in *Islam in the Media*.[78] However, the fact that a digital space such as *Mithly* was able to exist, for individuals to say who they are and what they think without shame or aggressiveness, despite the rise of the moralists in public life, is already a considerable achievement.

This analysis of the digital magazine *Mithly.net* is by no means exhaustive. Shifting to a broader frame, the emerging counter-hegemonic and youth discourses in Maghrebi digital media are under-studied for the moment, in particular given the dynamic nature of the sociopolitical context. Since the early 1990s, Morocco's mediascape has gone from being dominated by national TV stations, heavy with protocol news and interminable Egyptian soap operas, to pan-Arab broadcasting featuring scantily clad Lebanese starlets alongside religious figures with thick facial hair and bigoted opinions; romantic Turkish mega-series, contemporary love stories and panoramas of a glorious Ottoman past compete for audience attention, while a micro-series such as *In bed with Le Couple* can win huge popularity for its ironic vision of the Moroccan home. The internet, controlled in Morocco only for internal security reasons, provides an unprecedented level of access to discourses and data. Of the local broadcast media, only the radio has really opened up in terms of discussion of sexuality.[79] In this context, questions of the relationship between media, gender and sexual identities will continue to evolve. Doubtless, new paths through which to share and enjoy intimacy will emerge, in part because reproductive objectives no longer may be paramount. At the end of the

2000s, despite the arrival of *Mithly.net*, it was certainly premature to write of a social movement focused on the creation of a new form of sexual citizenship.

The situation will surely evolve, perhaps more rapidly than might be expected. With respect to research, long-term ethnographic work is called for to better understand individual and group trajectories, as people mobilise and make choices to shape their futures. With the continued spread of individual digital devices, communication will be characterised by a multitude of micro-identitarian projects. Where this leaves marginal communitarian initiatives, such as *Mithly.net*, is unclear. Work in the field will be the best way to grasp shifting discourses and practices, as they form and dissolve in the incessant digital flow.

Notes

1. Ayla Mrabet and Jules Cretois (2014) 'Moeurs: La transition sexuelle', *Tel Quel*, 28 February, pp. 26–33.
2. See the website of the Fédération Internationale des Droits de l'Homme: www.fidh.org; also Adrian Tippets (2010) 'The Most Dangerous Place on the Planet', *Winq* (Spring), p. 30.
3. Hassam Bahgat (2001) 'Explaining Egypt's Targeting of Gays' in *Middle East Research and Information Project* (MERIP), 23 July. Available at www.merip.org/mero/mero072301 (accessed May 2011).
4. In Morocco, the 2007 Ksar el Kébir affair, which saw a handful of men branded as 'perverts' following a same-sex drinking party, will be discussed later in this piece. Although on a much smaller scale, it too led to legal proceedings being taken against individuals due to their lifestyle choice.
5. Joseph Massad (2007) *Desiring Arabs* (Chicago, IL: Chicago University Press), p. 184. Extracts from this work, considered by its critics as more of a polemic than an intellectual history, now feature in various gender and regional studies courses in American universities.
6. Soumaya Guessous (1997) *Au-delà de toute pudeur: La sexualité féminine au Maroc* (Casablanca: EDDIF).
7. Abdessamad Dialmy (1997) *Jeunesse, SIDA et Islam au Maroc: Les comportements sexuels*. Report to the Ford Foundation (Casablanca: Ford Foundation).
8. Mohktar El Harras (1998) *Facteurs socio-culturels affectant les comportements en matière de démographie*. Rapport préliminaire (Paris: Projet International UNESCO/FNUAP).
9. Liz Ercevik-Amado (2003) 'Sexual and Bodily Rights as Human Rights in the Middle East and North Africa: A Conference Report', *Reproductive Health Matters* 12(23): 125–8.

10 Mahi Binebine (2010) *Les étoiles de Sidi Moumen* (Paris: Flammarion); Mohamed Nedali (2003) *Morceaux de choix* (Casablanca: Le Fennec)
11 Carla Makhlouf-Obermeyer (2000) 'Sexuality in Morocco: Changing Context and Contested Domain', *Culture, Health and Sexuality* 2(3): 239–54, p. 239.
12 Ibid.
13 Mehdi Sekkouri Alaoui (2009) '"La situation des homosexuels s'est améliorée"'. Interview with Samir Bergachi', *Tel Quel*, 7 March, pp. 28–9; Ziraoui, Youssef (2010) '"Les homos ne vivent plus dans la peur"'. Interview with Samir Bargachi, fondateur du site gay Mithly', *Tel Quel*, 10 July, pp. 6–7.
14 Aïcha Akalay (2010) 'Gay Proud', *Tel Quel*, 24 April, pp. 58–9.
15 Emblematic of the conservative mindset of the Moroccan establishment was the 'Satanic Rock' affair of early 2003. Journalists, bigoted politicians, the police and the judiciary came together, not fully by any grand design, to have a handful of guitar-playing teenagers locked up on very weak charges. The press portrayed the young heavy metal adepts as 'satanists'. Parents and their supporters demonstrated, and the charges were eventually dropped. See articles by Driss Ksikes (2003) 'L'inquisition près de chez vous', *Tel Quel*, 1 March, pp.15–16, and 'Notre 11 Septembre culturel', *Tel Quel*, 15 March, pp. 24–37.
16 Arab Press Network (2008) '"Maroc, les médias de la haine pourraient déstabiliser le pays". Entretien avec Saïd Essoulami', 20 February. Available at http://arabpressnetwork.org/articlesv2.php.?id=1915&lang=fr (accessed 10 November 2011).
17 The *Temara* case. While sitting in a parked car in the Atlantic coast town of Temara, two young men were arrested by the police, and Article 489 was invoked in the charges brought against them.
18 The notion of *hchouma* was notably analysed by the anthropologist Lilia Labidi. Lilia Labidi (1989) *Sabra, hachma* (Tunis: Cérès Editions).
19 Abdellah Taïa is a Moroccan writer and filmmaker. In 2006 he became the first openly gay Arab writer. His novels have been translated into many languages.
20 Kawtar Bencheikh and Hicham Houdaïfa (2006) 'Génération cybercafes: Comment Internet a changé la société marocaine', *Le Journal hebdomadaire*, 4 April, pp. 20–7.
21 Exotic elsewheres are a central theme in the 'autobiographical fictional' work of the Paris-based Marrakchi writer Rachid O., notably (1996) *Plusieurs vies* (Paris: Gallimard) and (1998) *Chocolat chaud* (Paris: Gallimard).
22 Read: government policy regarding the integration of the provinces of the Far South, brought back into Morocco from Spanish colonial rule in 1976 and 1979.
23 Taïeb Jamaï (2004) 'Courrier des lecteurs: la OLA de Tétouan' *Aujourd'hui le Maroc*, 18 June. Available at www.aujourdhui.ma/actualite-details16101.html (accessed 1 November 2011).
24 Florence Bergeaud-Blackler and Victor Eck (2011) 'Les "faux" mariages homosexuels de Sidi Ali au Maroc: enjeux d'un scandale médiatique', *Revue des mondes*

musulmans et de la Méditerranée, 16 July. Available at http://remmm.revues.org/index7180.html (accessed 16 November 2011).

25 Omar Dahbi (2007) 'Ksar el Kébir: arrestation de 8 personnes dans l'affaire du prétendu mariage homosexuel', 28 November. Available at www.yabiladi.com/article-societe-2213.html (accessed 1 October 2011).

26 The notion of 'technologies of the self' was presented by Foucault at a seminar at the University of Vermont in autumn 1982.

27 Ricky Bluthenthal (1998) 'Syringe Exchange as a Social Movement: A Case Study of Harm Reduction in Oakland, California', *Substance Use and Misuse* 33: 1147–71.

28 Peter M. Nardi (1998) 'The Globalization of the Gay and Lesbian Socio-political Movement: Some Observations about Europe with a Focus on Italy', *Sociological Perspectives* 41(3): 567–86.

29 Stephen Brown (2010) 'Con discriminación y represión no hay democracia: The Lesbian Gay Movement in Argentina', in Javier Corrales and Mario Pecheny (eds) *The Politics of Sexuality in Latin America: A Reader of Lesbian, Gay, Bisexual and Transgender Rights* (Pittsburgh, PA: University of Pittsburgh).

30 Chris Berry, Martin Fran and Audrey Yue (eds) (2003) *Mobile Cultures: New Media in Queer Asia* (Durham, NC: Duke University Press).

31 Tom Boellstorff (2004) 'Zines and Zones of Desire: Mass-mediated Love, National Romance and Sexual Citizenship in Gay Indonesia', *Journal of Asian Studies* 63(4): 340–67.

32 Tom Boellstorff and William L. Leap (2003) *Speaking in Queer Tongues: Globalization and Gay Language* (Urbana, IL: University of Illinois Press). In this book, the article by Denis M. Provencher, 'Vague English Creole: (Gay English) Cooperative Discourse in the French Gay Press', pp. 23–45, is of particular interest.

33 Lila Abu-Lughod (2000) *Sentiments voilés*, trans. Didier Gille (Paris: Edition des Empêcheurs de Penser en Rond).

34 Saba Mahmood (2009) *Politique de la piété: Le féminisme à l'épreuve du renouveau islamique*, trans. Nadia Marzouki (Paris: Editions de la Découverte).

35 Jérôme Vidal (2011) 'Agency and Empowerment', *Revue des Livres* 1: 62–3.

36 Mark McLelland (2000) 'Is There a Japanese "Gay Identity"?', *Culture, Health and Society* 2(4): 459–72.

37 Boelstorff, 'Zines and Zones of Desire', pp. 340–67.

38 Karim Samti (2010) '*Khiyanat al-mustalah*' ['The Betrayal of a Customary Term'], *Mithly* 3, July. All translations of Arabic quotations are by the author who has tried to keep the flavour of the original without resorting to literal translation.

39 Ibid.

40 Ibid.

41 Catherine Miller (2011) 'Usage de la *darija* dans la presse marocaine, 2009–2010', in *L'Année marocaine* (Rabat: Centre Jacques Berque).

42 The site *yagg.com* was set up as an online generalist gay medium by a former *Têtu* journalist.
43 The media group Presse Directe S.A., owner of the popular news magazine *Tel Quel*, launched a sister weekly news magazine, *Nichane*, with content in both Moroccan dialect and modern formal Arabic. The magazine was short-lived, largely because it failed to attract sufficient advertising revenue to cover costs.
44 The sample of texts studied here pre-dates the Arab uprisings. Since spring 2011, new sites expressing political demands have appeared, including *24mamfakinch.com*, *talkmorocco.com* and *lakome.com*. Some of these sites have been short-lived. Whether they are blogs, chat, news sites or videos, a variety of languages are used, determined by the social class, training and place of residence of the main contributors.
45 Anonymous (2010) 'Aridha maghribiya li-ilgha al-madda 489' ['A Moroccan Petition for the Abrogation of Article 489'], *Mithly* 3, July.
46 Ibid.
47 Mohamed Sassi (2010) '*Al-fasl 222*' ['Clause 222'], *Mithly* 3, July.
48 Ibid.
49 Ibid.
50 Samir Bargachi (2010) '*Baqbaqa fi zaqzaqa*' ['Useless Prattle'], *Mithly* 1, April.
51 Ibid.
52 Ghulam Abou Nawas (2010) '*Al-Mithliya, amrun tabi'i am la*' ['Homosexuality, Natural or Not?'], *Mithly* 1, April.
53 Ibid.
54 Sami Hamaoui (2011) '*Ana mithly … ana souri*' ['I Am *mithly* and I Am Syrian'], *Mithly* 6, February.
55 Ibid.
56 Ibid.
57 Ibid.
58 Friedrich Nietzsche (2007[1882]) *Le Gai savoir*, trans. Patrick Wotling (Paris: Flammarion)
59 Karim Ziyad (2010) 'Coming Out', *Mithly* 1, April.
60 Anonymous (2010) '*Ana mithly wa ana mawjud*' ['I Am *mithly* and I Exist'], *Mithly* 3, July.
61 Zayra (2010) 'Mon mariage, mes larmes et mon sourire', *Mithly* 4, August.
62 Ayman (2010) '*Rihat al-rijal*' ['The Smell of Men'], *Mithly* 3, July.
63 Anonymous (2010) '*Al-hubb fi alam al-haram*' ['Love in the World of the Forbidden'], *Mithly* 5, September.
64 Ziyad, 'Coming Out'.
65 Anonymous, '*Ana mithly wa ana mawjud*'.
66 Ibid.
67 Note that only one interview, with a Moroccan star, was written specifically for *Mithly*, the remainder being drawn from French gay media or Agence France Presse.

68 Julien Choquet (2011) 'Halim Corto', *Mithly* 5, January. (Article first published in *Têtu*.)
69 Mourad Haddad (2010) '*Dardasha maa al-fannan al-maghribi Hakim*' ['A Chat with the Moroccan Singer Hakim'], *Mithly* 3, July.
70 Omar Brouksy (2011) 'Abdellah Taïa, un écrivain marocain qui 'assume' son homosexualité', *Mithly*, 6, February. (Article first released by Agence France Presse.)
71 Ibid.
72 Sébastien Letard (2011) 'En Tunisie le vrai interdit c'est de se dire homo, pas d'avoir des pratiques homo', *Mithly* 6, February. (Article first published in *Têtu*.)
73 Anonymous (2010) 'Mohamed', *Mithly* 2, June.
74 Letard, 'En Tunisie le vrai interdit'.
75 Ziyad, 'Coming out'.
76 Samir Bargachi (2010) 'Editorial', *Mithly* 2, June.
77 Ibid.
78 Edward Said (2011) *L'Islam dans les médias: Comment les médias et les experts façonnent notre regard sur le reste du monde*, trans. Charlotte Woillez (Paris: Sindbad).
79 On air since 2011, Hit Radio's interactive evening programme, *On t'écoute*, is popular for its frankness, with a certain Doc Samad answering listeners' questions. However, there are limits to the sort of intimate practices which can be openly discussed.

Bibliography

Abu-Lughod, Lila (2000) *Sentiments voilés*, trans. Didier Gille (Paris: Edition des Empêcheurs de Penser en Rond).
Akalay, Aïcha (2010) 'Gay Proud', *Tel Quel*, 24 April, p. 58.
Al-Ghazali, Karim (2010) '*Al-sadma, al-hurriyat wal-fardiya*' ['The Clash, Freedoms and Individualism'], *Mithly* 3, July.
Allali, Reda (2003) 'L'enfer du décor', *Tel Quel*, 22 March, p. 22.
_____ (2010) 'Zakaria Boualem risque-t-il de se retrouver homosexualisé s'il assiste au concert d'Elton John', *Tel Quel*, 17 April, p. 90.
Anonymous (2010) '*Al-hubb fi alam al-haram*' ['Love in the World of the Forbidden'], *Mithly* 5, September.
Anonymous (2010) '*Ana mithly idhn ana mawjud*' ['I Am *mithly* and So I Am Present'], *Mithly* 3, July.
Anonymous (2010) '*Aridha maghribiya l-ilgha al-madda 489*' ['A Moroccan Petition to Abrogate Article 489'], *Mithly* 3, July.
Anonymous (2010) 'Mohamed', *Mithly* 2, June.
Anonymous (2010) '*Musharaka maghribiya bil-ala'ab al-ulimbiya al-mithliya*' ['Moroccan Participation in the Gay Games'], *Mithly* 4, August.
Anonymous (2011) '*Nass thawri*' ['Revolutionary Text'], *Mithly* 6, February.

Arab Press Network (2008) ' "Maroc, les médias de la haine pourraient déstabiliser le pays". Entretien avec Saïd Essoulami', 20 February. Available at http://arabpressnetwork.org/articlesv2.php.?id=1915&lang=fr (accessed 10 November 2011).

Ayman (2010) *'Rihat al-rijal'* ['The Smell of Men'], *Mithly* 3, July.

Bahgat, Hassam (2001) 'Explaining Egypt's Targeting of Gays' in *Middle East Research and Information Project* (MERIP), 23 July. Available at www.merip.org/mero/mero072301 (accessed May 2011).

Bargachi, Samir (2010) *'Baqbaqa fi zaqzaqa'* ['Chatting and Cheeping'], Mithly 1, April.

_____ (2010) 'Editorial', *Mithly* 2, June.

Bencheikh, Kawtar and Houdaïfa, Hicham (2006) 'Génération Cybercafes: Comment Internet a changé la société marocaine', *Le Journal hebdomadaire*, 4 April, p. 20.

Bergeaud-Blackler, Florence and Eck, Victor (2011) 'Les "faux" mariages homosexuels de Sidi Ali au Maroc: enjeux d'un scandale médiatique', *Revue des mondes musulmans et de la Méditerranée*, 16 July. Available at http://remmm.revues.org/index7180.html (accessed 16 November 2011).

Bernichi, Loubna (2006) 'Les homos débarquent', *Maroc Hebdo International*, 17 June, p. 34.

Berry, Chris, Fran, Martin and Yue, Audrey (eds) (2003) *Mobile Cultures: New Media in Queer Asia* (Durham, NC: Duke University Press).

Binebine, Mahi (2010) *Les étoiles de Sidi Moumen* (Paris: Flammarion).

Bluthenthal, Ricky (1998) 'Syringe Exchange as a Social Movement: A Case Study of Harm Reduction in Oakland, California', *Substance Use and Misuse* 33: 1147–71.

Boellstorff, Tom (2004) 'Zines and Zones of Desire: Mass-mediated Love, National Romance and Sexual Citizenship in Gay Indonesia', *Journal of Asian Studies* 63(4): 340–67.

Boellstorff, Tom and Leap, William L. (2003) *Speaking in Queer Tongues: Globalization and Gay Language* (Urbana, IL: University of Illinois Press).

Brouksy, Omar (2011) 'Abdellah Taïa, un écrivain marocain qui 'assume' son homosexualité', *Mithly* 3, February.

Brown, Stephen (2002) *Gender, Sexuality and Same Sex Desire in Latin America* (Thousand Oaks, CA: Sage Publications), pp.119–38.

_____ (2010) 'Con discriminación y represión no hay democracia: The Lesbian Gay Movement in Argentina', in Javier Corrales and Mario Pecheny (eds) *The Politics of Sexuality in Latin America: A Reader of Lesbian, Gay, Bisexual and Transgender Rights* (Pittsburgh, PA: University of Pittsburgh).

Choquet, Julien (2011) 'Halim Corto', *Mithly* 3, January.

Dahbi, Omar (2007) 'Ksar el Kébir: arrestation de 8 personnes dans l'affaire du prétendu mariage homosexuel', 28 November. Available at www.yabiladi.com/article-societe-2213.html (accessed 1 October 2011).

Dialmy, Abdessamad (1997) *Jeunesse, SIDA et Islam au Maroc: Les comportements sexuels*. Report to the Ford Foundation (Casablanca: Ford Foundation).

_____ (1998) 'Moroccan Youth, Sex and Islam', *Middle East Report* 28(1): 16–17.

El Harras, Mohktar (1998) *Facteurs socio-culturels affectant les comportements en matière de démographie*. Rapport préliminaire (Paris: Projet International UNESCO/FNUAP).

Ercevik-Amado, Liz (2003) 'Sexual and Bodily Rights as Human Rights in the Middle East and North Africa: A Conference Report', *Reproductive Health Matters* 12(23): 125–8.

Ghulam Abu Nawas (2010) '*Al mithliya, amrun tabi'I am la*' ['Homosexuality, a Natural Thing or Not?'], *Mithly* 1, April.

Guessous, Soumaya (1997) *Au-delà de toute pudeur: La sexualité féminine au Maroc*. (Casablanca: EDDIF).

Haddad, Mourad (2010) '*Dardasha m'a al-fannan al maghribi Hakim*' ['A Chat with the Moroccan Singer Hakim'], *Mithly* 3, July.

Hamaoui, Sami (2011) '*Ana mithly ... ana suri*' ['I Am *mithly* ... I Am Syrian'], *Mithly* 3, February.

Houdaïfa, Hicham (2006) 'Coupable d'homosexualité', *Le Journal hebdomadaire*, 1 June, p. 34.

Jamaï, Taïeb (2004) 'Courrier des lecteurs: la OLA de Tétouan' *Aujourd'hui le Maroc*, 18 June. Available at www.aujourdhui.ma/actualite-details16101.html (accessed 1 November 2011).

Ksikes, Driss (2003) 'L'inquisition près de chez vous', *Tel Quel*, 1 March, p. 15.

―――― (2003) 'Notre 11 Septembre culturel', *Tel Quel*, 15 March, p. 24.

Labidi, Lilia (1989) *Sabra, hachma* (Tunis: Cérès Editions).

Laby, Nady (2007) 'Kingdom in the Closet', *The Atlantic*, May. Available at www. theatlanticonline.com/doc/print/200705/gay-saudi-arabia (accessed May 2010).

Laurent, Erick (2011) *Les chrysanthèmes roses: Homosexualités masculines dans le Japon contemporain* (Paris: Les Belles Lettres).

Letard, Sébastien (2011) 'En Tunisie le vrai interdit c'est de se dire homo, pas d'avoir des pratiques homo', *Mithly* 6, February.

McLelland, Mark (2000) 'Is there a Japanese 'Gay Identity?', *Culture, Health and Society* 2(4): 459–72.

Mahmood, Saba (2009) *Politique de la piété: Le féminisme à l'épreuve du renouveau islamique*, trans. Nadia Marzouki (Paris: Editions de la Découverte).

Makhlouf-Obermeyer, Carla (2000) 'Sexuality in Morocco: Changing Context and Contested Domain', *Culture, Health and Sexuality* 2(3): 239–54.

Martel, Frédéric (1968) *Le Rose et le noir: Les homosexuels en France depuis 1968* (Paris: Seuil).

Massad, Joseph (2007) *Desiring Arabs* (Chicago, IL: Chicago University Press).

Miller, Catherine (2011) 'Usage de la *darija* dans la presse marocaine, 2009–2010', in *L'Année marocaine* (Rabat: Centre Jacques Berqu).

Mrabet, Ayla and Cretois, Jules (2014) 'Moeurs: La transition sexuelle', *Tel Quel*, 28 February, p. 26.

Mrabet, Ayla, Layachi, Fatym and Oulmouddane, Hicham (2010) 'Scandales "Made in Morocco" sur Internet', *Tel Quel*, 1 May, p. 44.

Nardi, Peter M. (1998) 'The Globalization of the Gay and Lesbian Socio-political Movement: Some Observations about Europe with a Focus on Italy', *Sociological Perspectives* 41(3): 567–86.

Nedali, Mohamed (2003) *Morceaux de choix, les amours d'un apprenti boucher* (Casablanca: Le Fennec).

Nietzsche, Friedrich (2007[1882]) *Le Gai savoir*, trans. Patrick Wotling (Paris: Flammarion).

O., Rachid (1996) *Plusieurs vies* (Paris: Gallimard).

_____ (1998) *Chocolat chaud* (Paris: Gallimard).

Ouahbi, Jamal (2005) '*Kharitat al-choudh al-jinsi fil Maghrib kama tuhadiduha mawaqî iliktrouniya*' ['The Map of Homosexual Perversion in Morocco as Defined by the Electronic Sites'], *Al-Sahifa al-maghribiya*, 23 December, p. 30.

Proth, Bruno (2002) *Lieux de drague: Scènes et coulisses d'une sexualité masculine* (Toulouse: Octarès).

Provencher, Denis M. (2003) 'Vague English Creole: (Gay English) Cooperative Discourse in the French Gay Press' in Tom Boellstorff and William L. Leap (eds) *Speaking in Queer Tongues: Globalization and Gay Language* (Urbana, IL: University of Illinois Press).

Said, Edward (2011) *L'Islam dans les médias: Comment les médias et les experts façonnent notre regard sur le reste du monde*, trans. Charlotte Woillez (Paris: Sindbad).

Samti, Karim (2010) '*Khiyanat al-mustalah*' ['The Betrayal of Custom'], *Mithly* 3, July.

Sassi, Mohamed (2010) '*Al-fasl 222*' ['Clause 222'], *Mithly* 3, July.

Sekkouri Alaoui, Mehdi (2009) '"La situation des homosexuels s'est améliorée"'. Interview with Samir Bergachi', *Tel Quel*, 7 March, p. 2.

Shahani, Parmesh (2008) *Gay Bombay: Globalization, Love and (Be)longing in Contemporary India* (New Delhi: Sage Publications).

Slimani, Leila (2011) 'Radios marocaines: libre antenne' *Mithly* 6, February.

Taïa, Abdellah (2009) 'L'homosexualité expliquée à ma mère', *Tel Quel*, 4 April, p. 20.

Tippets, Adrian (2010) 'The Most Dangerous Place on the Planet', *Winq* (Spring), p. 30.

Vandal, Julie (2010) 'A Dakar les gays sont traqués', *Libération*, 17 May, p. 4.

Vidal, Jérôme (2011) 'Agency and Empowerment', *Revue des Livres* 1: 62–3.

Vuylsteke, Catherine (2008) *Onder mannen: Het verzwegen leven van Marokkane homos* (Antwerp: Standaard Uitgeverij/Manteau Meulenhoff).

Zayra (2010) 'Mon mariage, mes larmes et mon sourire', *Mithly* 4, August.

Ziraoui, Youssef (2010) '"Les homos ne vivent plus dans la peur"'. Interview avec Samir Bargachi, fondateur du site gay Mithly', *Tel Quel*, 10 July, p. 6.

Ziyad, Karim (2010) 'Coming Out', *Mithly* 1, April.

Notes on Contributors

Ramy Aly is Assistant Professor of Anthropology and Mellon Postdoctoral Fellow in Anthropology at the American University of Cairo, Egypt. He is the author of *Becoming Arab in London: Performativity and the Undoing of Identity* (Pluto Press, 2015) and received his PhD from the University of Sussex.

Jamal Bahmad is a British Academy Postdoctoral Fellow at the University of Leeds, UK. His current research project explores youth, social change and the politics of realism in contemporary Maghrebi cinema. He specialises and has published widely in francophone and North African Cultural Studies with a focus on cinema, literature, cities, memory and youth subcultures. Among his recent publications are 'Casablanca Unbound: The New Urban Cinema in Morocco,' *Francosphères* 6(3) (2013); 'Naked Nation: Youth, Masculinity and the Coming Revolution in Nouri Bouzid's *Man of Ashes* (Tunisia, 1986)', *Africa's Lost Classics: New Histories of African Cinema* (eds David Murphy and Lizelle Bisschoff, Legenda Books, 2014); 'Rebels with a Cause: Youth, Globalisation and Postcolonial Agency in Moroccan Cinema,' *Journal of North African Studies* 19.3 (2014). His forthcoming monograph is entitled *Casablanca Belongs to Us: Globalisation, Everyday Life and Postcolonial Subjectivity in Moroccan Cinema*.

Donatella Della Ratta is a postdoctoral fellow at the University of Copenhagen, Denmark, where she obtained her PhD on the politics of Syrian TV drama. She is a former postdoctoral fellow at the Annenberg School for Communication, University of Pennsylvania, USA, and an Affiliate of the Berkman Center for Internet and Society, Harvard University. She has authored two monographs on Arab media and curated chapters on Syrian media and politics in several collective books. Her most recent publication is *Arab Media Moguls* (co-edited with Naomi Sakr and Jakob Skovgaard-Petersen, I.B.Tauris, 2015). She has managed the Arabic-speaking community of the international non-governmental organisation Creative Commons for five years. She has co-curated several exhibitions about Syrian emerging creativity in the context of the uprising, and is a co-founder of the web aggregator SyriaUntold.

Dictaphone Group is a research and performance collective that creates live art events based on multidisciplinary study of space. Tania El Khoury is a live artist working in London and Beirut. She creates immersive and challenging performances in which the audience is an active collaborator. Her solo work has toured in several international festivals. Abir Saksouk is an architect and urbanist. Her interests focus on multidisciplinary research on space, with projects including the history of production of the informal suburbs of Beirut, and understandings of public space in Lebanon. Petra Serhal is a performance artist who works as a performer, maker and producer. In her work she is interested in the performing body, and the relationship between the performer and the audience.

Tarek El-Ariss is Associate Professor of Arabic and Comparative Literature at the University of Texas at Austin, USA. His research interests include contemporary Arabic literature, visual culture and new media, eighteenth and nineteenth-century French and Arabic philosophy and travel writing and literary theory. He is author of *Trials of Arab Modernity: Literary Affects and the New Political* (Fordham University Press, 2013) and editor of the forthcoming MLA anthology, *The Arab Renaissance: Literature, Culture, Media*. He is associate editor of *Journal of Arabic Literature* and edits a series on literature in translation for the Center for Middle Eastern Studies at the University of Texas Press entitled 'Emerging Voices from the Middle East'. His new book project examines new media's effects on Arabic artistic and political practices by exploring the way that modes of confrontation, circulation and exhibitionism shape contemporary writing practices and critiques of power.

Heba El Sayed is a visiting fellow at the London School of Economics, and a visiting academic at the University of Manchester, UK, leading two research projects based in Cairo: one investigating Egyptian youths' consumption of New Information Technologies; and the other – co-hosted with American University in Cairo – focusing on street sexual harassment in Egypt and the media's role in fuelling this national epidemic. She completed her PhD in Media and Communications at the London School of Economics in

2012: her thesis involved an ethnographic account of Egyptian youths' consumption of transnational television as a daily resource through which local and cosmopolitan identities are articulated. Her forthcoming publications include a chapter in a volume on Arab feminist media, and a special edition paper for *Media, Culture and Society* on media and religion.

Rayya El Zein is a PhD candidate in Theatre at the City University of New York, USA. Currently she is conducting fieldwork for her dissertation, 'Performing el rap el 'Arabi: Feeling Politics and Affecting Possibility amid Neoliberal Incursions in Beirut, Ramallah and Amman'. In this study, she develops alternative models for understanding resistance in contemporary Arab cultural production, using Arabic rap concerts as its main site in three cities of the Levant.

Justin McGuinness has lectured in Communications and Urban Studies at the American University of Paris (AUP) since 2001. His BA degree at the University of Cambridge was in Arabic and Islamic History (1985). Subsequently he taught at the University of Tunis before undertaking a PhD on urban renewal in old Tunis at the Faculty of Architecture, Landscape and Planning, University of Newcastle-upon-Tyne. At the AUP, Dr McGuinness has developed a range of cross-disciplinary courses touching on media, society and urban space in the Arab world. Returning to his original training, he also teaches more traditional courses in early Islamic history and communications history. Justin McGuinness' contribution to the present book, based on discourse analysis, reflects an interest in the evolving culturescapes of North Africa. He is currently undertaking research into cultural meaning, heritage planning and daily life in the historic neighbourhoods of Fès and Tunis.

Nisrine Mansour is a researcher and documentary filmmaker with a PhD in Social Policy from the London School of Economics, and an MA in Documentary Filmmaking from the University of the Arts London, UK. Her interests include media, gender, family law, forced migration and civil society in the Middle East. In her work she seeks to document the voices of people living at the political, social and cultural margins in the Middle East. She has written several publications on women's subjectivity and family relations, civil society and counter-terrorism, Palestinian and Iraqi refugees and stateless Bedouin populations and cultures of representation in Arab media. Her filmography includes *Strata Artist* (Producer, shortlisted for best short documentary at the Open City Film Festival) and *Hues of Love* (Director, official selection at MESA FilmFest). Currently she is directing *The Morganti Rebels*, a documentary film on activist art after the Libyan Revolution.

Augusto Valeriani is Assistant Professor of Media Sociology in the Department of Political and Social Sciences, University of Bologna, Italy. He was awarded his PhD from the University of Siena. His main research interests focus on digital cultures, journalism, political communication and Arab media. On these topics he has authored and co-authored articles in international journals, including *Journal of Computer-Mediated Communication*, *New Media & Society* and *Middle East Journal of Culture and Communication*. He has also published several book chapters and three monographs. His latest book is *Twitter Factor* (Editori Laterza, 2011).

Sami Zubaida is Emeritus Professor of Politics and Sociology at Birkbeck, University of London, Fellow of Birkbeck College, Research Associate of the London Middle East Institute and Professorial Research Associate of the Food Studies Centre, both at SOAS, University of London, UK. He has held visiting positions in Cairo, Istanbul, Beirut, Aix-en-Provence, Paris, Berkeley, CA and New York, written and lectured widely on themes of religion, culture, law and politics in the Middle East, with particular attention to Egypt, Iran, Iraq and Turkey. His other work is on food history and culture. His books include: *A Taste of Thyme: Culinary Cultures of the Middle East* (edited with Richard Tapper, 2nd edition, I.B.Tauris, 2000); *Law and Power in the Islamic World* (I.B.Tauris, 2003); *Islam, the People and the State: Political Ideas and Movements in the Middle East* (3rd edition, I.B.Tauris, 2009); and *Beyond Islam: A New Understanding of the Middle East* (I.B.Tauris, 2011).

Index

9/11 46, 126
1908 Young Turk Revolution 131–3, 135–6
1967 Arab-Israeli War 3, 47–8, 57, 100

A Jamaâ (*The Mosque*) 222–3
Abbas, Edd 105
Abbas, Wael 65
Abdulemam, Ali 72–4
absolutism 8
Abu-Lughod, Lila 28, 91, 233
activism 12, 32, 34, 44–5, 48, 56–7, 62, 66, 70, 74–5, 77–8, 94, 114, 116, 119, 192, 199–201, 203–4, 224, 226, 232, 236
Adorno, Theodor W. 1
aesthetics, subcultural 177, 182–9
Agamben, Giorgio 89, 180
Ahmed, Sara 202
al-Ādāb 45, 48
al-Afghani 133–5
Al-Hariri, Rafiq 116
al-Jabarti 127
Al-Jazeera 71
Alaidy, Ahmed 46–8, 50, 57
alcohol 138–42, 166, 169, 230, 239
Alexandria 12, 127, 129–30, 141–2
Ali, Ben 65, 71, 78
Alsanea, Rajaa 53–6
Amamou, Slim 65
anthropology 4, 9, 27, 115, 201
anti-essentialist philosophies of transgression 10

Applebaum, Jacob 74
Arab Spring 22–3, 34, 46, 49, 57, 62, 156, 174, 228
Arendt, Hannah 88–91, 95
army 3–4, 49, 100–10, 116, 118–19, 132–3, 139
art 4, 6, 12, 19–22, 24, 28–9, 48, 88, 93–5, 104, 107, 114, 117–19, 121, 141
Assange, Julian 49
athaqafa al-fare'eya al-arabeya (Arab subcultures) 5
avant-garde, Arab 3, 12, 48

Bargachi, Samir 226, 231, 238, 244
Beirut 11–12, 45–6, 73, 88, 94, 96, 98, 100–3, 105–6, 113–15, 119, 124, 129, 198, 203–4, 206, 208, 215, 239
Berkman Center for Internet and Society, Harvard University 73
Bloggers Conference, Arab 70, 73
body 14, 89, 157, 164, 168, 196, 198–217, 232
Boellstorff, Tom 233–4
Bölükbaşı, Riza Tevfik 136
Booth, Marilyn 53–7
Bouazizi, Ali 78–9
Bouazizi, Mohammed 78
Bourriaud, Nicolas 118
Brown, Wendy 88, 93

Cairo 12–13, 18–23, 46–7, 50, 55, 65, 71, 94, 129–30, 141, 144, 146, 152–74, 224

Campbell, John L. 77
capitalism 30, 32, 88, 90, 92–3, 128, 158, 180, 190, 225, 228
Casablanca 13–4, 177–9, 181–93, 229
Castells, Manuel 64, 68–9, 79
Catholicism 213–14
Caubet, Dominique 189
censorship 71–2, 94, 116, 130, 145, 147, 162
Centre for Contemporary Cultural Studies, University of Birmingham (CCCS) 2, 10, 26–7, 29, 31, 67, 90
Certeau de, Michel 181, 186–7
Chanan, Michael 202
change, social 3, 10, 23, 25, 31–2, 69, 74–5, 79, 82–3en, 178, 229
Chicago School 2, 3, 5, 10, 26–7
cinema 14, 177–8, 182, 184–6, 188, 190–3, 196, 204, 214
Civil War, Syrian 199
class 2, 6, 24–5, 28–30, 45, 67–8, 90, 97–8, 101–2, 108en, 115, 138–9, 146, 152–74, 185–7, 193, 204, 249en
class struggle 13, 28, 45, 108en
Cohen, Stanley 28–9, 90–1
colonialism 27, 32, 57, 134, 182, 186, 210, 228
commitment (*engagement*) 45–6, 48
commodification 30–1, 34, 52, 185, 190, 193
confrontation 99–104, 106, 159
consumption 13, 26, 29, 145–6, 155, 157, 160, 178, 192
Corner, John 216
Corrigan, Paul 91
Corto, Halim 241–2
cosmopolitanism 12, 68, 126–8, 131–3, 135, 137–8, 141–7, 166

counterculture 20, 24, 30–2, 34–5
Creative Commons 66, 68, 75, 83en
creativity 66, 79, 87, 91–5, 255
cultural studies 2, 4, 7–8, 26–8, 32–3
cultural studies, Arab 8–10, 28, 33–6, 87
culture, digital 11, 14–15, 62, 64, 66–7, 69–70, 75–7, 83en, 184, 222–46
culture, participatory 62–3, 66
culture, popular 27, 29, 189–90, 257
culture, youth 2, 3, 5, 10, 13, 22–34, 90, 94, 154, 185, 229, 242

de Saussure, Ferdinand 6
Deleuze, Gilles 77
Derrida, Jacques 5, 23 *see also* writing, fear of
determinism, class 13, 154
determinism, technological 11, 66
Dictaphone Group 12, 113–21
discourse analysis 15
documentary 14, 196, 198, 201–2, 204, 210, 214–17
double-critique 8, 10, 34–5

El Khoury, Tania 12, 113–21
End, The 13, 177–93
Esler, Anthony 24
ethnography 13–14, 29, 65–8, 79, 88, 95, 100, 102, 154, 159, 202, 246
ethnography, political 11, 88, 100, 102
exclusion, social 13, 154
exposure (faḍḥ) 11, 46–8, 52, 54–7
expression, freedom of 65–7, 71, 73–4, 223

Facebook 62, 64, 75, 77–8, 157, 227, 236 *see also* media, social
fadihah (scandal) 11, 44–5, 48–9, 53–7

family 71, 143, 153, 156–7, 159–60, 163–5, 173–4, 197, 199, 207–13, 229, 232
Fanon, Frantz Omar 1
Fattah, Alaa Abdel 65, 70–6
feeling, political 11–12, 87–8, 95–107
Foucault, Michel 23, 52, 92–3, 232
'Free Ali' 72–3
freemasonry 130–8, 147en
Friends 161

Gallery 68 48, 59en
Gelder, Ken 90
gender 13, 31, 94, 117–18, 153–5, 156–8, 160–2, 171–2, 205–7, 223–4, 231, 245
'generation of the Defeat' 47, 58en
Gharbia, Sami Ben 65, 70–1, 73, 76–7
Girls of Riyadh 53–5
Global Voices 68, 71–3, 82en
globalisation 4, 30, 67, 145, 153, 157, 177, 181–93
Green Zone 19, 21
Grierson, John 215
Griffin, Christine E. 67–8
Guattari, Félix 77

hacking (*fadh*) 11, 47–9, 54–5, 57
hacking rites 49–53
Hakim, 241–2
Hall, Stuart 20–1, 26, 28–9, 33, 66, 90
Hamaoui, Sami 239–40
Hamas 94, 106, 109en
Hammad, Omar Ben 244
Hassan II, King 178–83, 185–7, 191, 225
Hassan, Manal 71, 75
Hazen, William 3–4
Hebdige, Dick 3, 7–8, 29, 34, 90, 158

hegemony 26, 30, 128, 172, 182
Helem 199–200
hermeneutics 9–10, 36
Hesmondhalgh, David 28, 31
Hobsbawm, Eric 187
homosexuality 12, 14–15, 144, 196–217, 222–35, 238, 242–5
Hues of Love 14, 198
Human Condition, The 88–9
human rights 24, 66, 71, 73, 156, 183, 196, 199, 231, 237

Ibrahim, Sonallah 48, 58en
identity 13, 28, 35, 67–9, 72, 74, 99, 126, 131, 134, 138–9, 153–5, 158, 160, 162–3, 165, 173, 197, 208, 215, 222–46
ideology 2, 21, 25–6, 28–30, 46–7, 53, 57, 113, 119, 126, 129, 132–3, 135, 142–5, 153, 155, 158
Idris, Suhayl 45
iltizām (political commitment) 11, 45–6, 48, 53, 57
imagination, cosmopolitan 155, 158–60, 164
imperialism 27, 29–30, 57, 127, 141, 225
imperialism, cultural 27, 29–30
individualism, networked 68–9, 79
information politics 76
internet 44, 46, 50–1, 54, 62–6, 68–9, 73, 77–9, 145, 226, 231–2, 243, 245
Islam 9–10, 94, 106, 136, 126, 129, 133–6, 138, 140, 142–5, 159, 163, 166, 170–1, 212, 226–8, 230, 237–8, 241, 244–5
'Islamist Winter' 22
Istanbul 12, 127, 129–30, 133–4, 138, 140, 142

Ja'far 96–8
Jargon File 49
Jenkins, Henry 63–4
John, Elton 238–9

Katibeh 5, 11, 97, 100–2
Kemal, Namik 129–31, 139, 140–3
Khal, Abdo 44, 50–1, 53
Khoury, Raif 46
Klemm, Verena 45

language 1, 3–6, 8, 10, 15, 26, 29, 55, 66, 69, 75, 78, 97, 103, 127–9, 146, 152, 168, 177, 184, 227–8, 231, 234–6, 244
language, non-academic 8
Lasri, Hicham 177–8, 182, 184–5, 188–93
Lessig, Lawrence 64, 78, 83en
Lévi, Pierre 64
literature 40–5, 47–8, 52–4, 56, 184, 198, 226
Lukács, Georg 1

magazine *see* press
Maghreb 229–46
Mahfouz, Naguib 51–2
Manaala 71
Manovich, Lev 78
Marxism 2, 26–7, 30, 90, 215
Massad, Joseph 197–8, 209–10, 215, 224–6
Massumi, 202
meaning and being, gap between 8
media 9, 13, 28, 49, 73, 75, 79, 119, 128, 145–6, 155–63, 168, 172, 174, 198–200, 203–4, 207, 216, 226–7
media and communication studies 9, 27

media, social 44, 62–3, 76–8, 94, 120, 174, 197, 203, 216 *see also* Facebook *and* Twitter
Meikle, Graham 76
memes 72, 78, 84en, 87
memory, collective 121
Merton, Robert 25
Mithly.net 14, 222–46
modernity 35, 47, 128–9, 134, 136–9, 142–3, 181, 198
movement, social 11, 24, 31, 62–3, 65, 67–8, 75–6, 79, 232–3, 246
Mouvement Autonome pour les Libertés Individuelles (MALI) 236–7
Mouvement du 20 Février (M20) 223
MTV 177–8, 185, 189
Mubarak, Hosni 47, 65
Mughisuddin, Mohammed 3–4
Murdoch, Rupert 49
music 1, 3, 6, 20, 22, 24–5, 29–30, 47, 87, 94, 96, 101, 103–4, 141–2, 155, 157–8, 163, 167–9, 173, 189, 238–9 *see also* rap

Naâmane, Soumaya 225
naming rather than meaning 6
nationalism 11, 127–33, 137, 142–5, 239
nationalism, banal 182
Nawaat 71, 77, 82en
Nayda 178, 185, 189
'neo tribe' 25, 30–2
neoliberalism 13–4, 32, 34, 92–5, 102, 104, 107, 114–15, 117, 178, 181, 185, 192–3, 203, 245, 256
New Left 24, 29
New Urban Cinema 186, 192
newspaper *see* press

Nietzsche, Friedrich Wilhelm 240
non-originary beginnings 7
Nothing to Declare 116–17, 119, 122–3
Nuwas, Ghulam Abu 239

O'Reilly, Tim 63
Orwell, George 78
Ottomans 129–32, 134–9, 142, 144, 245

pan-Arabism 9, 11, 45–6, 48, 69, 75
performance 115, 118–21, 162–3
performance studies 12
phone, mobile 49, 59en, 162–3, 230
pictorialism 14, 216
popular music studies 28
populism 32, 143
post-modernity 2–3, 7, 30, 33–4, 52–3, 55, 191, 215, 217
post-subculturalism 2, 13, 21, 25, 30, 154
postcolonial studies 4, 256
power 4, 7, 21–7, 30–1, 35, 44–4, 47–8, 51, 54, 56–7, 79, 91–4, 102, 107, 119, 128, 155, 164–5, 181–3, 186, 193, 201–2, 207–10, 226
Pratt, Mary Louise 4
pre-moment 7–8
press 4, 22, 29, 139, 141, 144, 160, 225, 222, 226–32, 235–6, 238, 242–5, 247
'Professional Whiteners' 20
protest 10, 18–19, 22–4, 32, 49–50, 57, 63, 72–3, 92–3, 115–16, 157, 159, 173–4, 179, 182, 187, 190, 196, 200, 204, 238
public sphere 15, 35, 44, 57, 90, 223
punk 30, 34, 77, 90, 158

queerness 14, 196–217
Qur'an 127, 171, 237

race 13, 31, 154, 172, 241
radio 105, 179, 181, 230, 245
Rakha, Yussef 50–7
Rancière, Jacques 89
rap 11, 25, 27, 30, 87, 96–7, 100–1, 103, 105, 168, 189
refugee 96, 100–1, 109en, 199, 257
relativism 8
religion 12–13, 68, 94–5, 101, 126–8, 131, 133–43, 145–7, 153–5, 157–8, 160, 162–4, 166, 170–2, 201, 213, 223–4, 237, 239–41, 244
remix culture 64, 67–8, 76–9
Renov, Michael 202
resistance 10–11, 21–5, 27–9, 32, 44, 56, 88, 90–2, 94–5, 99–107, 154–5, 157, 165, 168, 187, 236, 238–40

Saksouk, Abir 113–17, 119–21
Samti, Karim 235
Sandberg, 200–1, 217
Sartre, Jean-Paul 45, 57
Sassi, Mohamed 237, 241
scandal (*fadihah*) 11
Schumpeter, Joseph 93
semiotics 2, 6–7, 20–1, 24–5, 28–30, 66
Serhal, Petra 12, 113–17, 120–1
'Sha3beh' 105
Shahine, Selim 157
Shoenberg, Arnold 1
Shukry, Ghali 46
smiley face 19–22, 35–6

space 3, 9, 11–5, 20, 22, 25, 35, 45, 51–4, 64, 88–9, 99–100, 103–6, 113–16, 119–20, 127, 153–74, 178, 180–2, 184, 187–93, 214–15, 224, 227, 229–31, 236, 240, 242–3, 245
spectacular subculture 28, 30, 36
Spinoza, Baruch 202
status quo 3, 25, 66, 94
street art 19, 20–2, 24, 78, 87, 94
subcultural studies 5, 67, 87, 90
subculture, definition 5
Sufism 135–8
Sullivan, Chris 19–20
Syad, Daoud Aoulad 222–3

Tahrir Square 18–20
Taïa, Abdellah 229, 234, 241–3
Tarmī bi-Sharar 44
Techies, Arab 64–70, 72–6, 78–9, 80en
teleological discourse 9, 12
television 46, 54, 56, 145–6, 157, 160–3, 180, 183, 185, 192, 203, 230–1, 245, 254
theory 1–3, 13, 25, 63, 79, 87–8, 91, 95, 106, 224
theory, political 12
theory, post-colonial 87
theory, trans-subcultural 3
This Sea is Mine 114–16, 118, 120, 123
Thornton, Sara 7–8, 68
tolerance 12, 88, 93–5, 126–7, 242
tourism 145–6, 203, 234
trade unions 24, 65, 78
tradition 9, 16en, 27, 32–3, 45, 48, 52–3, 129, 142, 162, 166, 168–72, 181, 199, 228
transition, sexual 223, 226
translation 3–10, 13, 30, 34–5, 53–6, 71, 145, 154, 178, 214

translation, epistemic 6
translation, ethnographic 6
transnationalism 13–14, 21, 34, 72, 143–5, 155, 157–8, 165, 168, 173, 177–8, 256
'trash aesthetics' 13
Tubman, Harrabic 103
Tuszynski, Marek 74
Twitter 44, 50–1, 53–4, 57, 62, 64, 75, 157 *see also* media, social

uprisings, Arab 6, 11, 18–19, 24–6, 62–3, 65–6, 71, 73–6, 79, 87, 106, 156, 223, 236

Vaughan, Dai 198
Vidal, Jérôme 233
violence 19, 25, 28, 44, 47, 92, 96, 99, 107, 138, 177–81, 185–93, 198, 235

Web 2.0 63–6, 70, 74, 76, 80en, 223, 229–30
writing, fear of 23 *see also* Derrida, Jacques

York, Jillian 72–4
YouTube 230
Youth Culture Studies 26, 28, 30, 33, 34 *see also* youth studies, Arab
youth movements 24–5, 36
Youth Studies, Anglophile 26–7
Youth Studies, Arab 10, 18–36

Zarcone, Thierry 135–7
Ziyad, Karim 238, 240–3
Zuckerman, Ethan 73